To Amy
Teaching means
changing student's lives.

When Mongrel Dogs Teach

Enjoy!

William J. Burghardt

12/9/2016

Copyright © 2016 William J. Burghardt
All rights reserved
First Edition

PAGE PUBLISHING, INC.
New York, NY

Originally published by Page Publishing, Inc. 2016

Cover art and design by Wanda Platt

This is a work of fiction. Names, characters, places and incidents are products of the author's imagination and any resemblance to persons, actual events or locales is purely coincidental.

ISBN 978-1-68348-175-1 (Paperback)
ISBN 978-1-68348-176-8 (Digital)

Printed in the United States of America

*In a soldier's stance, I aimed my hand
At the mongrel dogs who teach
Not fearing I'd become my enemy
In the instance that I preach*

—Bob Dylan, "My Back Pages"

Contents

1. The Magic of Maps 9
2. "I Met a Young Girl, She Gave Me a Rainbow" 21
3. "What the Fuck Is Wrong with You People?" 28
4. Laramie 33
5. The Business of Changing Lives 38
6. The Day the Berlin Wall Bricks Ring....................................44
7. The Chick Character Assassination Conspiracy 50
8. Thick as a Rubric; Students in Boxes 54
9. Suffering the Beauty of the Drake Shuffle 60
10. How to Build a Ticktock Swamp 66
11. Storm Clouds 71
12. "I Got Your Back"..75
13. "The Whole World Is Watching" 80
14. Losing My Bedroom: The Myth of Standardized Testing 91
15. The Platonic Conception of Self..97
16. Amy Knows about Zimmerman in Real Time 113
17. "So You're the Kind Who Likes to Be Beat First" /
    "The Pros from Dover"..118
18. A Sticker on a Briefcase...124
19. Captain Canary Sings 135
20. The Lessons No One Observed: Great Chain of Being 141
21. The Lessons No One Observed: Transcendentalism...........148
22. Surrounded by Morons Making Millions...........................153
23. Lights Fade, Curtain Drops 159
24. Contracts, Stipends, and the Art of Ultimate Frisbee 167
25. "You're Very Well Read, It's Well Known" 172
26. The Plot to Assassinate Huckleberry Finn..........................176

27. Biff, Max, *Deathtrap*, and *Oswald*:
    The Actual Interrogation 187
28. In the Heat of the Storm..193
29. "Paranoia Strikes Deep, Into Your Life It Will Creep" 200
30. "Clickety-Clack, Clickety-Clack. If You Go,
    You Can't Come Back" 204
31. Tits..212
32. "Chasing Paper; On Our Way Back Home".........................221
33. When Rubrics Become Maps..231
34. Hypostatization 238

Appendix: The Anatomy of a Strike 241
About the Author...270

To Maggie Fredricks, who instinctively reaches out to
change lives, and makes life itself worth living

CHAPTER 1

The Magic of Maps

Why is my hometown of Park Forest, Illinois, a southwest suburb of Chicago, meriting a two-page spread—with a semidetailed rendered map—in a high school textbook?

WILLIAM J. BURGHARDT

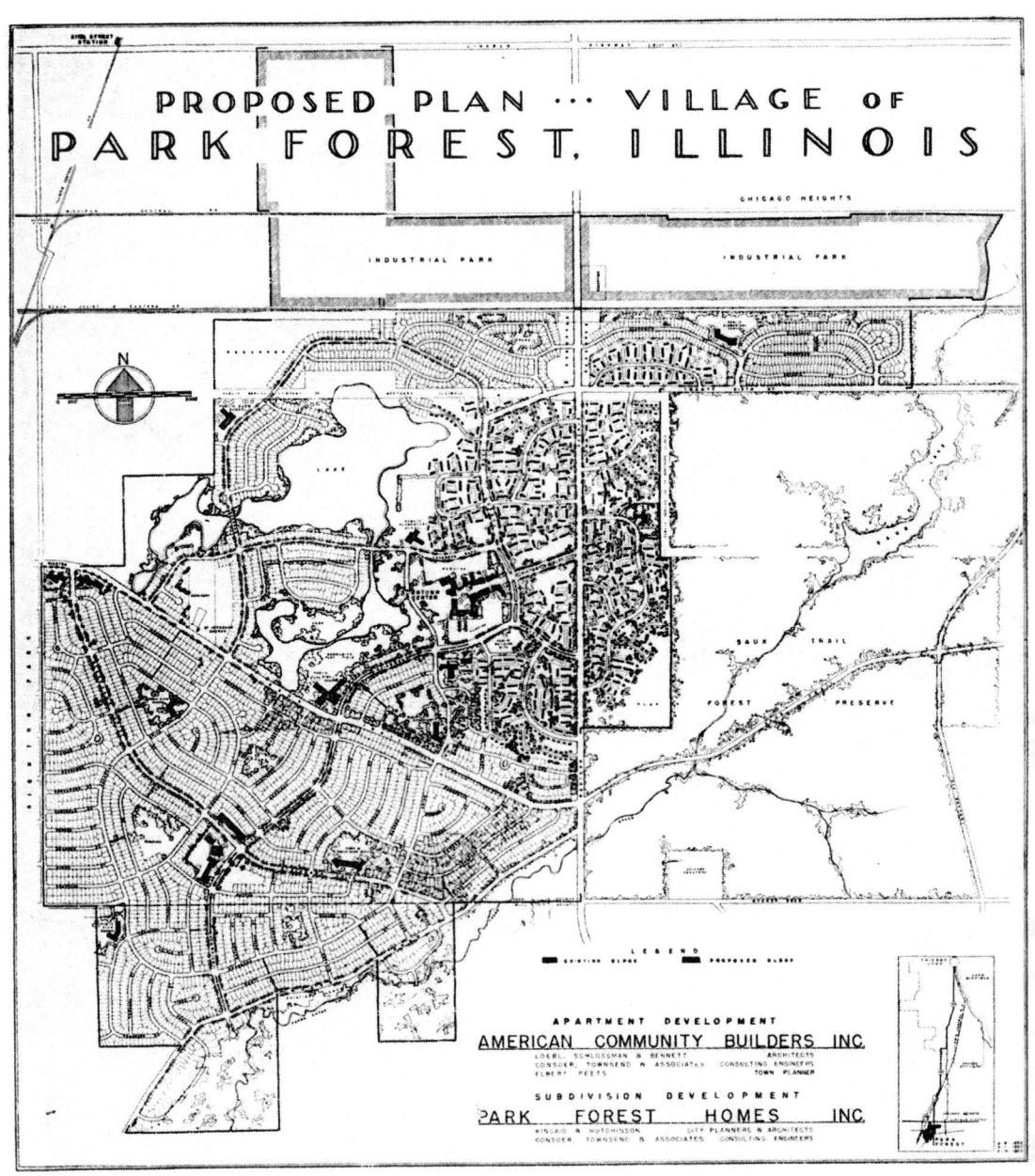

Illustration Courtesy of Park Forest Historical Society

I am sitting on a desk in the classroom, flipping pages in this history book, and there's the town. Headline: "The Road to Suburbia" in big blue letters and an aerial map, drawn circa 1950, showing the streets, the layout of the town, the parks, the churches, the shopping center, the houses. The visual shows what you think it shows. What I see is different from what someone else might see. That's the magic of maps.

I find my street. I can see my house. I can almost see my backyard. I didn't live there when this replica was made—it's actually an artist's rendering—but I am wondering why my hometown is included in a high school junior history book.

Later, I go online. I find an aerial photo. With a magnifying glass, I can make out the ditch behind my backyard and the curved sidewalk that leads to my elementary school. I remember it as it happens: Where a kid named Woody tells me, after I'd gone home for lunch (just have to cut through the backyard), as we wait for the bell to ring to allow us to enter the imaginary portal to school—I remember, I was waiting at the sidewalk, Woody tells me President Kennedy had been shot; he heard it at his house when he went home to lunch.

"Oh, you mean just in the arm or something like that," I say.

He says, "No, in the head."

The map of Park Forest in the old history book doesn't really tell you much, but to me, it creates a memory avalanche. It's where I grew up. I look at the aerial photo and find Rich East High School. My dad taught there for a while. It was he who encouraged me to become a teacher. He died in March 1997. At the time, I was working as a journalist. A year later, I quit the newspaper, and by February, I was taking classes to become a certified teacher.

I remember the first class I took. I needed to take a Multicultural class and wanted Religions of the World, but the only one I could get into was Music of the World. I remember that first day; me, at forty-four, with a bunch of twenty-year-olds in this music class—and they were all stoned. The teacher played a Nepalese *dutar*. I freaked out. I literally teared up and thought, What the hell have I done to my life? But I got through it, student teaching and all, ending up here: a second-year high school teacher.

I later learn that a guy named William Whyte wrote a best-selling book called *The Organization Man*. Park Forest was discussed big time in that book. Whyte's book matched the fictional best seller of the period, *The Man In The Gray Flannel Suit* by Sloan Wilson in inspiring criticism that "those Americans inspired to win World War 2 returned to an empty suburban life, conformity, and the pursuit of the dollar."

"You know we don't use that book anymore." A voice pulls me out of my memory. It's Conrad, my team teacher, a man I connected with the moment I met him. "We use the Howard Zinn book."

"What are you looking at?" he asks and comes over. "Park Forest," he reads out loud.

"My hometown. I grew up there."

He scans the pages. He summarizes the information. Park Forest was one of America's first model communities. During the 1950s, after the war, these little towns sprung up and started to grow, but Park Forest was different. It's in the history book because they built the whole town before anybody lived there; then they sold the houses. Other towns start small and grow as the population dictates. One day, Park Forest was an idea in the heads of some developers and architects. It was a large tract of pristine prairie. Two years later—*poof!*—it was a town, magically created out of dust. "A complete community for middle-income families with children," says the book. People leapt at the chance to move their young families to a town that was created just for them. My family was one of them.

"You know," I say, "I remember something like that, but nobody really talked about it. We just lived it."

It dawns on me. "You know, Park Forest was a map before it became a town. That's what this book is saying."

Conrad just stares. There is an awkward silence.

We haven't really talked about the class much; he did not click with the other teacher who team-taught this class last year, and so I am here. This guy is younger than me by about fifteen years but has taught about, I don't know, ten years. The class we teach is called American Studies; two periods, two teachers, English and History together. What I find out is that my partner, Conrad, the History guy, knows a lot of literature; and I, the English guy, know a lot of history. It will make our class click. We become a very good teaching team; we often complete each other's sentences. We're both liberal guys; well, I'm liberal; I eventually find out Conrad is politically to the left of Castro. Or so he pretends. It's hard to get a feel on what Conrad really thinks—this I learn as we continue working together.

"The town's a shadow of itself now," I tell Conrad. "My mother still lives there. Right there. But the town is dying." I refer to the aerial photo. "They built a mall nearby and killed the shopping center, the plaza, which was an outdoor string of eclectic stores and shops, big and small. The plaza, right here, was the center of action, hundreds of stores, and they are all gone. All of them."

I don't know if Conrad is empathetic at all about the death of the Park Forest plaza. "Marshall Field's—dead! Goldblatt's—dead! Sears—dead! Kresge's—dead! Clothing stores like Richman Brothers, Lytton's, Rothschild's—all dead!"

I'm doing my John Belushi imitation from *Animal House* (Niedermeyer—dead!) or the Al Pacino mantra from *The Godfather* as he tells his soon-to-be-executed brother-in-law Carlo about all the guys he killed that day as the Corleone family "settles all its debts." Barzini—dead! Philip Tattaglia—dead! Moe Greene—dead! And so on. I see Conrad begin to smirk. Ah, a small breakthrough.

"I sold clothes at Rothschild when I was in high school. Hell, we had a candy store where I used to take my twenty-five-cent weekly allowance. We used to go down to Sears every Friday to pick up the new WLS Silver Dollar Survey with the top forty songs, and you could get a 45 record for a buck."

He shows me a bulky paperback book. "We use this, as I think I told you." He says it, not snotty, but with an I-know-how-to-teach-this-class-and-you-don't-you're-new attitude subtly tucked behind the remark.

Conrad continues to hold the book up for me to see, as though it's a Bible he got in fourth grade from the Pope, personally addressed and autographed. Which it is, by the author, with a personal salutation. Howard Zinn is a scholar of some renown with an admitted liberal bent, and his tome is titled *A People's History of the United States*. I have heard of it before. I think for a second, and I remember; it's in the film *Good Will Hunting*. Matt Damon is looking at the books in Robin Williams's office and says something like "You read all these books? All you people, you're reading the wrong fucking books. You should read Howard Zinn's *A People's History of the United States*. Now there's a book that'll knock you on your ass."

"That's mentioned in *Good Will Hunting*," I tell my partner and explain. He didn't know this. I know something he doesn't. More silence. I try again.

"Zinn? I don't know it, but what's wrong with this book?" I'm holding the book with Park Forest in it.

"Number one, who wrote it? You look at the authors and they list like sixty people. Whose voice is writing this book? It's by committee, like most text books. And look at the supposed point of view. Here. The Boston Massacre. You know that, right?"

I nod. "Well, is it a massacre? No. It's a stupid skirmish that went out of control. Some British officers panicked after being pelted with snowballs. It's a freaking snowball fight gone bad. Five people were shot. You know who defended the British soldiers at the trial? John Adams. So the Boston Massacre is no massacre. And then here, you want to read about a massacre?"

My partner begins flipping. "Here. The Battle of Wounded Knee. Last assault on the Native Americans. Was it a battle? No. Now that was a massacre, but this book calls it a *battle*. Some three hundred Indians slaughtered. It was a horrendous massacre. In the purest sense of the word. The Native Americans were 'ghost dancing' or something and the cavalry panicked and this—now this was a massacre. Hundreds of Native Americans killed for no reason. The Boston *Massacre*, right, and the *Battle* of Wounded Knee. A battle implies fighting on both sides. It's bullshit. That's why we use the Zinn book. This book changes the way people think because they've been taught a shaded truth."

The Zinn book became a life changer for me. I love maps. The Zinn book has no maps. But in the first chapter, he talks about maps, and it's the way he talks about maps that clarifies how we all look at the world, life, the whole human experience.

For Conrad, Zinn is a life changer, a true scholar, someone he fervently wants to share with our students.

For me, my life changer is J. D. Salinger, well-known author of *The Catcher in the Rye, Nine Stories, Franny and Zooey,* and *Raise High the Roof Beam, Carpenters and Seymour: An Introduction* I know everything about Salinger. Conrad knows everything about Zinn. We are both passionate about what we know, and our passion clicks, making our team the most wonderful educational teaching experience I will ever have.

Zinn begins by focusing on Columbus. He mentions an award-winning Harvard historian named Samuel Morison who wrote a book called *Christopher Columbus, Mariner*. Now, Zinn says there's nothing really wrong with the Morison book per se. The text's point of view supports what it wants to, which is to focus on the art of navigation. Morison focuses on Columbus's expertise as a seaman and so on and so forth. In one sentence, he mentions that Columbus murdered thousands of Arawak Indians and committed genocide.

One sentence.

Zinn says his chapter on Columbus focuses on nothing but the genocide and barely mentions Columbus, the mariner. Morison wrote that book and decided what he wanted to focus on—seamanship. I remember reading somewhere that there is a statue of Samuel Morison on the Harvard University campus (it's mentioned in the Pulitzer Prize winner, *The Goldfinch* by Donna Tartt). Zinn says he wrote his chapter and decided what he wanted to focus on—genocide. As far as I know, Harvard boasts no statue of Zinn.

What's the better picture of Columbus? Each man has his bias. Zinn begins his book by openly stating his: he is going to write the history of the United States from the point of view of the underdog, the disenfranchised, the downtrodden. Zinn doesn't apologize for this; he wants the reader to know where he is headed.

And then he talks about maps.

Different maps serve different purposes. Flash forward to the day we teach Zinn's introduction to the American Studies class. I tell our students we are taking a field trip on Monday to Alfie's, a local hamburger joint (I'm lying, but they don't know it); and after they stop cheering and screaming, I tell them, "We need to show you guys how to get there." And to make sure everyone knows where Alfie's is, I pull down from that roller-type-jobby-map-conglomeration-doodad hanging in the front of the room with tons of maps you can pull up and down, and I show them a full-blown Mercator map of the world. I make a big deal of trying to find Alfie's on this map. This goes on for a while, and I eventually say, "This map sucks." The kids finally speak up.

The world map doesn't suck, we learn, it's just the wrong frigging map for what we want to do. I pull down other maps. Also no good is a map of the United States. So is a map of Illinois. So is a map of Chicago and the suburbs. There is nothing wrong with these maps. They just aren't helping us today. What we need is a very local map showing the streets and the specific route to Alfie's. That's the map we need. And it's not here.

So the Zinn book is one "map" of Columbus, and the Morison book is another "map" of Columbus. Which map is right? Or does it matter?

I begin to think about maps from various angles. Often they reflect life and death.

The Park Forest map shows a town, not busy being born, as Bob Dylan once warned us, but busy dying. I'm thinking, *Nobody really left.* There are no little kids there anymore. Almost all the schools are shut down, though the Rich East Rockets are still alive. As I said earlier, we used to go down to Sears every Friday to pick up the new WLS Silver Dollar Survey with the top 40 songs and you could get a 45 record for a buck. The first record I bought was *Touch Me* by The Doors. Jim Morrison, he's also dead. Let's see, that's got to be 1968, eighth grade, maybe freshman year.

I think, okay, both Morison (Samuel), and Morrison (Jim) are dead. So is Buddy Holly, Jimi Hendrix, Janis Joplin, Elvis, and John Lennon. Lennon, shot by a kid inspired by Salinger's *The Catcher in the Rye* to shoot a man he saw as a phony. That's the book I love to teach and know it backward and forward. In the English department, I'm known as the "Salinger czar."

A digression: my favorite thing to teach in *Catcher* is page 80. Holden Caulfield wonders and worries about Jane Gallagher, a girl he knew at fourteen but is now sixteen and is out with his "unscrupulous" roommate Ward Stradlater, a sex fiend who he is afraid will ruin Jane's innocence. He says he doesn't think Jane would let Stradlater get to first base with her. I talk about first base, knowing Salinger is a baseball guy. (The character in *Field of Dreams* played by James Earl Jones was originally Salinger in the book on which the film was based,

Shoeless Joe by W. P. Kinsella; the final chapter, when Salinger walks into the cornfield, is entitled "The Rapture of J. D. Salinger.")

First base, second base, third base, home run. They all know what it means. I know what it means. My parents know what it means. My grandparents know what it means Definitions vary, but we all know what it means—It's weird the things we pass down outside of the classroom. And in its own way, this particular euphemism is a map all its own (like *cooties*; how do things like that get so effectively passed on to each generation? It's not in the classroom).

I ask what the most exciting play in baseball is, and I lead them to the inside-the-park home run. Ball hits an imperfect niche on the outfield wall, caroms off, the outfielders run like madmen to get the ball, the batter is flying around the bases, and the throw-in goes where? To the cutoff man. And then where? To the catcher, whose job is to protect the home run from becoming reality. How is the catcher different? He blocks home plate. He *protects* home plate. He is dressed in a lot of equipment: cup, chest protector, shin guards, mask, and particularly for the 1950s, when the book was written, he is dressed differently how?

I always pause for effect.

"He has his hat on backward. He is the catcher. And who else wears his hat backward? Holden Caulfield. 'The catcher in the rye.'"

The kids go nuts. "You made that up." "Salinger didn't put that in. How do you know?"

I don't, I tell them, but it's there. It is a valid literary criticism. Whether Salinger meant it or not is irrelevant. The kids just stare like I'm nuts. But they see it. It's a great teaching moment. And I lead them to the discovery.

I watch few serial television shows but was emotionally drawn to *The West Wing*, created by Aaron Sorkin. The series focuses on life and decision-making in the administration of President Josiah Bartlet, a liberal from New Hampshire, brought to life on the screen by a long-time favorite actor of mine, Martin Sheen.

In one episode, the president's staff was forced to listen to obscure, out-there radical requests from the American populace. Press Secretary C. J. Cregg attended a presentation on maps from a group of avid and forward-thinking cartographers. This episode was a great evolutionary step in my map-enlightenment odyssey.

The presentation by the fictional group Cartographers for Social Equality focused on the visual inaccuracies of the traditional Mercator map, flattening a round object, whereby for instance, Greenland appears to be way larger than South America, among other anomalies. But the real head turner comes when the presenters unveil and explain a dichotomy in the economy of our world—that a large percentage of impoverished people in so-called third world countries existed below the equator, and the lion's share of the richest, most economically developed countries existed above this arbitrary dividing line.

The group claimed this was due to one reason. The maps were wrong. They showed north up and south down. The society claimed that this showed an undeniable, flat-out universal bias became everyone views "up" as good, as "winning," and "down" as bad, as "losing."

"What's the score? How many are we up?" I mean, people don't approach you and say, "Hey man, what's down?" They say, "What's up."

In that episode, the Society for Cartographic Equality wants President Bartlet to flop all maps by presidential decree; in fact, flip globes so that south is up, and north is down. They believe the map change would undoubtedly stimulate growth psychologically in what is now the southern hemisphere.

What? Or to quote C.J. Cregg "You guys are freaking me out."

But consider the idea and how this affects how we view the world—both individually and sociologically—through the unintentional bias of maps.

I once heard that the term "the Orient" came about because that portion of the world was, in those days, the top of maps, or the place from whence one could "orient" their current location (like those minimaps at malls that state "You are here.") Orient has its roots in a word meaning "east," which, if you don't know, is where we all say the sun rises and the direction many people in the Old World (white people in Europe) believed where the Garden of Eden was located.

Whenever I study the hawk's-view of my hometown, there's no knowing what this photo might be hiding. The satellite view is a photo, so there's no mistake on the page. There is actually nothing hidden there, but still I look, trying to find—what? Like the "Seek and Find" page in *Highlights for Children*; where's the hidden upside-down animal? Where's that fuzzy figure on the Grassy Knoll or the Mystery Tramps with their polished shoes and neat CIA haircuts, like the visuals seen in JFK assassination conspiracy books?

This map represents my Monopoly "Go" square, where my Scottie dog (that token survived the ax when Monopoly redid its playing pieces—the Scottie dog lives!) starts as he walks his way around the colorful streets and avenues of the game board. And now I'm back at a high school, the last place I left on my old map.

And it helps explain my fascination with the Park Forest maps.

But is this not how we view life, view the world? Through a specific lens? What is your lens? And mine? Or anyone's? In any individual's head, what map do people use to figure out the world and their lives? And where to go? And where not to go? And when to move?

In the days that lie ahead, I often find myself picking up the abandoned history book with the misnomered Boston *Massacre* and the *Battle* of Wounded Knee, and study the architectural rendering of my hometown along with the aerial on-line photo I use as a bookmark. I find the high school, home of the Rich East Rockets. It's like I find something new each time I look at it. The Rich East lagoon (our yearbook was named *The Lagoon*) where I caught a catfish that I kept as a pet. It died in a bucket after one day. I didn't understand fish need room to move, to live their lives. I'm moving, and hopefully, unlike the fish I caught, I'm busy being born and not busy dying.

And now I'm back at a high school, with Conrad, Salinger, and Zinn.

The semesters go on.

One day, thanks to Conrad's and others' efforts, Howard Zinn speaks at our high school. He's treated like a rock star.

On January 27, 2010, Zinn moved on to a spiritual map and left us behind. Conrad organized a kind of memorial in our class, and during those lessons, I would walk back to my desk and look at my computer and, for not the last time in my life, I would freeze and tear up. I look at Conrad, who sees something's happened, and he comes back, looks at my screen, and says, "Wow. Man, I'm sorry." We share a moment. On January 27, 2010, Howard Zinn died. On the same day, J. D. Salinger, who had not published anything since 1965, also died.

The same day.

Did they have coordinated maps?

WILLIAM J. BURGHARDT

Where am I going now? Where are we all going? And how do we get there, particularly if we are all carrying different maps? Maps we carry around in our personal and invisible automobile glove compartments, guiding us, often without knowing, toward places that are up and down roads we should or should not travel.

How do we know what is up—or down—with that?

CHAPTER 2

"I Met a Young Girl, She Gave Me a Rainbow"

I had an anxiety attack on November 8, 2005. It started for no apparent reason in a class I was teaching with Conrad. There were about ten minutes left in the class (we taught first and second hour), and—after sort of realizing what was happening. I thought I could get through it. There was a fire drill scheduled during third hour which I had off. I was kind of okay through that; but afterward, it came on like a wave. I couldn't stop it. I could not stop hyperventilating; I wasn't crying, but tears were flowing down my face, an embarrassing condition especially for a teacher in a classroom. The nurse was called. My friend Ms. Pick was there. They brought a paper bag to breathe in and out of, but that didn't work, and I went to the hospital. Ironically, one of the ambulances that was there as part of the fire drill was the same one that took me to the hospital, and the attendant recognized me and said, "Why didn't you just crawl in when we were here earlier?" A real wit.

At the time, the high school summer play I had directed a few months before, Lanford Wilson's *Angels Fall*, was being considered for inclusion at the Illinois State Theatre Festival, an honor akin to going "down state" for the athletic teams. This would be the third time I had taken our school to this academic distinction, if we were selected. We were to find out Friday, November 25, the day after Thanksgiving, when the state theater honchos would make the final call. They usually picked about fifteen schools out of three hundred, so it was kind of a big deal.

Two years earlier, our school was the first in the state to perform and be recognized for *The Laramie Project*, the Moisés Kaufman-led Tectonic Theater Project reporting and staging of the horrific events surrounding the torture and murder of Matthew Shepard, a gay University of Wyoming student who was chained to a fence and left to die.

On the evening of November 20, 2005, a shy, blossoming young actor named Caitlyn, one of my favorite students—a theater kid, a junior who was one of the five students cast in *Angels Fall*—was at a dance performance and collapsed, had a heart episode and died. She was seventeen years old. The doctor later said he thought he had saved her but then suddenly lost her. I knew Caitlyn's family quite well; Caitlyn's older brother Biff was one of the actors in *The Laramie Project* and went on to win the John Belushi scholarship at the College of DuPage, and then to study theater and film at the University of Southern California.

I believe the anxiety attack twelve days before Caitlyn's death was a spiritual premonition. It was a foreshadowing, an alarm of sorts, and I knew at the time it was some kind of signal, like "Warning: Falling Rocks" on a road sign going through the mountains.

Whatever it was that happened on November 8 was definitely related to what happened on November 20, and it led to major life changes, doors opening and closing, roads taken and not taken, that are still affecting me to this day.

To write about a death of someone so young, so totally not a person you would expect that to happen to, usually requires a barometer of how special that person was; to describe a life that way strives for an emotional, maudlin reaction, the way the unexpected death of a young one deserves.

Caitlyn was so unassuming, so "I don't want to be the center of attention," filled with carefully crafted dreams of the stage, ballet, and theatre, but shy. She treated the arts with a reverence I have and I feel. The part in *Angels Fall* was her first major acting performance, and she was gone before she heard her final cue. "Lights Up."

I can't explain it all, but you know what you know what you know.

When someone dies, many people are affected; it may sound selfish, but all I really know is what affects me. Particularly when it's life-changing and spiraled into so many more events that changed so many things; I hope these events, still ongoing, will lead to some kind of enlightenment, a Zen Buddhist satori moment so prevalent in the characters Salinger wrote about: Holden, Franny and Zooey Glass, Sergeant X, and others.

The days between the anxiety attack and Caitlyn's unexpected passing are a blur to me now. After my attack, I remember going to the hospital where they dripped drugs from a pole to calm me down. It was a slow process that took several hours, and it was done in an emergency room at the hospital. My wife came right away. She was concerned, cautious, curious, and wondering, I'm sure, what the hell was going on with me.

We talked about things. Our lives were good, our marriage sound, but there was an unspoken atmosphere in that room that somehow, someway, a transition had occurred, a line crossed leading "maplessly" to a place neither of us could sense or see.

They reached my regular doctor, a gruff, tell-it-like-it-is physician named Marks I liked because he was a total nonbullshit kind of guy. The way Marks became my doctor deserves a few paragraphs.

In 1989, I was acting in a play, David Mamet's *Glengarry Glen Ross,* a 1984 Pulitzer Prize-winner being performed at a local community theatre with quite a prestigious reputation. I had the role of Williamson, the office manager, a real mean son of a bitch. Our final performance was on a Saturday, and we struck the set on Sunday. In the course of doing that, I had carried a Chinese restaurant booth used in the play to a storage area down a twisty staircase and noticed later that I had chest pains.

I worked in Chicago and the next day, the pains became stronger, worse, and with a long history of heart issues in my family, I made one of those decisions that some of us wrestle with—should we call the ambulance? I decided to take a train home and walk a few blocks to the clinic.

They checked me out, I gave them a detailed blow-by-blow of my family's heart history, and out of caution, they sent me by ambulance to Central DuPage Hospital. My wife and two kids met me. They were young enough (aged five and three) to be freaked out by Dad lying there with a plastic doohickey up his nose amid the austere hospital surroundings.

At that point I had no regular doctor, so they "group-observed" me I think for about 24 hours and I was eventually randomly assigned to Marks. The memory is vivid. Marks walks in and takes one look at me and exclaims, "You're that guy! You're that mean guy!" I have no idea what the hell he is talking about. He's just staring and pointing at me and telling me I'm "The Mean Guy," and I am about to rip all the hook-ups and syringes and whatever else they got me wired to and bolt out of the hospital.

What I didn't know was that Marks had seen *Glengarry Glen Ross* the previous Saturday. I was flattered my performance was so life like he thought the guy whose heart he was checking out was that mean son-of-a-bitch Williamson. Obviously, I had brought my character to life so much my new doctor didn't know the difference. Or so actors tell themselves. From then on, Marks and I become close friends.

The whole initial episode with Marks ended with a stress test, among other procedures, and was finally and officially diagnosed as atypical chest pain. It had always been my belief I had pulled some pectoral muscles moving the Chinese restaurant furniture down those rickety theater stairs, but hey, you can't be too careful. Marks ended up seeing all the plays I was in.

End of digression and back to the 2015 anxiety attacks. A young doctor came in and said, "Who's your doctor? He kept telling me to give you a stress test and why hadn't I already done it and where did I learn how to be doctor ... a real ballbuster." Yeah, that's Marks. We did a stress test right there (normal), did another the next day at Central DuPage for some reason (again, normal), and I made an appointment to see Marks in a couple of days. The anxiety continued; I found myself breathing heavily, shaking, with tears rolling down my face and no chest pains. It was just pure *panic*. I met with Marks, to talk about what was happening. It was not physically driven. He said in his usual in-your-face style, "I think you gotta go see a shrink."

The first guy I went to—and the only place I could go to because of insurance reasons—said, after talking to me for about ten minutes, that I was, in no particular order, definitely bipolar, the most nervous guy he had ever seen, probably with one foot in the grave, was grossly overweight, physically dependent on both sugar and other stimulants, and, after I gave him my family history, said he felt my grandfather had been murdered—possibly by my mother or my grandmother or both together—and it obviously deeply affected my mother's ongoing guilt complex, which in turn affected me.

"This is a textbook case," he explained. All this in fifteen minutes.

What. The. Fuck?

Before I fired him (actually, after two sessions, their entire office was shut down), he prescribed Klonopin as a "relax pill" that he instructed me to take immediately, under my tongue, the second I felt an anxiety attack approaching. He also prescribed Zoloft. As I recall, I took the Zoloft but didn't take the Klonopin because I wanted to talk to Marks about it; obviously, I wasn't going to take a pill because some guy thought my grandfather had been murdered, possibly by both my mother and grandmother, and that I was textbook bipolar.

Time gets mixed up for me here. The sequence is fuzzy. I do remember on the night of the twentieth, I received a phone call from Conrad. He called first to say a girl from our high school with Caitlyn's last name had died, but it was not Caitlyn, and that several people told him to call *me* so I wouldn't freak out. Two minutes later, he called, apologized, and said it was, indeed, Caitlyn. The principal called me and said he was with Caitlyn and Biff's mother and did I want to say anything. I could not speak. All I can remember is saying something like "So it's true." The principal waited for more, but all he heard from me was silence, so he said he'd convey my sympathies to the family and hung up. Some drama kids, mostly alumni, called me and asked something like, "So what are we going to do now?" They were crying. All of them.

I have no recollection of what I said. I do remember that I kept phone numbers of cast members on my phone for emergencies like changing of rehearsal dates and the like. I called Caitlyn's cell phone, listened to her voice message and broke down. I don't remember any more from that night.

The next day at school, I was in the counselor's office to help kids grieve. Many alumni showed up, and at one time, I think we had thirty kids down there, crying, reminiscing. I remember I had my Klonopin but didn't take any. The counseling staff must have asked me ten times if I was okay. I said yes, I had medicine, whatever—and it was all a lie. I was not okay. And they knew it. In a school, stuff like that spreads fast. The next day, Tuesday, was the last day of the week for the students because of the upcoming Thanksgiving break. Also, teachers had a half-day institute on Wednesday. So by the end of the day, a decision had been made by Ms. Leaffler—a former teacher and now interim chairperson of Communication Arts—that I should go home once the kids left and not return until the following Monday; in other words, go home, get your act together, and come back Monday, ready to teach.

I don't remember how all this happened, but it did. Now I started to take the Klonopin on a daily basis. No more than three in twenty-four hours. I cut them in half. I monitored my intake of caffeine. I was a regular Cabernet drinker, often as many as three or four glasses a day; it was all a balancing act if you found the right groove, even though mixing that pill and alcohol is frowned upon by the medical profession. And if an attack was coming, I put one pill under my tongue, and within ten minutes, the anxiety went away, making everything tenable. I was able to teach. This feeling came and went, but it was there—whatever it was—ticking. I knew when it was coming and had made a network of a few other teachers who I knew, like Ms. Pick, who could take my class for a few minutes, if need be. If I took two pills, I found I didn't give a shit about anybody or anything.

We had Thanksgiving. One of my sisters, who was also on Zoloft, said she'd never seen anyone so anxious in her life.

On Friday, November 25, the state theater folks called. *Angels Fall* had been selected to be featured at Theatrefest in January. Short an actor, I didn't know if the kids even wanted to go. I didn't know if I wanted to go. No, I did want to go. Of the other four kids in the cast, three definitely wanted to go, and they convinced the fourth. A courageous sophomore girl took Caitlyn's role.

I had to re-rehearse them and, in early January, presented the show to the school as a fund-raiser for the trip to Theatrefest and as a memorial for Caitlyn. The auditorium was packed. I had personally purchased expensive jerseys with numbers and the kids' names on them, just like the football team. For the curtain call, the five kids came out and put on their jerseys (the grand unveiling). I came on stage, made a speech, and introduced Biff, who wore Caitlyn's jersey, number 15. I don't remember what I said, but I do know my voice cracked, and I remember Biff and I sharing a moment on stage at one time, some kind of a supportive hug. I was crying, so was Biff. Afterward, the principal came up to me and said he couldn't have done what I just did.

We did go downstate.

But something had been taken from me, chipped off like a sculptor with his chisel, never to return; and, as it goes with things like that, I felt scarred, wounded, with no apparent hope on the horizon to heal.

CHAPTER 3

"What the Fuck Is Wrong with You People?"

As I related before, I started my teaching career at forty-five in August of 1998. My dad was a coach, teacher, athletic director, dean, and assistant superintendent, and had always told me I would be a good teacher. I had even guest lectured on reviewing theater as an award-winning journalist as well as lessons on *The Catcher in the Rye* and the JFK assassination, mostly on the college level. I was comfortable teaching, was able to effectively use my theater skills, comfortable in front of a group, knowledgeable, funny—I was good.

All my interviews went well, and I was in demand because I was at the low end of the salary schedule. I had a lot of real-life experience, and I was certified to teach the following subjects: theater, journalism, speech, and English, which gave me a tremendous amount of flexibility. On top of that, in 1989, I had won the Peter Lisagor Award for Outstanding Journalism Accomplishment in the area of Arts Criticism, a distinction awarded by the Chicago Headline Club, a competition that covered the seven-county Chicagoland area. Also, I had acted in or directed some forty theatrical productions for our semiprofessional community theatre (where Marks had seen *Glengarry Glen Ross*); so not only did I have the certifications for four different classes, I had the experience outside the classroom at a very high level. And from a school's point of view, I was a cheap hire, and I was not some twenty-one-year-old kid. I found a job pretty quickly.

The man who interviewed me was leaving the school in the fall, but one of his last assignments was to hire new teachers for the openings the next school year. None was in theater or journalism, but he said things change pretty quickly in the educational environment, so who knew what the future might hold.

One of the most interesting things we discussed was whether I would be willing to teach a "skills" class. I asked what that meant, and he began to talk cryptically about students who "learned at a slower rate," students who required "more time to complete the lesson" that I would have to teach slower than I might expect. I thought I could do that. He gave me the number of the teacher who had taught these classes the year before, who was to be on pregnancy leave, and she could give me the lay of the land.

These classes were called Social Communication-Skills, and I was surprised when I saw the rosters and discovered that out of nineteen students in one class and twenty-one students in the other one, there were only two girls in each class. Those class numbers were low. By contract, the largest they could give a teacher in that district was something like thirty-one, but I relished the chance to teach a small group of ready, curious minds. I went in to these classes somewhat blind, and it took me three weeks to figure out what I had on my hands, which really pissed me off at the school, the district, and the asshole who hired me, who was comfortably living the retired life on some North Carolina beach.

Of nineteen kids in class one, seventeen were "behavior disordered"; in class two, nineteen of twenty-one were the same. These students were not necessarily "slow." These kids had major issues at home, were constantly getting in fights, violent, smart-asses, and they grouped all these kids together. There I was, a first-year teacher, with the biggest discipline problems in the entire sophomore class. I later learned it was rumored to be the worst group of angry children ever assembled in one classroom in the school's history—and no one told me. They gave it to me in code. Will you take a "skills" class?

The forms started arriving. These kids were on various "plans." I talked to some other teachers, and they recommended "Keep writing them up. Send them to the dean." I became an expert at writing referrals; that first semester, I averaged ten a day. Nothing happened. I called these kids' homes. If I did get through, a mom would say "I know, I know. We can't do anything with him, can you?" I thought to myself, I'm not raising your kid.

Fights broke out daily. I kicked kids out, food was thrown, and very little education was going on. In retrospect though, at the time, I remember thinking, I'm doing pretty well with these assholes. That was until I was "observed" by a vice principal who told me I had to call every kid's parent every day to get control of the class. One day, I reached a Mrs. Columber, who told me to bring Eric's homework to the dean's office. The head counselor told me, "You spoke to Mrs. Columber? You should get a medal. I've been trying to reach Mrs. Columber for three years and have never had a conversation with her." I showed my class lists to the head dean, who said, "All these kids are in the same class?" I said, "Yeah, and I'm a first-year teacher." She looked at me for about ten seconds and just shook her head.

The climax of this opening adventure into my world of lighting up young minds occurred one day as I was talking about some book—I believe it was S. E. Hinton's *The Outsiders*. I turned to write something on the board and a red pen sailed about two inches over my head and smacked into the chalkboard, ricocheting to the floor. I smashed the podium to the floor and screamed, "What the fuck is wrong with you people!?"

And then I sat at the desk and said nothing for about twenty minutes.

The kids eventually started to freak out. "Teach us!" "We're just bad kids!"

I just sat there and stared at the kid I was pretty sure hurled the red pen. I said nothing. The bell rang. They left.

I talked to some teachers at my sister's school—she was on her thirtieth year of teaching junior high—and I was amazed to discover that there were teachers *trained* to teach children with behavior disorders. One teacher my sister introduced me to was a specialist teaching three to five kids at a time who said, "I would be thrilled to have a class like that." But when I talked about this back at the high school, there was very little support.

The thinking at the time was, if these kids were sprinkled throughout a bunch of regular classrooms, they would distract or hurt the mainstream students. As a result, they put them all together in a skills class; and rather than hire a person like the woman I had met, who would be thrilled to teach a class of these challenged kids, they throw them in an erratic, bizarre group to some new gullible sap like me. But they don't tell you what you're headed for—"It's just a skills class."

I solved this problem by finding a study area where I could spread everybody out. Two kids at a table. I would roam from table to table, giving them what I could and trying to keep things cool. Some days, we would do nothing.

One day, a fight broke out. I got between the two pugilists and tried to calm things down. I asked what was going on, and one kid started yelling, "He called me a Jew! He called me a Jew! I'm not Jewish! I'm Italian!"

There were some successes. A student named Jackie wrote a twenty-five-page paper on Kurt Cobain. It was handwritten, about four lines of writing per page, in purple and pink ink with drawings in the margin containing huge misspelled words, run-on sentences, and many indecipherable sections, but it was filled with passion. I could tell she worked hard on it, and I read some of it to the class. I gave her an A; probably the first she ever got. She was thrilled. She dropped out the following year and, last I heard, was picking an electric bass in a garage band playing both Limp Bizkit and Korn.

I gave another kid an A for a speech about how he squirted lighter fluid on himself and set his leg on fire to win a bet because he didn't think it would ignite on his skin. He even showed us the scar, rather proudly. Another kid wrote a paper about how his dog died running into one of those invisible wireless fences. I'm not sure if his family sued, but I do remember his passionate retelling of the dog hitting the wire barrier, being thrown back, shaking violently, and then dying. He teared up as he read this to the class.

The guy who interviewed me—the guy who asked me if I minded taking a "skills class" before skipping town—was right about one thing; things did change. In November, a woman who had just been hired to run the theater program resigned, giving two weeks' notice. She couldn't handle the workload. Some kids in the know went to the woman serving as Director of Student Activities—a Mrs. Sad—and strongly recommended me for the job. I interviewed and, with my extensive experience and the urgency of the situation, was hired as the theater director at the highest salary level possible. I had one demand. I wanted the leaving teacher's remaining classes: three mainstream junior American Literature classes and two Acting classes in addition to selecting, casting, and directing the fall and spring plays. My life was about to change.

I think I did reach that group of behaviorally disordered kids. On the day of the final exam, one kid—who had actively been chasing a very attractive student teacher by loudly whistling whenever she walked down the hall—accidentally shot some Silly String on the floor. I was about to kick him out when he begged me, literally, to let him stay. Once the kids handed in their exams and it was time to dismiss them, they all stood up, surrounded me, and "assassinated" me with nineteen rounds of Silly String, covering me head to shoes. The vice principal commented later, "You reached them. It was the only way they knew how to thank you."

CHAPTER 4

Laramie

The summer after I secured the drama-teaching gig, and escaping from the madness of these other first-year anomalies ("Just wait, it gets better," everyone I told about the experience reassured me), the next summer, I began a master's degree program at Roosevelt University. This degree was called a Fast Track in Directing Theater and designed specifically for high school drama teachers. The program was demanding—three intensive summer sessions, 9:00 a.m. to 7:00 p.m. Monday through Thursday, and Friday night, with the commitment to watch and discuss performances at prominent Chicago theatres, like the Goodman, Steppenwolf, and Drury Lane. Over the three years, I was able to incorporate many lessons from the program into my high school classes, and as I was studying with some thirty other teachers from around the country, I was able to tap in on their collective ideas for techniques and more contemporary plays I could stage.

One show I had my eye on was Lanford Wilson's *The Rimers of Eldritch,* a great ensemble work with a large cast. Directors were always pressured to have large casts so that as many students as possible could participate. The only problem I foresaw, and one I thought I could easily get away with, was that the main character in Wilson's play was a social outcast named Skelly, who was eventually run out of town and killed by a mob because he supposedly liked having sex with sheep.

No big deal, right?

I even presented the idea to my peers at the master's class; I assumed these stage professionals from all over the country were—as I myself was—comfortably living on the edge, pushing the proverbial envelope whenever possible.

"Are you nuts?" they almost universally exploded. "You wanna get fired?" Even the lead professor of the program thought I was drinking Woolite, though a few of the professional directors brought in to teach our classes—many from the Goodman—said, "Go for it." But they weren't high school teachers.

I did try to do just that, give it a go as it were; and as these things fatefully go, we got a new principal, and Mrs. Sad, the student activities director, went on pregnancy leave. When I returned later that summer, I met the new guy, a man named Fainero, who quickly informed me, "That sheep sodomy play is dead, so what play are you going to do?" The tone was unmistakably aggressive, one of those I'm-new-and-I-am-in-charge statements, so I calmly looked him in the eye and immediately said *Our Town*. I love that play. It was totally safe, and I actually ended up producing Thornton Wilder's masterpiece twice at that high school, each time with females in the lead role of the Stage Manager, a casting decision you rarely see when that show is staged.

The next summer at the master's program, I met a gay male teacher from Colorado. There were about thirty or so teachers each year in the class—one-third completed the program each summer, one-third replaced those graduating—at least thirteen of approximately fifteen teachers were openly gay, as well was most of the faculty. Such is the nature of the world of theater. I told my new friend I wanted to do something new and edgy at the high school, and he turned me on to *The Laramie Project*.

As noted earlier, the play focused on the 1998 murder of Matthew Shepard, a gay student attending the University of Wyoming in Laramie. Matthew was beaten severely, tied to a fence in an obscure part of the area, and left to die. Kaufman had taken his Tectonic Theatre troupe to Laramie to interview residents about what happened. He captured it all, and created a very effective piece of ensemble theater. Kaufman carefully stayed neutral, but he had a built-in villain in Fred Phelps a pastor of a church in Westboro, Kansas, who had gained some homophobic notoriety in creating a website called godhatesfags.com. This site, which was updated daily, featured a graphic of Matthew Shepard's face burning in hell and an ongoing count of how many days he had been there, sent by a God who condemned all homosexuals. It was the first thing my friend asked me to look at even before reading the script, and it was repulsively frightening.

The entire *Laramie Project* experience was a life changer for me, the students, and a lot of other people. We got some flak, to be sure, from the religious right, but the kids wrote their own letters to the editor of our local paper and were easily winning whatever kind of argument that existed.

I thought I might receive some resistance from the school. Quite the opposite. There was a half-assed version of the play on video made-for-TV that I got my hands on, but it told the story well enough to show it to some people. I gave it to the new student activities guy—that would be Fainero—who takes a role in this story later. Anyway, Fainero watched just a portion of the tape before he literally grabbed me in the hallway and said as vehemently as our first conversation, "Not only *can* we do this play, we *must* do this play!"

It was an incredible time. Not just in my life, but in the landscape of American history, and that's no hyperbole. When I asked my lead senior about the play, he panicked and said, "Oh no, we can't do this. No one will let us do this." I had him against the wall and said we had to do it because he was the leader, and if he was on board, the rest of the actors would follow.

Later that year, right in the middle of our doing *The Laramie Project*, that same student appeared on the cover of the *Chicago Tribune Sunday Magazine* as one of the first high school students to openly come out. There is no doubt in my mind that the catalyst was our production of Kaufman's play.

The swift shift in the world's attitude toward the gay population was very quick, and nearly miraculous. It was unlike any other major changes in societal attitudes toward any other oppressed group, and it all started with the millenials (loosely defined as "those born after 1982"), the generation evolving while I was teaching.

A vocal number of them quite frankly didn't give a shit about who was and was not gay.

Yes, I still heard in my classes "your shoes are gay" or "your shirt is gay," and I would always stop class and grill the student who said that and ask if they were implying that a specific shirt had a sexual preference or if those shoes had a sexual preference. Other kids stopped these kids. A Gay-Straight Alliance club was popular at almost all schools.

This movement came from the kids. I watched it, and the way the school as a whole rallied around *The Laramie Project* was just one of many reasons why.

In 1985, I lost my brother-in-law, Jeff—a brilliant lawyer who used his wonderful tenor voice in several church choirs—to the AIDS virus. He had come out to my wife and me the summer before, but no one else in the family knew. We started getting calls from Albuquerque that "somebody better get out here quick," and the next phone call was to inform us that Jeff was no longer among the living.

The doctors, who wore men on the moon costumes whenever they brought him a meal, said Jeff died of pneumonia. We flew out, and my father-in-law flew in from Florida, not knowing his son was gay, and ready to "sue the hospital because no one dies of pneumonia in this day and age." He sat down, and I watched a double sledgehammer to his psyche. *Gay. AIDS.*

This is a man who lost one son to suicide in 1968. Now his second son was dead. His third son deteriorated into a psychotically induced life of alcohol and drugs, and he also died, but that happened after the old man himself passed away. How did he survive all this loss?

We had our one-year-old daughter with us on that trip, and she stands as legacy to Jeff, who left her an insurance policy that eventually paid for her four-year degree at the University of Wisconsin-Madison.

After 1985, President Ronald Reagan finally was convinced to recognize the epidemic in a half-assed way. The hard-hit theatre community rallied with fund-raising efforts like Season of Concern and also responded with brilliant plays reflecting the destruction of this startling phenomenon, first and most notably Larry Kramer's

The Normal Heart, and Tony Kushner's *Angels in America*—both parts 1 and 2—and after that, *The Laramie Project*.

Matthew Shepard was an outgoing gay student who may or may not have hit on two local Laramie men, as he supposedly was not afraid to "flaunt his gayness." These two men used the defense of "gay panic" as validating the beating of Shepard to pulp then tying him to a fence where he was left alone for almost eighteen hours before he was found. He was airlifted and later died at a Colorado hospital.

Kaufman's story is powerful, and the kids quickly caught the message and its importance. I had my best actors ever, and we performed the show downstate at the University of Illinois's Foellinger Auditorium to two full houses of around twelve thousand students, teachers, and parents. Later, by request, we performed the play for an encore at another local high school.

Downstate, directors from leading high schools sought me out, congratulating me and the cast. Each student had three to four different Lamarians to play, from bartenders to gay cowboys (shades of *Brokeback Mountain*) to ministers from every delegation, from Baptist to Unitarian. Not to any surprise to me, nine of the twelve high school kids in the show went into professional theatrical vocations, from producing in Los Angeles to teaching in New York, and pursuing acting on all levels in Los Angeles, Cleveland, New York, and Chicago. I just saw one student from the show on a Chicago-based police television series.

The story here is more than twofold or threefold or however many folds you want to divide this global experience into.

For starters, it changed my life, it changed the students' lives; the whole country was changing, and I watched homophobia—and kids calling anything they didn't like as "so gay"—slowly, but steadily, go away: from my brother-in-law's death and AIDS and open hostility toward gay men and women, to the Supreme Court signaling the unstoppable legalization of same-sex marriage—all in thirty or so years. The legalization of gay marriage went from unthinkable, to inevitable, to done-and-done as of June 26, 2015.

Think about that.

Did you miss it? I sure as hell did not.

CHAPTER 5

The Business of Changing Lives

These next events intersect like a jigsaw puzzle created by a malfunctioning, drunk cardboard cutter, but I'll try to recall this as straightforward and truthfully as I can. I won't stoop to Nick Carraway's claim in Fitzgerald's *The Great Gatsby* that I am the most honest man I have ever known. There is some literary license here, but about 90 percent is exactly how I remember this. It will be out of order in some cases and events, and people have been blended and combined. The purpose is to tell a story, not an expose. The purpose is to enlighten, to bury pain, to instruct both in and out of the classroom arena.

Caitlyn suddenly died, and I ended up with a psychiatrist Marks recommended named Duke, who was extremely booked, but on Marks's recommendation, he added me as a patient. Ironically, Duke later told me he didn't even know who Marks was. Marks later told me someone else had recommended Duke for Marks's own mother. Weird, yet provident; serendipity at work from somewhere.

Duke was great. He had teenagers who knew some of the kids I taught in the drama program as his son was in a theater-related curriculum at a neighboring high school. As I explained things to him, which took several sessions, the immediate concern were the tears rolling down my face suddenly, unmotivated, for no reason, as I taught class, plus the anxiety or panic attacks that continued periodically over the stupidest stuff. The attacks and the tears would occur both independent of each other and concurrently, with no discernable pattern.

Once, I had to hook up a slide projector to a computer, and I couldn't make the wires fit into the right holes. The clock on the wall was ticking down the beginning of class. The closer we were to the bell, the more frustrated I got. Then the symptoms began, and I couldn't really complete the task. It was not a hard thing to do. I had done it before. I'm no tech wizard, but this is basic stuff. Couldn't get the thing to work. Hand shaking heart racing tears collecting, *Ticktock, ticktock.*

So I'm freaking out. Fortunately, a sympathetic co-worker at the time, a woman who really was a tech wizard, walked by, saw my distress, fixed it in about twelve seconds, and calmed me. At this point, my ongoing condition was just starting, and I hadn't let a large number of people know about it, but I saw the need for the network of support so often spewed to the afflicted; a group of human beings that I now accepted as colleagues in some secret team photo.

A fellow teacher, the aforementioned Ms. Pick, was my first line of defense; so whenever I felt an impending incident, I would alert a student I could trust to go find Pick immediately, and she would take the class while I took the drug "the Duke" gave me. Within five minutes, everything calmed down. What was annoying and frustrating were the tears streaming down my face. I wasn't crying, actually, because I didn't feel bad or sad or mad or glad. I just had this warm, salty water gushing from my eyes, noticeable to all. You can't teach a class when that happens.

Another time, we were at all-staff meeting in the cafeteria. All the departments sat together at long tables while the powers that be droned on about things they thought we all had to know. Two guys across from me were writing notes on a yellow legal pad, and I was adding my two cents when one guy wrote, "You will die at exactly 9:59 a.m. today" with an arrow pointed at me. I looked at the clock, and it was like 9:41. Then 9:42, 43, 44, 45, and here came the symptoms. *Ticktock, ticktock.* I'm in a huge room where many people could see me, and the closer we got to "my final minute," the more upset I got. The hyperventilating started, the water started falling, and I bolted out of the room. The school nurse and Pick had noticed my attack beginning, and they followed me to give me some isolation. I took the two pills, and in five minutes or so, I was calm but felt dumb. Everybody saw this, or so it seemed. The morons who wrote the note apologized. Was this, again, just something stupid I should handle? I had no answer. I had no choice.

In Illinois, when you achieve certification to instruct students, you have to take a number of specific courses and receive endorsements in subjects you can teach. Between my previous college years and my most recent eighteen months to complete the classes, I needed to complete certification (like the aforementioned Music of the World multicultural requirement). I was endorsed in Speech, English, and Journalism. Theater fell under English. I later added that master's degree in theater, so eventually, I was endorsed in four subjects. A strong resume.

I had been a journalist for over fifteen years (this becomes important later), but I had never taken a journalism class; therefore, I was not officially endorsed until I went back to school for the second time—which was ironic because I had to take eight hours to be certified (two semesters of classes), and I had ten times more experience than the dude teaching the classes. The college only offered an Introduction to Journalism class (which I basically co-taught), so the second semester, I took an independent study class with the same dude where I had to write an extensive investigative piece on a topic of my choosing.

Ironically, a nearby high school district had just settled a very divisive and intense teachers' strike. That's what I investigated. I interviewed over twenty educators and administrators at four high schools in the district, but the school board members refused to talk to me. In fact, when I formally went through the press contact for the district, the school board held a special meeting and officially agreed that no one on the board would talk to me or anyone else about their negotiations with the teachers union, and everybody was ordered to sign it.

Keep in mind that school board members are not educators. They are elected from the community. One board member was a minister at a church around the corner from where I lived, and he really wanted to talk to me, but wouldn't. At any rate, it was a kick-ass piece of work, some thirty pages in length, and fulfilled my journalism endorsement. That piece of writing is included as Appendix A.

I am now going to digress from this digression (Mr. Vinson from Holden Caulfield's Oral Expressions class at Pencey Prep would really be pissed at me). People who go into the education profession, once employed, have the opportunity to take additional classes and earn advanced degrees. You got your Type 75 teaching certificate, and you got your Type 73; the latter is for school counselors; the former is for administrators. These certificates, often earned online or with a minimum of a dozen classes, enable you to become the Instructional Coordinator/Department Head of a department like Humanities or Communication Arts; and these positions, which have very little to do with teaching or education, attract bureaucrats and climbers, those not really interested in anything but getting ahead.

Yes. Climbers—easy to spot and, in most cases, care little for students (one exception was my father). And it is at this level, in my opinion, where there is a tremendous waste of public money, politics, and the kind of games I had experienced for twenty or so years in the real world business community and not in the so-called playground bubble of public education. This was where a basic problem arose for me because of my age, my peers, and the fact that I was not your traditional teacher following the traditional road map to madness.

I know I was and am a good teacher, but I had no interest in pursuing the road to a department head or guidance counselor or principal. And that's where the big money really is, and that's what happens. What I quickly witnessed is what you actually end up with—a faculty comprised of two different kinds of educators. You end up with those who are motivated to teach and those climbers who are motivated to move up. The two groups are not mutually exclusive: of the other; the people who pursue the map to administration-land are the easiest to spot.

A perfect example of a climber is my father. Another perfect example was our principal, who plays a very important role in my odyssey. His name was Storm.

The evaluation of teachers is a very hot issue at this writing, and as Storm once told the entire faculty, the people doing the evaluating take these extra courses, but it doesn't really qualify them to evaluate anybody. And this is a universal educational miasma. Principal X may say to all Department Heads A through Q that when evaluating, be sure to follow District Procedure 302Z-99, and all evaluation scenarios "must follow the Pythagorean Theorem."

Obviously, what I just wrote is bullshit, but the whole process is bullshit. And once you're indoctrinated in the bullshit, principals change, districts change, superintendents change, and then there is new, improved bullshit. Very little of this bullshit relates to classroom reality—all the system does is smother the passionate teacher in theory—multiple theories of bullshit. So you try and employ the theory and quickly realize it is version "pie-r-squared" of the same historic bullshit, so you end up chucking the bullshit and do what you, as a passionate professional educator, know how to do—motivating teenagers and, hopefully, changing their lives.

I imagine Jack Nicholson in *A Few Good Men*, in my educator's version, lecturing me and my colleagues, "We are here to *change* lives, son, it's that simple. And Santiago's death, while tragic, put *changing* lives in danger ... we are in the business of *changing* lives ..."

You get the drift. Colonel Jessup, Jack Nicholson, said "saving" lives, but the point is hopefully made. It's all about changing these kids' lives.

And the people implementing this bullshit—those who do nothing to inspire students—the people whose only purpose is to improve test scores, these people do not believe this bullshit either. But they willfully, annually drag out the bulldozers and spread the bullshit around, and why? For what? This practice justifies their existence. This practice gives them something to do.

I am reminded of an example from my corporate life when I sat in a meeting of about twenty people in our department, and listened to a Senior Executive Vice President, who was probably making half a million per year, read a fifteen-word sentence that was the company's new Mission Statement. He made it such a big deal. Ten guys making six or seven figures went off to some retreat for a week and came back with this sentence that was going to revolutionize our industry.

I immediately knew it was pure bullshit. "This is the game plan," he said. "This is what we are all about."

Of course I couldn't resist raising my hand and asking, "So the top people in our company went off for a weekend retreat and came back with this sentence?"

He replied, "You don't know how hard it was. We debated every word."

Guess what? In a month, that mission statement changed four times, and all four versions were pure, cosmically unadulterated bullshit. Bullshit with bows on it. See the pretty bullshit? Well, it's still bullshit.

You know what's not bullshit? After I'd been suspended with pay for a period (preview of coming attractions), I got a call from a woman who used to teach in our district. She apologized for calling me at home, but she explained I had her son in my third period American Literature class. "I don't know why you are on paid leave," she said, "but I know how political things can be in our profession." She continued, "I wanted you to know about Robbie, my son who is in your class." There was a pause. I knew her child; one of those quiet, unassuming kids who just manage to get by. "Well," she went on, "Robbie has not read a book since third grade. I teach at that grade level. Nothing—and I mean nothing—has ever motivated him to read a book." Another pause. "The other night, his light was on quite late and I checked on him and he was reading *The Great Gatsby.* Now I didn't want to make a huge deal of it with him, but I asked him why he was so interested in this book.

"It's my teacher," he said. "He just makes the book come alive. He makes it exciting. You know, Mom, I think I might want to be a writer."

Long pause. She said, "As a teacher, I just wanted you to know that. I wanted to personally thank you for that." More small talk, I thanked her for sharing, and we hung up.

You want to talk about changing lives? *That's* changing lives. No bullshit.

CHAPTER 6

The Day the Berlin Wall Bricks Ring

A key incident occurred, and I want to say this is August 2006, I'm not sure, but Pick had gone to Ireland to revolutionize the educational system in some way. We had an unofficial meeting about who would be the next, what, "rescue person" in the case I had an uncontrollable anxiety episode, and we had decided, Pick had decided, we all had decided that the best candidate was Ms. Sorinski. She was relatively new, but she got the concept. She was sympathetic, and we had a meeting the previous June before Pick went to the rolling hills of green, but I had no idea how quickly I would need her the following August.

The other important thing here is, I had a new boss, the aforementioned Ms. Leaffler, a young woman who I considered a friend though I totally disagreed with her teaching methods and her not-so-subtle biases. She was cited on the Rate My Teacher website as a person who favored female students and looked down on male students. This Rate My Teacher site is about as unscientific as it gets because kids vent all kinds of bullshit. However, there is some truth in what they post; in cold, hard fact, a lot of truth.

Her first year as supervisor must have been 2005 because when Caitlyn died in 2005, as I mentioned previously, she was the one who came down to the guidance office and told me to come back after Thanksgiving. I remember that distinctly. At that point, I think her title was Interim Instructional Coordinator for Communication

Arts. Even though I disagreed with her about a myriad of things, she was perfect for the boss job if only to get her out of the classroom. She embraced theory. She loved teaching concepts. She was also afraid of parents. She was afraid of a lot of stuff. She wasn't a bad person, and she was undoubtedly promoted too quickly. She was also a climber. We had a rocky first year, which ended with her writing me a note apologizing for "being such a bitch," which I still have and carry with me from time to time. When exactly she penned that self-confessional ditty in this sequence of events, I cannot recall, but she wrote it, I have it, and I will always keep it. Somehow, it helps me understand these events.

In American Studies, Conrad had come up with a very cool lesson where kids chose people off a list to illustrate "What does it mean to be an American?" The list included people as diverse as Chief Seattle to Huey Newton to Bobby Kennedy to Bob Dylan to Leon Pelletier to Helen Keller to Mother Jones to Margaret Sanger to Cesar Chavez to Rosa Parks to Billie Holiday to Gloria Steinem to John Lennon (whose fight to become an American citizen qualified him for the list). We were always adding to the list. One I added was Larry Kramer, author of the play *The Normal Heart*. He deserved to be on the list as the first vocal voice for the gay community, alerting us all to the AIDS crisis and, most importantly, why it was happening. He was an extremely vocal guy who woke up America. I think of him whenever I think about my brother-in-law Jeff. He had his voice heard years earlier.

Students studied these people and actually dressed like them for a year-end tea complete with snacks and beverages. The kids interviewed each other and then chose three or more to write about for their final exam, answering the question "What does it mean to be an American?" as viewed from these various perspectives.

They also had to make a visual of some kind to enhance the assignment. Examples we had saved included a baseball bat with a Jackie Robinson motif, which we eventually had to get rid of because one kid threatened to bash someone's head with it. We also saved an elaborate large oil container with John D. Rockefeller quotes and symbols all over it. Again, very well done.

One passionately conservative student had chosen Ronald Reagan, and his visual, which we had saved because it was cool, was a collection of broken bricks symbolizing the collapse of the Berlin Wall. The Reagan-enthused student brought us the Berlin Wall bricks he created. On one side, he spray-painted *Freedom*, and the other side had something else, maybe "Mr. Gorbachev, tear down this wall." The bricks were cracked but still hung together. It was excellent work.

And the bricks are key to this particular pinnacle-incident in my teaching career because my American Literature class room was the same room where I taught American Studies, and the bricks were there, off to the side, majestically posed on a bookcase.

The student Armando was Turkish or Montenegrin, and he suffered severe ADHD. Because his parents did not believe in medicine, they treated his abnormalities with orange juice. He seemed somewhat normal at first, just your typical frustrated student loudmouth. I "classroom-managed" him in the opening days and quickly came to realize two of Armando's friends were also in the classroom.

Even in my brief experience, handling three malcontents—or better yet, children crying for some kind of attention—was doable. Four was a gang, pure and simple.

Early in the semester (we started in mid-August), you learn the feel of a class. This one was clearly going to be a challenge.

One day, all my suspicions came to fruition. In the middle of some lesson I don't quite remember, a cell phone rings. The sounds seem to emanate from all over the room. This is a larger room as it is two rooms together, the same room used in the American Studies class.

I stop class, look around, and this sound keeps ringing and ringing from some undisclosed place. My dramatic skills kick in; I pretend amusement, I look around, but I got nothing. The phone starts ringing and then stops, eliciting nervous laughter from the class. I fear I am losing control a bit here. I keep thinking, I can find this, but the more it continues to ring, the more I can't seem to figure out where the sound is coming from.

Ticktock, ticktock. Anxiety is setting in. I should take a pill, but I don't think to, and I can't in front of the class anyway. It starts to ring again and then stops and goes on for a while, and I got nothing. I sit. I think. I go around the class. "That your phone? Yours? You know whose it is?" I keep looking. I can't find it. I may be losing control of this group of teenagers I have to face every day.

The day's lesson is shot. This is what pisses me off. Some sixteen-year-old has fucked up my schedule. And I can't fix it. I suspect it's Armando and then I know it's Armando. I can tell just by looking at him. I know. He knows I know. Yet he smiles. I think he looks like Alfred E. Neuman on the cover of *Mad* magazine. He even has the gapped tooth. I must regroup. He asks to go to the bathroom, and I let him.

Ticktock, ticktock, ticktock.

Now he's not even in the room, and the phone rings again. Sounds like it's been moved. But I got nothing. And the anxiety begins to kick in.

Finally, one student, a kid from the drama group I had cast as a freshman but later had a falling-out with, comes up and says, "The phone is in the bricks." The Berlin Wall bricks, the ones the Reagan-enthused kid made for his project. I look over there and read the word *Freedom* mocking me from the bricks' place of honor. The phone is supposedly hidden there. Okay. I wait. I don't want to blow the kid's cover who told me the phone's location. I think.

There's a white button on the wall you can push to call a dean for help. Deans are important people, just below the principal. They can suspend students. So the button is generally used only for major reasons,—when fights break out, that sort of thing. But I don't want to use it now because Armando's back from the can, and I don't want to tip him off that I'm on to him. I want a dean there to catch him in the act. So I slowly make my way to the back of the room, tell the kids to read a brief section in their book for tomorrow, and I use my phone to call Mrs. Grudge, the Department Secretary/Assistant/Admin, whatever they call her.

"Listen," I whisper on the phone, "I got a problem here in my room, and I need a dean. Can you call down there and have them send up Stevens or O'Connor?" I have good rapport with these two.

Pause. "That's what the button on the wall is for," she replies.

Mother of God! I try again, "Look, I need help here." The anxiety is moving up a notch. *Ticktock, ticktock.* "Just call down there, will you?"

"No, push the button, that's what it's there for."

Now this really pisses me off. All right. I go to the Berlin Wall bricks to get the phone. My plan is to find it, bring it to the front of the room, place it gently on the desk, then stand on the desk just like Robin Williams in *Dead Poets Society*, and stomp that fucker to dust.

But the phone's not there.

I signal the drama kid over, and he says, "He moved it." I ask him to come out in the hall for a second. He's hesitant, but I leave him no choice. See, I want to catch Armando in the act.

"He did this last year with Mrs. Gorman."

"What?"

"Yeah, he did it last year for months."

Gorman was an elderly woman, fragile. I suspected she drank at work, and she had retired last year. She got in trouble once for telling a student from Saudi Arabia, who wore the scarf thing on her head, the bursa, that she looked like a terrorist.

"He did it all year. Phones ringing every other day. Gorman said she must be hearing things. She thought she was imagining it. Drove her crazy. Literally."

"And no one ever told her?"

He shook his head.

Now I am extremely and utterly pissed. Gorman was a teacher who shouldn't have been teaching, but to torment her like that. The phone starts ringing again. Okay, fuck it. I press the button on the wall, and the loud speaker comes on, so everyone including Armando can hear. I ask for a dean to come to my room.

"For what? Is there danger? Is it serious?"

"Just send a dean please."

"Well, why?"

I disconnect. Fuck! *Ticktock, ticktock, ticktock, ticktock, ticktock.* I look out the door at the back of the class, and I see Leaffler in a meeting with one-third of the department. It's all the freshman teachers. They are having a grading day, whereby all teachers grade a bunch of different students' work to see if they are all on the same page. The boss isn't grading though, just supervising.

Suddenly, two Campus Supervisors burst in. The kids call them NARCS. Now I am shouting.

"Take Armando to his dean and let him explain why I am sending him down! Tell the dean, Armando, how you rigged a phone to ring in here to disrupt MY CLASS!"

Armando goes ballistic. "It wasn't me! You have no right. That kid finked on me. He's a fucking liar, and he put the phone there, not me!"

I'm breathing heavier, and I consider maybe he's telling the truth; but I don't think so, and I yell at the NARCs, "Just take him!"

But I figure I have to get down there myself. There's only ten minutes left in the day, and I have gotta explain the whole fucking story as I hear Armando yelling as they take him down the hall. *Ticktock, ticktock, ticktock.* So I go across the hall and politely, as cool as possible, ask Leaffler if I can see her. I need her, but she says, "I can't right now, I'm in a meeting." And again I can't fucking believe these assholes, so I try again, "Hey, Ms. Leaffler, listen to the tone of my voice. I need your help *now.*" And it's again, "I can't *right now*" and I see Ms. Sorinski, who is in this meeting, rise and start my way because she knows what the fuck is happening—*ticktock, ticktock, ticktock, ticktock*—and I say, "Hey—" and the boss says "What is it? What's so important?" and I'm fumbling for pills, but Sorinski gets there too late, and I go "Mother of God. I told you, I need some"—*ticktock, ticktock*—"fucking help" and the water is rolling down my face and I'm thinking about Armando and the dean and the phone, which I think is still ringing, and the water is rolling down my cheeks and I'm sitting on the floor in the hall, taking the drugs, and Sorinski tries to calm me and the boss walks into my class, and I see O'Connor, the dean, and then I don't remember, and the bell rings.

School is out for the day.

CHAPTER 7

The Chick Character Assassination Conspiracy

I have a nagging to explain my attitude toward women because it affects so much of this piece and has caused many self-introspective moments in rereading what I have written so far and where I am aiming to go. Some readers have suggested I am sexist. I am not.

I think women are great, wonderful people—at times, confusing to understand. I have been told in at least one conversation that "Oh God, you are so male." Not sure what that means. I have noticed that women when collectively alone, explore events and experiences many men just don't get. This is the proverbial "girl talk," "girls night out" type of thing. There are two specific issues I wish to focus, call it big picture and little picture. First, issues relating to fairness and equal rights and so-called political visions. Women should be free in society, and in every other way imaginable, to do anything and everything men are allowed, permitted, legally protected to do.

I voted for George McGovern in my first eligible Presidential election and, to this day, consider the man to be the wisest and most humane politician I have ever had the pleasure to hear (I was fortunate to be in the audience to see him one magical night at the University of Illinois in Urbana-Champaign at the same Foellinger Auditorium where we would perform *The Laramie Project* some twenty years later). George McGovern's politics are mine and were mine and, barring some unforeseen ideological intervention, will always be mine. This extends to my support for the women's liberation as it was once known and for laws protecting women from sexual harassment, unequal pay and gender discrimination.

I became further enlightened about women, when I began to understand how the decks were initially stacked intentionally or not by Constantine around AD 400. I'm no scholar in this stuff, but I did minor in Classical Civilization, studying the lives of the Greeks and the Romans, their beliefs, cultures, and so on. Two things happened, as a result of seeds planted by Constantine and his boys to try and solve certain cultural conundrums.

Once Christianity caught on, the powers that be needed to meld the two existing belief systems—Christianity and the Greco-Roman deities. While that happened slowly over time, the bottom line is that Saturnalia, the end-of-the-year solstice celebration, was replaced by Christmas, and Easter, originating in part by the Anglo-Saxon goddess of spring, Astarte, reflected the cheering on the return of the robins and the grass and blossoming trees. This made a perfect tie-in for the celebration of the Resurrection. This is the CliffsNotes version from my memory, but you get the drift.

Now as far as God was concerned, the Greeks and the Romans had a slew of polytheistic pagan deities in their heavenly team photo, but the Judaic-Christian tradition only has one, or three if you throw in the Holy Trinity, and Catholicism pushed Mary, Mother of God (an alleged virgin who gave birth to God's son, swaddling). Bottom line there was no room for Greek deities. They had to go. As a result, women got screwed. Lost were strong female archetypes like Athena, goddess of wisdom, or Artemis, goddess of the hunt, and Aphrodite, goddess of love, and so on and so forth. So who replaced them?

I don't want to go all Dan Brown *Da Vinci Code* here, but when they put together the New Testament, female role figures were left on the cutting-room floor. Remaining were Mary, the Mother of God, and Mary Magdalene, who they turned into a whore. Now Magdalene is not depicted as such in scripture and is mentioned more times in the New Testament than any apostle, *and* she was notable enough to be there for the crucifixion and the resurrection. But something else happened to her over time; she was confused with, first, Mary of Bethany and, second, the woman who anoints Jesus's feet with oil. A real culprit in this character assassination was Pope Gregory the Great in AD 591, creating, as Richard Hooper describes in his book *The Crucifixion of Mary Magdalene,* this cosmic mathematical equation: Jesus's feet + ointment + hair + Mary of Magdalene + Mary of Bethany + sinful woman = Mary the whore! QED. Throw in Eve, the instigator, for good measure, and you are left with a very thin choice of female role models.

This lesson has been hammered home *ad nauseam* for eons—women are pure and virtuous or they are whores and devious. Throw in the Islamic curricular wing of female scholarship, and what you have is a public relations spin of cosmically universal proportions that is impossible to overcome. Eve is the bad person in Genesis, menstrual cycles are a God-ordained curse, sex is original sin per Matthew Brady in the Scopes "monkey" trial, and women have had to fight this barrage for centuries.

Athena—dead! Aphrodite—dead! Artemis—dead! Not that I am promoting a polytheistic belief system, but from a female perspective, all these strong images/role models were replaced, probably by a bunch of whiskey priests at the Conference of Nicaea, into the Virgin Mother of God or prostitutes. Choose! Pick! What a menagerie of options.

We are all victims of this belief system which grew through time into the Great Chain of Being, on which I will elaborate later. Through this Cosmic Chain, everything on Earth is connected to God and everything in heaven.

Women who remain unmarried are somehow off the chain. They aren't married, they haven't found a man, so what's up with that? Well, they become witches, another outstanding female option. Once this stuff becomes ingrained in your belief system, it is very hard to get it out. The Salem witch trials were 1692. Ever read Arthur Miller's *The Crucible*? It's all right there.

As I said, we are all victims of this, men and women, me and you. I met my spouse in 1972, and we were married in 1976, but I asked her to marry me on our second date (people didn't really date, it was just "hanging out," but I asked her quite quickly). Why?

Because I was blessed at just that moment with a spiritual insight that impressed on me *this is it*, as well as my distaste for the entire ritual of courting. Did he call? Did she call? Am I going too fast or too slow? What is he or she really thinking, really feeling? It's a bullshit experience, particularly if you're a teenager overwhelmed with insecurities about self-image and being deluged with impressions like the cover of Seventeen or Cosmopolitan magazine, which not so subtly sends the message "If you don't look like this, you suck."

For me, I have found there are limits, case in point when my wife finally said yes (she had never said no, but waited), I knew she would keep her last name. I was fine with this, realizing that society had evolved by treating women as pieces of property and requiring them to take the last name of her new "master." I knew the phrase "rule of thumb" began to describe the legal width of a branch with which you could beat your wife. I knew the term honeymoon comes from a one-month span of time where caveman Org knocks his favorite chick on the head and drags her to a cave for thirty days of indoctrination. So many ways women got screwed once those seeds were planted.

However, my wife also stated that because she was not a piece of property, she would not let her father walk her down the aisle to give her away. While sympathetic to the underlying philosophy, I saw the pain on her father's face because to him, this was a treasured moment, and he didn't get the point of not letting him go through with the ritual. In fact, I tried to talk her out of it because I sympathized with him. The man was crushed and I thought this was unfair. On our wedding day, my wife and I walked down the aisle together.

The second part of this lesson occurred when our newly printed checks arrived in the mail. Our names were in the upper left-hand corner; my wife's full name was on top. My name was under hers. It was not even alphabetical. I looked like the butler. I confronted my wife about this, and I insisted we reprint the checks. She couldn't believe it, but I couldn't live with it, so the checks were reprinted.

What does that tell you about the evolution of male and female roles?

CHAPTER 8

Thick as a Rubric; Students in Boxes

The first inkling of trouble for me was the forced introduction of rubrics. I'd never heard of them, didn't use them, thought they were counterproductive, taught students nothing, and their primary purpose was used as a cop-out for teachers who were (A) afraid of parents questioning their assessments or (B) lacking the confidence to grade an assignment.

This all started before Leaffler was promoted to Instructional Coordinator—a position, incidentally, I encouraged her to go for—a position into which I thought she would quite nicely fit. We had been equals before this, but I encouraged her to become my boss. We had never had anyone in that position full time, but I thought she'd be great. She was hesitant, insecure, but there was only one other candidate, an ex-marine type, and I thought she would be just fine.

All this occurred, of course, before the phone-behind-bricks incident and after the Caitlyn tragedy; and even with my intermittent anxiety issues, I thought she'd be okay—and most importantly, we'd be okay. I thought she was perfect for this kind of theoretical job because it got her the hell out of the classroom where her ongoing fear and distrust of males dominated her teaching techniques.

One memory that stands out particularly strong is her fear of parents criticizing her grades. That's why she so readily embraced the rubric concept of grading, which was somehow being pushed on all teachers from all corners.

A rubric is nothing more than a matrix—a square visual presentation up one side and down the other that puts student achievement in a box. For example, down the left side of the box, you might have categories for a written composition: Thesis, Development, Support, Transitions, Mechanics, and some overall Total. Across the top of this box, you might have Excellent, Very Good (trendier teachers might substitute "Almost There"), Meets Minimum Requirements, and Needs More Work. These categories are totally fucking arbitrary and are supposed to let the students know how they did, where they can improve, and to easily grasp the result of their efforts on the assignment.

For teachers, the box concept made grading much easier because you could quickly read the paper, circle the appropriate box for each concept, and lay on the grade. Leaffler allayed her fear of parent criticism by relying on the circled boxes to justify any grade in case someone criticized her analysis (like the parent of some young male she punished because she did not like him) by—*ta-da!*—showing them the rubric. "Look," she might say, "here's how the grade was determined by this rubric." Of course this was all bullshit.

The whole rubric concept was very convenient, very formulaic, and ultimately a total waste of time. Most importantly, the rubric is unsound educational practice. I used to openly say in department meetings that "Rubrics are used by teachers who do not know how to grade papers." While cementing my reputation as a maverick, it caused some tension among my colleagues. So be it; they were being sold a crock of educational cow manure.

While this was never explained to me mano a mano—or to a lot of other males in our department—somehow the women all knew the rubric boxes were designed to replace the standard approach of grading students, writing meaningful and witty comments in the margins, and at the end, writing a meaningful paragraph thoughtfully commenting on the students' ideas. Why witty? Because that's what they'd read.

I have been accused of being sarcastic or even mean to my students, but I knew I'd connect. They called me by my last name, which I couldn't correct because they'd say, "No way, man, you're one of us." I might say out loud to a student whose paper contained nonsensical sentences, "Hey, Henderson, were you stoned when you wrote this? Yeah? Maybe? Tell you what, I'll give this back to you—you can turn it in tomorrow for full credit, and we'll call this a rough draft, dude. Deal?"

If a student is a flower growing and ready to bloom, the rubric system uprooted the tulip or the daisy or the rose and brought it into a dark, greenhouse laboratory to be analyzed by scientific fertilizer aficionados when all that was really needed was the personal attention of a good gardener.

That's the difference between the two systems of learning.

Anyway, students would read your comments and ignore your boxes. I continually asked the kids, holding up some rubric, "Are these helpful? Do these make learning easier?" The answer was almost a universal "no." Over time, I created an unofficial "focus group," and the results rejected the boxes. Students did not get the mumbo jumbo that was written therein.

Not to be overly technical, but for example, take box one, "Thesis." Under "Excellent," you might read "Thesis is excellent, clear, concise, and is fully supported throughout the paper"; this same sentence would change across the boxes to "mostly clear and some support" to "somewhat clear with some support" to "weakly" and, finally, to "nonexistent." They would just change a few words going down this academic evaluation ladder, and you think the kids didn't get this sham? Hell, I spent hours in meetings where we would argue the right choice of words, as if our collective expertise would somehow find the right words to revolutionize contemporary education. I will use a cliché here: all we were doing was annually rearranging the deck chairs on the *Titanic*.

See the boxes. See your work analyzed. See the bullshit. Watch whatever lights were in your eyes dim. All flowers beware: sunshine is limited, and fertilizer is abundant. And you wonder why American education sucks?

Say a student turned in a paper, as I once received, with virtually no capitalization. The rubric teacher would circle the box under "Mechanics," which would say "Basic grammatical rules need improvement"; and if said teacher was powerfully motivated, a comment might be added off to the side, "capitalization." What I would do is circle each and every uncapitalized letter and write, "Please go back and visit your second grade teacher to review rules on capital letters." If same student, say, properly capitalized the name Abigail, I would circle the A and write, "Wow! Excellent use of capitalization! Way to go! Keep it up!" These were juniors in high school, for God's sake.[1*]

And the result? They'd laugh. I made sure they got the humor. I remember, in this case, the paper circulated throughout the cafeteria at lunch and was read by about half the student body. I was considered "cool" and the kids got the drift and dug the humor. I treated them like adults, and they appreciated it. And they learned.

Better yet, Conrad was on my side. In team meetings with the other American Studies team, which included Leaffler and another history guy, Conrad asked, "You know, I went through college for four years plus, and I never once heard the word rubric. What makes it the thing to do now?"

"Neither did I, and I just finished my teacher certification classes about a year ago. No mention of *roo-brick*," I added with a splash of sarcastic emphasis.

Leaffler responded with some mention of a workshop we had all attended, and I said, "But nobody said we had to use it. There

---

[1*] This capitalization business is the focus of study guides and grammar manuals, yet there is another way to look at it. Capital letters can be used for emphasis, or code, or for whatever the writer aims to do. For example, I am reminded of a statement made by Bob Dylan in D.E. Pennebaker's documentary *Don't Look Back*, which focused on Dylan's 1965 tour of England. When being interviewed by an overmatched magazine writer, Dylan springs a verbal harangue on the interviewer on many topics but also includes the following.

Dylan: "Every word has its big letter and little letter. You know the word know... the word k-n-o-w... you *Know* the word capital K-n-o-w? Like each of us really *Knows* nothing. I'm saying you're gonna die, you're gonna go off the earth, and you're gonna be dead, it may be twenty years from now, it may be tomorrow. So am I. We're just gonna be gone and the world will go on without us...."

See the full exchange at:

https://www.youtube.com/watch?v=mnl5X5MQKTg

was no dictum sent from on high. So who's pushing this now?" "It's the way education is going," she replied. She seemed, even then, to be tuned to some secret society that she was in on but we weren't. I said, "I'm telling you, my kids don't like the boxes. It's impersonal and demeaning."

This toggle was one side of my backstory with Leaffler; the other side was my role as mentor. For whatever reason, she would often ask me what I thought or what I would do about a whole gamut of topics, from discipline to the dress code to lesson ideas. That I was older was part of it—some twenty-plus years—but somehow, her insecurities locked on to my bluntness and decisiveness as a soundboard to quell her fears. And we often fought together for the same causes. I remember we were both adamant about moving the Peter Weir film *Dead Poets Society* to the junior curriculum from the sophomore because the themes are perfect for the Nature and Transcendentalism unit about freethinkers like Henry David Thoreau, Ralph Waldo Emerson, and Walt Whitman. Also, the school had some arcane rule that students could not see the same film twice (in four years of high school—horrors!), but Leaffler and I got that changed.

Sometime later, after Leaffler had been promoted to the boss, *Dead Poets Society* was a catalyst for a parental call to one of our three principals about a scene in the film where Charlie "Nuwanda" Dalton, holds up, a *Playboy*-esque picture of a buxom naked woman, while he reads a poem on the other side. The film is set in 1959, and the action of Nuwanda and the boys is quite typical of the time and setting—a private boys school with no girls. For a parent to be upset about the brief scene, let alone a principal, was ridiculous.

But, ironically, that wasn't the parent's concern. Instead, it was the exploitation of women; that the use of a nude foldout was demeaning to women and that the scene in the film should be skipped. She was furious of the depiction of women as sex objects. Who "woulda thunk"?

So Leaffler had to talk to the principal about how to respond to the parent, and she sought me out first because, as she said, "My first thought was 'What would you do?'" I advised her to tell the principal that we had shown the film for years with zero complaints, to reinforce how the film beautifully fit the lesson, and basically to tell the principal to take a chill pill. I also offered to call the parent myself. I was continually astonished how a phone call from a parent could instill such fear in my peers.

Whether it was over a grade or a film or anything else, the standard answer from me was that we were the experts when it came to educating young adults. Leaffler once asked me if a parent questioned a grade I gave a student, and I didn't use the rubric, how I would I handle it. Answer: Identify the concerns, offer to let the student rewrite the paper at no penalty, but the bottom line I would strongly communicate is that I am a professional educator, no different from a lawyer or a doctor, that I know how to evaluate and establish student grades, and if they wanted a conference to talk about it, come on in. I strongly believe this, and that's why I think teachers are just like lawyers and doctors and should be paid accordingly.

Not everyone can be an effective teacher. The best teachers are specialists like lawyers and doctors. And yes, there are ineffective people in all three vocations, but I rarely hear people screaming that doctors and lawyers are overpaid. (They are, for what they contribute to humanity as a whole, and are, for the most part, a dime a dozen. Not so with the effective teacher.)

Because if you are changing a young person's life, what price would you put on that?

CHAPTER 9

Suffering the Beauty of the Drake Shuffle

I was in seventh grade when I was first exposed to the Drake Shuffle. I was the manager of the basketball team (the guy who sets out the ball racks for practice and picks up the towels), and the coach was, no kidding, a guy named Bob Hope. He taught the team—and me, by just watching—the Shuffle, used, as you will see, when the team has no dominant scorer. It's the kind of thing that works for a team with five quick guys of no big size who share the ball and the points. It's a totally fascinating strategy of movement that is complex in its simplicity and also has a Zen flavor to it, emphasizing movement without the ball and total selflessness. An article in *The New York Times Magazine*, written by Sam Anderson about Phil Jackson's book *Eleven Rings*, describes the beauty of the Shuffle. Anderson writes:

> Of the many plays that Phil Jackson diagramed for me, the one I couldn't stop thinking about was something called the Drake Shuffle. The scheme was invented in the 1950s by a coach in Oklahoma, to be used by teams that lack a dominant scoring threat— no Wilt Chamberlain or Shaquille O'Neal or Michael Jordan to dump the ball to and get

out of the way. Jackson described it to me as a "continuous offensive system," which means that—unlike many plays, which have a definite endpoint or morph into something else when they get too much pressure—the Drake Shuffle never stops. You could run it, theoretically, forever. All five players move in coordinated motion, taking turns with and without the ball, until they've exhausted an elaborate cycle of screens and cuts and passes—at which point the play doesn't end but starts all over again, with each participant now playing a different role within the same cycle. Everyone on the floor keeps moving, probing, trading off.

The Drake Shuffle sits at the center of a particularly Jacksonian nexus of ideas. It's a scale-model democracy, a metaphor for the life cycle, a parable of the Buddhist idea of rebirth, one of the Lakota Sioux's sacred hoops. Jackson's career itself, with its endings and renewals, its retirements and unretirements, seems like a kind of existential Drake Shuffle, played out over 45 years. He's gone from player to coach to retiree to whatever it is he's doing now: cooking, writing, gardening, hiding, self-promoting, advising weary pilgrims from his sacred mountaintop, tantalizing struggling teams, driving endless Internet rumors. He's in, he's out, he has the ball, he doesn't have the ball, he's moving, he's moving, he's moving."

And that was me, too, going from business to journalism to freelance writing to teaching—constantly interrupting my life. It's a beautiful thing to be part of, but, I discovered, a terrible thing to have done to you.

A superstar arrived at our school in the persona of Ms. Mazona Drake, a rather tall athletic redhead teacher who once asked me if I wanted to box—she actually held her fists up—and who was also assigned the role of girls' basketball coach. Everyone loved her, including me. Everyone wanted to be her friend. She was outgoing, vivacious; students and teachers adored her. It was because of her name that the Drake Shuffle popped back into my brain. One day, I found some articles explaining how to teach the players the ballet-like movement of the Shuffle. I copied them, put them in a folder, and gave them to her as if I was bestowing on her presents of gold, frankincense, and myrrh.

Sometimes it was so hard to get her attention; you felt like you were standing in line. When I had a free moment and a lane opening, I drove directly to her and dropped the Shuffle package in her hands. I briefly explained it, suggested she might want to give it a go with the girls' hoops, and gracefully bowed away. She gazed at me with deep, mysterious blue eyes and merely nodded. Gift received, and I was, as they say in the educational game, dismissed.

At first, Ms. Drake seemed to be best buddies with Ms. Pick, who was my friend too, which I thought might endear me to the new phenom. She was buddies as well with Leaffler, who was a teacher when the phenom arrived, but eventually Leaffler became her boss. Drake was so good she "accidentally" was named Outstanding Teacher of the Month in our department four times in a row (this is from some thirty potential candidates), not because she did anything outstanding, but because she was—as Arthur Miller portrayed Willy Loman's greatest desire in *Death of a Salesman*—well liked. Not just "liked," but "well liked."

And oh-my-God did this four-award-in-a-row fiasco create a brouhaha because she was nominated by three different people who all claimed they didn't realize she had been previously a winner. These are meaningless honors, but they are done in front of the entire faculty, and it looked like the only person worth a shit in Communication Arts was Drake. I thought it was hysterical because this award was a certificate that meant absolutely zippity-doo-dah, a token, an "attaboy" pat on the back that let everyone else in the school know this person was, well, well liked. Comparatively, I was responsible for bringing our drama kids to the state festival four years out of eight when you can go only every other year, and I never got a fucking certificate. So there.

And then I began to hear things about the Drake. She'd be friendly and then ignore you. She had a smile for everyone, hiding a vicious temper. And, another member of the growing club, she hated men—or had been disappointed by men. You know, all this hoo-ha was floating around, but it was pretty much kept between the women in our department, who seemed to be growing like clones of a feather. You had to creatively eavesdrop or practice camouflaged lurking to be in on all the dirt.

Their clothes were like unofficial uniforms: tight short skirts with colored hose and, most importantly, stunning high heels in a splendiferous spectrum—turquoise, bright cherry red, Kelly green. The coup de grâce for me was when I went into Leaffler's office one day and found, in a high circle around the room, twenty-five framed drawings of various high heels. These were interspersed with blown-up covers from *To Kill a Mockingbird* and *The Great Gatsby*. It showed where her hidden priorities lay.

At the same time, these women, these educators, were all very attractive, or close to it. One, who appeared to be an airhead, was actually a semiprofessional ballet dancer who had taught at Oxford or Eton or some other upper-crust London school. She played the airhead but was undercover brilliant. And her buddy, a petite blonde who drove a flashy European two-seater, seemed to adore her and vice versa. (She once rose at a teacher's workshop, where we were given some mundane three-minute writing assignment, and read out loud an "Ode to Her Dancer," which left nothing to the imagination regarding her feelings.)

Another was a tall, brusque, humorless Germanic type who enjoyed arranging my bookcase in order and creating labels for each section; doing it, she told me, "because she liked it." In reality, she could not stand disorder. German also had a background in theater, (was she my replacement?), and I cringed in meetings when she brought out trite colloquialisms like "Let's get all these dead white males off the reading list."

These women also traveled together, usually to Florida over the December winter break or to Isle Royale in Lake Superior or, during the summer, on long Rocky Mountain adventures. But they usually went alone; no boyfriends or husbands allowed. It sure looked strange to me, particularly when little signs like "What happens in Florida, stays in Florida" began appearing around the Communication Arts cubicles.

Following Caitlyn's death, the school created a Performance Award in her name, given to the student who exemplified spirit and poise in any field of the arts. At the year-end award ceremonies for the students, I would traditionally present this award and served as a liaison with Caitlyn's family in choosing the recipient. This was always a highlight for me because I could speak knowingly about her, and why this person was chosen (in the beginning, it was often theatre kids), and I also had a flair for public speaking. I could make the kids listen. I was not afraid to tear up as I spoke (no kidding), and I would often get laughs from the group as a whole. In short, among the students, I was "well liked."

One day, I was informed I wouldn't be needed to present the award, that a new committee—made up largely of these women—were creating a more special way to present them. And again, oh my God, when year-end award day came, it looked like the Oscars or Golden Globes. All these women in strapless sequined gowns literally dressed in a Hollywood-wannabe grotesque "fashion." Granted, they had asked two stooges to wear tuxedos to not make it too obvious, but I was appalled. I remember saying something to Principal Storm that I was surprised there wasn't a banner overhead saying "Available for Dates." This display was not about the awards or the kids; it was all about them. As any prom-bound young lady knows, it's always about the dress. The next year, they got rid of it.

At one time, Drake summoned me to her classroom via e-mail for a private meeting. Her e-mail said to be there by three thirty. Recall we are on the same level, both Comm. Arts teachers, but I showed the e-mail around and the reaction was "Woooh," as in "Be careful." Pick was gone by then, but we had talked on and off when she returned to the States, and she had filled me in on how she and Drake "were the best of friends" until one day, Drake just cut her off. Pick even asked to meet with Drake to clear the air, but got nothing.

The final assessment was that Drake used people as far as she needed to and then, if they could do her no good, let them go. Others, per Pick, had the same experience.

I entered Drake's classroom. She shut the door.

"I want to talk to you," she said. "I don't like the way you treat students."

"Funny, I don't like the way you treat adults." Didn't miss a beat, and we were off to the races. Or I was because I exploded all over her. I told her she had treated Pick like shit. I told her that while she may not like the way I treat students, the students and their parents do, and who the fuck was she to criticize me—I had taught longer and was older. I told her she was a "classic climber"—sucking up to people just to get ahead, and she didn't give a shit about the kids. I had teared up by now, and I noticed she was crying, but I went on anyway. I told her she didn't appreciate or even acknowledge the Drake Shuffle, that she was rude and cold and unfeeling. The longer this went on, the more she recoiled, and I buried her with "You know, I used to think you were someone pretty special, that you had a real gift, but now that I really see who you are—now that we've gone beyond the high-heel sneakers and the Leopard-Skin Pillbox Hat, I see you in a whole new light. I see who you are. You're nothing but a fat girl with a lisp."

Somehow, the meeting ended, and there was a moment of "let's forget all this." Right.

After that, Drake was promoted to a Dean's position.

She was proving quite the successful climber.

CHAPTER 10

How to Build a Ticktock Swamp

Somehow, after the Armando-bricks-phone fiasco, things temporarily returned to whatever normal is considered to be. Leaffler was somehow appeased; as I recall, Armando's phone was taken away for a week. There were still two of his friends in the classroom, but as stated before, four could become a gang. I could handle three. And one day, a new student transferred from another American Literature class meeting the same hour as Armando's. This reshuffling of students happened frequently at the beginning of the semester, but it didn't take me long to realize this new student was not transferring for schedule reasons; he was changing classes because he had found his friends.

Let's call them Armando and the Mindbenders, alluding to the 1960s Manchester band Wayne Fontana and the Mindbenders (the band recorded a beautiful song called *Groovy Kind of Love* in 1965, later covered by Phil Collins), and let's call the Mindbenders Frick, Frack, and Frock. The new kid was Frock. What was a manageable mess quickly became a four-ring circus, and because I knew Leaffler had to approve any student transfers, I went to her to complain only to find she had not signed the transfer, but a counselor did—turned out to be Conrad's wife. We got along well, so I bopped on down to her office—where I met wall number one.

"Well, yeah, I signed it. But it was not my idea. I was told Frock was a good kid, wasn't connecting with the other teacher, and wants to 'find himself.' He wanted your class."

"That's very touching, actually, but he's not trying to find himself. He's trying to find his friends. And guess what, he's found them—Armando, Frick, Frack, and Frock. What was a potentially manageable three-student alliance has become a gang. I want Frock moved back."

Ms. Conrad paused and said, "Look, off the record, I signed it, but the request came from elsewhere—a higher up."

She looked and said nothing. The only higher up in this scenario was the Dean for her team, her de facto boss. He was a solidly built soccer coach who had played at the school back in the day, was a homegrown star, and was—in addition to being a Dean—the head soccer coach of the varsity team. And the team was good. He had his share of clout and looked it—a buff dude who regularly shaved his head; hence his nickname, Mr. Clean.

"Does Frock play soccer?" I asked her. Pause. Longer pause. Finally, she nodded, smiled, and pointed her pen toward the office of Mr. Clean. Without saying anything, she told me all I needed to know.

Mr. Clean was out for the moment, but I contacted him later in the week. Overall, he seemed decent. I once ran into a friend of his from way back when in a bar, who extolled his good-guyness.

When I found him, he initially tap danced around the Frock issue and said he had nothing to do with moving Frock to my class. This was an absolute and obvious lie and he knew it and I knew it and he knew I knew it. But then he brings out his hey-c'mon-buddy skills and elaborates about what a great kid Frock is. He actually says he didn't move the kid, but Mrs. Conrad did, and Leaffler. I mean, didn't I know Leaffler was the only one with the authority to move Frock? I watched this hand-washing Pontius Pilate routine as he went on and on about what a great kid Frock is and yada yada yada bullshit squared times yada cubed.

I went back to Mrs. Conrad, who confidentially said she'd love to see Mr. Clean say to her face in front of me that he didn't order the Frock change—of course he did—but technically, she moved him in but needed Leaffler's blessing. She kept emphasizing that "technically" Leaffler was the only one who could "officially" move him, so the Pilate hand-washing tap dance was growing into a minimusical.

So it's back to Leaffler. Yes, she approved the move because it had come from a Dean (though not really), and she was reluctant to move Frock back. "Okay, fine," I said. "Then let's move Armando back to Frock's old class." I kept emphasizing that three of these kids are manageable, but four are a gang, but Leaffler was hesitant to move my discipline problem to another teacher. I calmly explained that Armando minus Frick, Frack, Frock is very manageable and emphasized that the chemistry of the four together created a witches' brew of Macbethian proportions.

She wasn't budging. I said I wasn't finished with the issue, but I would talk to her some other time and put the whole thing in writing, which is exactly what I planned when I reached my desk. I visualized spelling out the whole scenario including Armando's phone-behind-the-Berlin-Wall shenanigans, and basically how three manageable students morphed into Armando and the Mindbenders, a quadruple quagmire.

Before composing this e-mail, I experienced a sudden moment of enlightenment. I made a quick visit to Armando's dean (there were four deans, and students were grouped by their last name, A to F, G to N, M to S, and T to Z). The guy I needed to see was a man named Mathis, who had had confiscated Armando's cell phone for a week following the singing bricks incident. Mathis was really sympathetic to the predicament and endorsed moving Armando to the class Frock left to even the playing field. He even took a moment to call Armando's counselor, who was also familiar with the amazing moving of Frock to my class, and she agreed moving Armando seemed logical. But—and this is a big but—neither one of them would put this agreement to my plan in writing. Mathis reminded me that the only person who could technically move Armando was Leaffler. Okay, fine. To further strengthen my case, I went next door to see Mr. Clean and Mrs. Conrad. They also endorsed the switch, but again reminded me that *a la* the boys in William Golding's *Lord of the Flies*, Leaffler held The Conch shell and was the only one who could technically move Armando. More yada yada yada bullshit yada.

So once more, it's back to Leaffler. I revisit the scenario, logically lay out the proposal but she says she won't move Armando unless Mathis—Armando's dean—tells her to move Armando, which I knew politically he wasn't going to do (unlike the bolder Mr. Clean who moved soccer boy Frock and defied convention) because Leaffler had to agree to okay the move.

Unbelievable! Leaffler wants the deans to do her job for her even though I bent over backward to lay the groundwork to make it simple to do, and persuasively showing it was the right thing to do—but noooo!

To review, Coach Mr. Clean moves soccer boy Frock into my class, unknowingly becoming the de facto creator of Armando and the Mindbenders, and Leaffler approves it. But when I explain how Armando and the Mindbenders have become the Hells Angels, she won't move Frock back—and she now also adds, a bit vehemently, that she won't move Armando either even with the invisible endorsements of all the relevant key deans and counselors, and even knowing of my growing anxiety issues—even when I lay out the fairness of the issue. War!

Leaffler goes on to say this is my class, and it is my job to manage the situation and I remind her that this is her department, and she is the only one to placate the entire hair-ball mess (*ticktock*) and that it appears she lacks the "testicularity" to make the move and (*ticktock*) that no one—and I mean no one—would care, and I mean *no one*, if she moved Armando out and (*ticktock*) she was just being frigging stubborn and was afraid to make any move at all (*ticktock*), and she was over her head in her job if she couldn't do something so easy, just signing a piece of paper and still, she said she wasn't moving *Anybody* out of my class, that it was my job to manage the switch and then I asked her why she made the switch in the first place and answered the question myself (*ticktock*), telling her that because she was new in her job, she was too chicken to tell a dean no *ticktock*, but was also too chicken to tell me yes (*ticktock*). When she stood up and screamed at me, "I'm not moving Armando!" I backed off and waited a few seconds.

And stared deeply in her eyes to see her soul, and there was nothing there but a dimming flame; so I very calmly said, "He goes or I go."

Very cool, very stoic, staring, watching her fear process. And walked out of her office knowing she was too afraid to make that big an issue of all this crap.

So on Monday, Armando was moved to a Mrs. Tanks, who was off that period, and stayed there for eight weeks. No problems with him or with my class.

Leaffler backed down, but I knew this was far from over. As an aside, student Frack wrote me a long note at the end of the semester how the unit on Transcendentalism (more on this unit later) made him realize he had been wasting his opportunities, disappointed his parents who had come to America from Korea to give him a better existence, and my class had changed his life. That's what we're about here—Changing Lives!

Ticktock.

CHAPTER 11

Storm Clouds

Principal Storm arrived in the middle of all this, well after Caitlyn's death, after the promotion of Drake to Dean, but probably right before the Armando's bricks event and the introduction of the Mindbenders, Frick, Frack, and Frock.

In fact, I think I met Storm before any other teacher. I was in the school in late July rehearsing a bizarre attempt at an experimental theatrical work, and the outgoing principal was meeting with Storm when I walked by the two and was invited in.

"This guy," said the man who was retiring and whose job Storm was assuming, "this guy puts on college-level quality theater, best high school productions I've ever seen. He's taken our plays downstate four years out of eight, and you can only go every other year." Storm's eyes lit up. "I love theatre," he said, and we shook hands. As I recall, he held on to my hand longer than was usual for a first greeting—and as I looked into his eyes, I felt an initial bond. The man had a soul.

The summer show that year (I'm thinking now this was the summer of 2010) was a vigorous compilation that included scenes from three Pulitzer Prize-winning authors, David Auburn, Lanford Wilson and David Mamet, which I entitled *Jupiter and Orion.* It was a haphazard display of short to medium to longish scenes, the anchors being Wilson's *The Great Nebula of Orion,* Mamet's *No One Will Be Immune,* and Auburn's *Fifth Planet* thus the *Jupiter and Orion* bow around the package. I won't get into how far out these were, but the theme of the state festival was "Master Class" or something close; but they were encouraging bold, experimental works, so I put this menagerie together. That show was the first one under my direction that Storm saw, and I remember his wistful post-performance comment: "Do you ever do plays with a cohesive plot?"

After that initial meeting, the bond was reinforced at a first-week awards ceremony in our school cafeteria; with all the seats available, Storm sat next to me. We joked around; neither one of us could read the program due to the small type the first time I wondered how old he was, and he displayed a marvelous sense of humor that matched mine—a rarity. Again, I sensed a connection.

The second show we did that year was *Macbeth*, an aggressive staging that stretched the actors, tech people, everyone to the max. I was sitting in the cafeteria with Biff before the show, and Storm walked in with an attractive younger African-American woman. Biff and I nodded at them—and collectively raised our eyebrows. It was an unspoken question communicated across the table: "That his wife?" I'd heard Storm was divorced, but no other information about his not-at-school life. No big deal, of course, but I wanted to find out, and later in the week, started creatively querying regarding Storm's marital situation. No one knew.

A couple of days later, at the beginning of my first period Acting class, Storm strolled in and came right up to me with a photo of an attractive young woman of color. Smiling, he said conspiratorially, "I understand you were wondering about this person. This is my daughter." And he gave me this wink and left.

This told me a few things: one, he made the effort to bring in the photo, and two, took the time to personally show it to me, but three, he had obviously heard I was asking about him, and four, once he heard, he was interested enough in my curiosity to personally explain who the person was. He didn't have to do any of those things, and through all the off-stage drama that was to follow, I found it important to keep that in mind; through it all, I always felt there was some kind of hidden karma between us even though I was to become disappointed with him from time to time.

Storm continued with these periodic little gifts for me; he knew I had a passionate interest in the assassination of John F. Kennedy, and one day, he walked in and gave me the *Saturday Evening Post* magazine from December 2, 1967, with a cover claiming *"Three Assassins Killed Kennedy."* The article was written by Josiah "Tink" Thompson, subsequently well known in conspiracy circles, and one of the first to question the Warren Report's conclusion of a single bullet passing through both JFK and Governor Connally, causing seven wounds, and coming out *pristine*—the word they used to explain the condition of this miraculous piece of ammunition, dubbed the magic bullet.

Hell, there were more bullet fragments left in Connally's wrist and leg than were missing from this magic bullet, also known as Commission Exhibit 399. I'm sure not a lot of this mattered to Storm, but for a conspiracy realist like me, this was treasure, a real collector's item. He said he was cleaning out his garage; the fact that he thought of me was a real charge.

At the same time, Storm gave me a painting one of his former students created of a pair of large eyes on a plywood board. Connoisseurs of *The Great Gatsby* will understand his offhanded comment that "I can't remember if this is supposed to be 'Owl Eyes (a minor character) or the eyes of Dr. T. J. Eckleburg"—in the novel, a billboard sign referred to as the "eyes of God"—"but either way," Storm continued, "I thought you might appreciate it."

Eventually, there was another connection; Storm knew I was a Salinger devotee, but it went—subconsciously, I assume—somewhere cosmically beyond that. In the summer between my graduation from Rich East High School in Park Forest and my freshman year in Urbana-Champaign, two buddies and I went on an odyssey to find Salinger in Cornish, New Hampshire. Though we never found Salinger (great road trip, but we didn't know the locals would send us in circles to protect the writer's sanctimonious privacy), it was during that trip, that I fell in love with New Hampshire and Vermont and the entire area. I made a promise to myself to settle there some day— hopefully next door to my new friend J. D.

Many years later, my wife and I celebrated our thirty-fifth anniversary by flying to Syracuse, New York, renting a car, and doing a semiplanned road trip of our own through the greenery of New England. We visited the baseball Hall of Fame in Cooperstown as well as checked the museum of Natty Bumppo's creator, James Fenimore Cooper, for whom the town is named. To my surprise, at the Farmers' Museum, the Cardiff Giant was exhibited. The 10-foot tall Cardiff Giant was one of the most famous hoaxes in United States history. It was a purported "petrified man" uncovered on October 16, 1869, by workers digging a well behind the barn of William C. Newell in Cardiff, New York. The hoaxers wanted to feature the "giant" as an actual fossil. P.T. Barnum got a hold of it, among others, who charged admission to see this unique archeological miracle. Mark Twain wrote a hilarious ghost story about the giant, showing the gullibility of human beings, and Conrad read the story to our classes every Halloween. I sent Conrad a photo of the "fossil" right on the spot. I had no idea the farcical piece of stone was in Cooperstown. An unexpected find.

We also hit Bennington, Vermont, to visit a friend of my wife's, and then into Southern New Hampshire, where we experienced Mount Monadnock from Thornton Wilder's *Our Town* and other small towns, before heading to Cornish.

When I was talking to Storm one day about this trip he told me he owned property in New Hampshire just down the road from a public library. When he retired, he hoped be the Head Librarian. I asked exactly where his land was and found it on our trip—a barren field with a red flag tied to a stake. I also found Salinger's driveway. He had recently passed away—but my wife wouldn't drive up the hill because it said "Private." I should have walked up myself, but didn't.

All this was later, of course, but it preceded the big incident that serves as the catalyst for this story.

CHAPTER 12

"I Got Your Back"

Every year, teachers at the school filled out goals. Depending on who was in charge of your department, this was a no-sweat bureaucratic formality or a hassle. This speaks again to the teacher evaluation process because it starts with goals then observations in the classrooms, forms and more forms, and culminates with an overall final rating of excellent, satisfactory, or unsatisfactory. When I started, the first three years (later changed to four) were key because that was the time given to decide if you were meant to be a teacher or meant to do something else. Before that period, a teacher could be dismissed—no questions asked. And again, this was taken seriously with new hires, the thinking being that span of time was enough for anybody to conclude that someone wasn't qualified to teach.

But after that—tenure! If you reached tenure in the education game, for them to get rid of you, you had to do something really bad. I mean really, really bad like repeatedly showing up for work drunk. The key word is repeatedly because if it happened once, you were instructed to go on the Employee Assistance Program and receive free medical help for your problem. You could get fired if you were tenured if you had sex with a student (happens more often than you think). Even then, you'd get suspended with pay and have to go to court. But you were done in the classroom. But if you turned into a shitty teacher or were not seen in the first three years to be a shitty teacher, you were pretty much set for life. And there were a lot of shitty teachers with tenure.

A lot of this had to do with who was doing the watching. Those in positions to evaluate—the climbers—or those interested not so much in teaching but more in making as much money as possible, such as your Instructional Coordinators, Deans and Counselors, Principals and Assistant Principals—these people with often little training to evaluate anything, clueless as to who was or wasn't a gifted teacher—these people could make horrendous decisions. Politics played a role. But still, if you were in that position and wanted to get rid of a tenured teacher, it would be easier to move the entire school across the street. This is what annoys the shit out of people not in education; they are used to the corporate lifestyle where building a case is easier—there is probably no union and no tenure. I once fired a guy in the private sector. If I was doing in the private sector what I have described here, I would have been fired several times.

The reason this does not happen in the world of education is because of the power of the teachers' union. That strength gives them a choke hold on a community because of the threat to strike. Some of the power is for reasons you wouldn't think of, such as an impending strike at a high school whose football team is predicted to be a powerhouse. If a strike results in the forfeiture of one game, the public suddenly gets very interested in the negotiations and will pressure school boards to settle so their kids' football experience will not be jeopardized. The fact is, the general public is more interested in the football team's record than the teachers' salaries; they see that as a comparatively smaller issue against Johnny's team taking a loss, dropping in the standings, and perhaps derailing a championship run.

Another issue that sticks a potential strike right in the face of the public is child care, particularly in districts that run kindergarten through twelfth grade. A few days of lining up immediate emergency childcare for two working professional parents presents huge problems, and again, whatever the teachers are striking about fades in comparison. The high school kids view a strike as extended vacation, and the youngsters are left to roam the streets en masse. Most parents of six-year-olds don't give a shit if teachers want a three percent raise. "Get the kids back in school, whatever it takes" becomes this group's mantra, and again, pressure is hammered on the publicly elected school board members to cool their jets and cave.

This is the strength of a tenured union, which negotiates strong contracts because their vocations affect almost everyone with children. Add on to that, that the teaching job is not easy, that teachers are, as a rule, underpaid for the stress and the hassle and the rigor of the job, in my opinion (as stated earlier, I believe they should be paid as specialists akin to doctors or lawyers), and you have an unmovable, unified working force.

This, then, ties in to the process of how teachers are evaluated. Underneath it is an implied evaluation process. And the only reason a teacher evaluation becomes an issue is if some moral line has been crossed or politics intervenes, and a few people decide to go out and "get" somebody. And this is where the process becomes downright nightmarish.

In 2010, I gave Leaffler my goals as per standard operating procedure. Quite frankly, I don't remember what they were, but I know they were pretty generic. For my two Acting classes, I wanted to better blend the kids in my class to make a stronger after-school drama club by performing rehearsed scenes after school with the drama club as the audience. For American Studies, Conrad and I wanted to work on stronger coordination with the other American Studies section—which Leaffler herself had just quit. This was a sore spot because Conrad and my section always had kids wanting in from the other class. Kids of ours assigned to the other class—at the semester, rosters would change to accommodate schedules, so you'd lose some kids and add new ones—these kids would corner me in the hall and plead with me to save them. Why? Because Leaffler and her successors made their class too boring, too rigorous, showed minimal interest in the students themselves, and failed to understand what it took to make lessons personally relevant and life-changing.

Counselors were always complaining that our section was in such demand that it had become a problem. This is when the movement began to break up Conrad and me—don't reward the section all the kids want, just break it up and make both classes boring. Anyway, that was one of my goals, to make both sections more in sync. I had something about American Literature, probably trying to incorporate more of the Harlem Renaissance, the period in the 1920s when African Americans moved to urban cities and rediscovered their culture—or invented it anew. Slavery allowed little room for culture, aside from singing gospel and the blues.

We went through these goals, and Leaffler out of the blue says, "I'm adding another goal—improving classroom management."

"Why?"

"Because of what happened last year when you freaked out about Armando and the phone."

"If you recall," I remind her, "a lot of that occurred because I got no help, and you wouldn't transfer Armando."

"Well, Storm is concerned, and he is going to personally observe you both semesters, as am I."

"I'm not scheduled to be observed."

"Too bad. There's a new sheriff in town, and he's concerned. I'm not the only one."

Ticktock.

"Wait a second, Storm is concerned about my classroom management? Why? Why is Storm concerned about that?"

"It's not just me."

"Why is Storm concerned suddenly about my classroom management? What did you tell him? Huh? Somebody told him something."

"I told him what happened and how you freaked out."

"You did, eh? Did you tell him that a lot of that was your goddam fault for not leaving a meaningless meeting when I needed help? Did you tell him I went to the hospital with an anxiety attack? Did you tell him I'm seeing a doctor and am on medication? Who brought this up? What are you trying to do?"

"It's not just me."

"You keep saying that. What does that mean? It's not *just you*?" Then it hits me—Drake. Mazona Drake. Sure. The two of them ganged up and told Storm I was a problem. Drake was a Dean now and Leaffler an Instructional Coordinator, and that was enough to force Storm to do something, especially if they both brought it up together in a group setting.

Unfortunately, it was at this time—as usual—I went into a full-fledged panic attack. Water flowing from the eyes. Hyperventilating. I wasn't done shouting at her, but I don't remember what I said. The bell ending school rang, I grab my briefcase, and I run downstairs to see Storm. He is in a meeting where he sees me through the glass. I walk in and ask him if I can see him, and we go to a vacant office and I scream, "You're gonna observe me? You're gonna observe me?"

Hands on my shoulders. "Yes. Calm down. I have to do this."

"Why? What the fuck happened?"

"You have got to settle down." So I do.

He says, "I got your back on this one. We'll observe you, and at the end, I want to be able to say '*Yes!* This man is a great teacher!' Relax. I got your back."

A moment of silence.

"I have to get back to this meeting. Pull yourself together and go home." And he leaves.

CHAPTER 13

"The Whole World Is Watching"

Storm let me know that the order of observation of my classes would be by him, the Activities Director—Mrs. Sad, and Leaffler. Here's how the whole observation thing works. You have a pre-conference where you bring in a filled-out form describing the makeup of the class, what the lesson is, your objective for the lesson, basically what you are going to teach in order, what "measurable" results you are aiming for (this was new—everything had to be measurable when evaluating teachers), and if there's anything in particular you want the observer to focus on like some troubled student or whatever. In my time at this school, these forms were handled rather loosely. In fact, when I filled out one for Storm, I printed mine in purple felt pen, untyped, asked if he minded, and he said, "No, these forms are ridiculous."

The worst, though, is the actual observation process. The observer comes in stealthily, supposedly not trying to be noticed by the students (yeah, right), bringing in a laptop computer, and types everything you say and do for fifty minutes. Where you go, who you call on, what the students say, who you don't talk to, where you look, how you transition from point to point, on and on, writing down everything, and I do mean *everything*, that happens in that class on that one day.

Think about that. Your boss comes in and watches everything you do, looking for anything to criticize, like someone looking up your butt with an electron microscope for any kind of dirt they can find. It is a humiliating and hellacious experience particularly for someone with an anxiety disorder.

I asked Storm at some point during this evaluation procedure, how would he like it if the Superintendent sat behind him all day and wrote down everything he said, did, if he sneezed or farted, and then nitpick the shit about the whole day—why did you do this, why didn't you do that, and so on. And Storm replied, "No, because that's what we do here." Insanity.

So think about your career in any fashion, and that's what they do—they take a snapshot in time of one brief moment and then decide who you are, what kind of a worker you are, all based on this random moment. It's *in-fucking-sanity*. And when you consider what you really should be doing—changing lives—this snapshot shit will not be able to capture those crucial skills.

I haven't said much about my psychiatric team support—The Duke and his team. Duke was a king in his field, and the more I needed to discuss and analyze my feelings, I was assigned to a counselor in his office, a perceptive gem at handling patients like me, named Canella. Her standard line after listening to me pour out my frustrations, fears, reaction to Caitlyn's death, and the unexpected anxiety issues was simply "I get it." She was sensational at taking the jumbled junk in my head and rearranging it in a way that made sense to me. She knew I had been through a lot, and when I eventually left her as cured as I could be, she remarked, "When you came through my door the first time, you looked like death. And the change I've seen in you going through this and surviving—and you are a survivor—is remarkable. The difference in the person I met and the one I'm looking at now is indescribable."

When I explained the observation strategy of Storm and all, her first comment was "It's like asking a man in a wheelchair to go up a flight of stairs and then give him a grade. It's probably doable, but how unfair."

Canella had an edge to her. She had been similarly victimized in a professional situation, and she not only understood what I was after—which was some kind of vindication, revenge, clarifying what the hell was going on—she supplied me with some readings that showed me she did indeed get it, including this one that I really liked, written by Claire Damphous.

French Revenge

Though you have hurt me, I will show you. I will get my life in order. I will heal. I will get well. I will become fabulous. I will surround myself with love and loving people. And I will love them. I will grow beyond you. And you know ... I might even forgive you.

No turn the other cheek there, boy. I loved the "I will grow beyond you" line because I felt that way in my gut, which helped me throw caution to the wind and fight for what I knew was right. Even if I went down—whatever that was going to be—I was going down making sure *they* knew that *I* knew I was right. I had reached that point after the observation game plan was announced and kicked in. I thought the people going after me were real lightweights, so lightweight, in hard cold fact, that there were times I felt sorry for all of them because they were just weak people on all counts: self-image, self-awareness, spiritually, morally, and all in all pathetic.

But when I had these softer moments, Canella kept me focused, on track, and fed the "I'm mad as hell, and I'm not going to take it anymore" ire that needed the occasional stoking in my soul. Canella wielded a pretty powerful poker.

I asked Duke to write a medical note describing the potential harm these observations could cause me because the panic attacks were still hanging around, and while the medications helped, there were still moments when I became watery-eyed and breathless. Even though I still had my network of support, I wondered if going through this shit—which these assholes had decided to make me endure—could possibly cause me some stress-related long-term harm, which I naturally wanted to avoid. So Duke readily wrote this letter to Storm.

> **To whom it may concern:**
>
> **I am writing this letter to you at the request of my patient. He is a teacher at your school. My patient has a diagnosis of a significant anxiety disorder. He is being treated for this and has been compliant with all aspects of treatment (therapy and medications).**
>
> **It has been brought to my attention by my patient that he recently has been "observed" as a tenured teacher more often than he has been accustomed to. This has caused him heightened anxiety and stress. It is my recommendation that this process be reconsidered for my patient, as this may contribute to his heightened anxiety symptoms.**
>
> **I hope this letter is of some service to you. If I can be of any further assistance, please do not hesitate to contact me.**

Sincerely, and Duke scribbled his signature. You would have thought this might force whoever was making Storm do this—and I still felt this was not his idea, but he was being pushed by Drake and Leaffler—to back off and come up with some other method to evaluate my performance, but no way. I wrote to Storm, urging him to reconsider this, but he wrote me back that by contract, they could observe me whenever they wanted and not tell me why, and furthermore, such a system was sound educational practice. I even told him that yes, contractually he could do whatever the hell he wanted, *but he didn't have to*. He said the observations would continue and even stated something to the effect that the doctor's note did not specifically say anything would happen, but just that it might and that anything could happen to anyone at any time, and that while he appreciated Duke's note, he wasn't swayed by it.

I had turned another corner. I was observed by Storm in my acting class, which was a breeze. I announced to the kids two weeks in advance he was coming and picked the outstanding kids to perform their scenes—

as the previous principal told Storm, this was college-level-and-beyond theatrical experiences. I had a feedback style for the observing students. They had to raise their hands to critique another's performance, leading with the question, "I have an opinion. Would you like to hear it?" That gave the students on the stage total power in the evaluation process.

We started class with a ball game to break tensions and build class camaraderie, which I had picked up from my master's work. Starting from the beginning of class, all students were required to memorize the opening to Shakespeare's *Henry V*:

> **O for a Muse of fire, that would ascend**
> **The brightest heaven of invention,**
> **A kingdom for a stage, princes to act**
> **And monarchs to behold the swelling scene!**

Every student had to memorize this. Every day, one by one, I marched the kids up on our stage, complete with our own little stage light set up and an actual stage, to recite until everyone had it cold. Then I would put them in a circle with a soccer ball, and they would set a pattern of who threw the ball to whom, randomly. Then they would cite one word at a time as they tossed the ball. This was done slowly at first and then faster and faster.

Over time, sometimes weeks, we would do this every day as a warm-up; and then one day, I added a second ball that would start with a different person, and later on, a third ball with yet a different person. So a student could, on ball one, have the word *princes*, on ball two, the word *O*, and on ball three, *invention*. Faster and faster the balls circulated among the group of about twenty students.

Then, hopefully, at some point, the sense of self would disappear.

These balls would be going so fast the circle and the balls would come alive—the individual was lost, but a greater sense of ensemble would literally be created. In my fifteen years of using this method, only two or maybe three times would that magical feel of selflessness be obtained. There's a Zen concept involved here, but man, oh man, when this would work, it was cosmic. The circle was alive; the self was invisible.

It was exactly like the Drake Shuffle. Ongoing, never-ending, pure kinetic energy, and built a group into a new creation. I still marvel at how this all works in all matters of life. Storm asked about this exercise after he'd observed it—believe me, he had no idea what the hell was happening—but I could tell he was impressed. I told him one class passed around four balls while, reciting the first four lines of the Chorus from *Henry V,* at the most rapid speed I had ever experienced. I am sure there are more levels to be found with this exercise.

I still run into alums, who, if I cue them with "O for a Muse of Fire," will immediately go into the entire Shakespearean stanza. If you think about it, that's a life changer too.

That was the first lesson of this new observation period. I had two more that semester. One was on Transcendentalism as part of a unit on the Romantics, which is fairly complex for anybody, not just high school-aged students. Mrs. Sad, the Student Activities Director, but former gym teacher probably thought Transcendentalism was a new category in a gymnastics meet. I will talk about this lesson in another chapter, but the only feedback I remember receiving from her was to write the assignment on the board.

Leaffler was next and, man, was I nervous for this one, knowing in advance I was going to get hammered. The subject of the lesson was the wrap-up on the poems of Robert Frost. Why I did this, I don't know, but when I went in for the pre-observation conference, she asked for the pre-observation form, and I didn't have one. "Don't believe in forms," I told her. "Even Storm thinks they're dumb." And she didn't say a word. She just wrote some things down and asked me if there was anything I wanted her to focus on. I said, "Student-centered lesson," which was a buzz phrase of sorts and just the thing I knew she would critique. This would both haunt and help me.

In retrospect, I think I was subconsciously setting up to fail because I knew there was no way to win. Why I did this, I don't know. I have a sixth sense sometimes about these things, and by coming off somewhat cocky and communicating what a waste of time this all was, I was somehow sensing that this was a good thing to do. Again, I don't know why.

The lesson was a bust, and I knew it from the get-go. I had twelve poems in all. Kids in groups of four presented—I knew the poems backward and forward my favorites being "Mending Wall,"

"Out, Out—," "Acquainted with the Night," and "Stopping by Woods on a Snowy Evening." I had given the kids some solid prep on interpreting the poetry. But group work is chancy because some key member of the group might be sick, or some kids just won't do anything, and other reasons. This lesson had some of all of these. At the same time, I hit a number of literary topics that I had previously introduced: context, comprehension, interpretation, allusion, and some others. I thought I had my bases covered.

Leaffler spent her time typing away, and at the end, she asked me how I thought it went. I said it could have gone better but, overall, quite well. She said, "Well, we will cover that at the *post*-observation meeting," and she left.

And then at that meeting, where she basically just asked me to read her remarks, she dropped this bomb in one of the evaluation boxes:

> **Be much more specific in how students should use reading strategies to determine meaning. The recognition of literary devices is actually a comprehension standard, and the use of them to form a conclusion is an interpretation standard, and the additional target of context presents another challenge. It seems the students were being asked to interpret and provide context (which is actually a 12th grade standard, not an 11th grade standard) for most of the lesson and it might have been clearer if students could see the progression more clearly ...**

I'm reading this aloud, and I say, "Wait a minute, wait a minute, let me read this again." Pause. "What the fuck does this mean? Who wrote this shit? It makes no sense. What are you trying to do? Someone else wrote this, right?"

"No," she said, "I wrote it."

"Well, my God, you know this is capital *B* bullshit, right? This is what's wrong with education. You lose focus on the big picture and get smothered by theory and … bullshit. It's the only word that describes this. How can you do this? How can you write this? And put your name to it? How? *How?*"

The meeting ended, I don't remember how, but I walked by my friend Rocket's class where five other males were eating lunch, and I said, "Guys, listen to this. This is from my latest observation." And I read it to them V*er-fucking-batim*. And their eyes just glossed. No one knew what any of it meant. "We gotta talk like that now?" one befuddled dude said. Five decent teachers, and they have no idea what this means. I looked in their eyes and I saw fear.

Then I immediately went to two female teachers and read it to them, and they knew exactly what it meant. "We came up with this over the summer," a person I considered a friend told me.

"Were there any men in these meetings?" I asked.

"No."

"Why the gender split?"

This all came to a head at the official review meeting in Storm's office about two days later. Storm, Leaffler, and Mrs. Sad—who, by the way, was my immediate supervisor in my role as the director of plays at the school—all attended with their filled out little review packets. I had read them all, and while the first two were relatively harmless, it was Leaffler's that was the most damaging to me. In the spirit of true apparent fairness, I was allowed to speak first and decided again to blast them with my pent-up frustration at this entire charade. In my own mind, I was somehow teaching my students a lesson in how to stand up for what you believe in, as we studied in the Civil Disobedience movement in our textbook, which focused on aforementioned Transcendentalists, Thoreau and Emerson as well as Martin Luther King Jr., whose "Letter from Birmingham Jail" was a key lesson in our literature book.

I said, "This whole exercise has been a sham from the get-go. I was told that I was to be reviewed by Ms. Leaffler on my use of classroom management skills due to an episode that occurred last year, where my well-documented anxiety condition—for which, I remind you, I was carted out of this building in an ambulance. This anxiety led to a breakdown in order in my eighth-hour American Literature class and I needed support from my department. This call for support landed on deaf ears. I asked for help several times. I received none, including from Ms. Leaffler and the office secretary. It was this issue, I was told, that you, Mr. Storm, had become aware of in a way that has never been fully explained to me. But what I have found out is this: You Mr. Storm, offered to make yourself available to review teachers who any of your upper management team—your Instructional Coordinators and Student Deans—deemed worthy of your *eyes*, so to speak, and two people, Ms. Leaffler here, and Mazona Drake, were both shouting my name. It was this spotlight brought on me that put you, Storm, in a position where you had no other choice but comply with these two requests."

"That is not entirely true—" said Storm, but I cut him off.

"It doesn't matter. What matters is what got this ball rolling. Now on these reviews, I got nothing, nada, zippity-do-dah about classroom management from anyone. In fact, I asked Mrs. Sad in our talk about my classroom management, and she said, 'Why do you keep asking about that? You're fine." And there is really no other mention of this anywhere. My Activities friend here did say something about "Writing the name of the lesson on the board—"

"Would it kill you to write the lesson on the board—" said Storm, but I cut him again as I was really rolling now.

"I will write the lesson on the head of a pin if it will make you all happy, but I will tell you *if* writing the name of the lesson on the board *is a must*, is *a requirement*, and I have noticed many teachers in our department doing just that, day in and day out, and I wondered who put the word out on this, did I get the memo? No one made a pronouncement saying, 'From now on, each and every day, all teachers will write the name of the lesson on the board, and failing that, you will go to hell." I got nothing on that, which brings me to this, Ms. Leaffler's evaluation, and everyone, please, listen to this—"

I then proceeded to read that raft of bullshit from Leaffler cited earlier in this chapter and went on, "Does anybody know what this means? You?" I looked at Mrs. Sad. "Or you?" I looked at Storm.

"I believe I recognize part of the standards for the American Literature curriculum—" said Storm, but I cut him again.

"News to me. And guess what? News to every other male in our department. I read this when they were all having lunch in the Rocket's room and to a person. Their eyes glazed over, deer in the headlights, they're like 'What the fuck?' But—but I go to several women in the department, and they know all about this interpretation, context is twelfth grade only, and isn't that ridiculous, but listen to the language. This is education? This is teacher evaluation? This is helping me improve classroom management?"

Leaffler finally spoke and said, "You opened the door on that when you asked me to focus on student-centered lesson as something to watch—"

"I did what? I 'opened the door?' What does that mean? I'll tell you what that means. It means you are trying to nail me on classroom management, but you can't, so you try to nail me on this other crap. And when did this become the law of the land? I found out that over the summer, a women's only grouping of teachers came up with this stuff and began implementing it, but told no one else about it. Why? Huh? Why? I'll tell you why."

It was at this point I pulled a highlighted copy of the Keirsey-Bates book on temperament entitled *Please Understand Me* and began to read a description of a certain personality type.

"This is Ms. Leaffler. She's the kind who doesn't tell anyone anything, who expects others to find out on their own what's going on, or if she casually mentions something one fucking time and you don't get it, you are out of luck. It's just the way she is, and that's fine. The world is made up of all different kinds of people, and that's what this book is all about—understanding why two people can drive each other nuts. And look here, this is my personality type, and guess what—our personality temperaments are the epitome of oil and water. But if you will read this, Ms. Leaffler, perhaps we can understand each other better and—"

"Enough." Storm cut me off. "I think this is insulting. I know if someone came to me and said, 'Here's your personality and here's mine,' I would find that very insulting." Then he shouted, "*After all, she is your boss!*"

"*Only on paper*," I topped him.

Storm again, "Here's what we are going to do. We are going to observe you again three times this next semester."

"NO!" I yelled and hit the table. "This ends now. This is over now. My doctors have told you what this process does. It's insane. No more observations."

"I will remind you that contractually we can observe you whenever we want, and we don't have to tell you why," said Storm.

"I know that. But you don't have to. You, Mr. Storm, should put an end to this charade right now!"

And I walked out. I recalled our union representative Barnum was in the building fielding questions from interested teachers, and he was just down the hall. Conrad was the teacher liaison, and I barged into this meeting and told him I wanted to file a grievance.

"You're not going to file anything," he said. I gave him the headlines on the last hour's discussion, and he said, "The first thing you are going to do is go down the hall and apologize to Storm for whatever he may be angry about. Then you'll keep quiet and write up what happened and send it to me."

Conrad was laughing, either half amused or half afraid; I could never tell with him. But I did it. I went back to Storm and apologized for my outburst and told him that is not the way I wanted the meeting to go.

He put his hand on my shoulder and said, "We'll keep talking. I told you I had your back on this one. I hope this doesn't lead to a lawsuit."

I looked at him. He looked away. I never found out what that meant.

That night, I went home, and the vision in my right eye felt fuzzy. I ignored it for one day, but then went to the local ophthalmologist who immediately sent me to a specialist, who quickly surmised I had macular degeneration in my right eye. My mother had it at the time, and he immediately proceeded to inject serum into my eye. In other words, he stuck a needle in my eye, echoing about the punishment for lying.

I lost total sight in my right eye that day. It has never come back. And I wondered if "they" had caused it.

I want to call a lawyer.

CHAPTER 14

Losing My Bedroom: The Myth of Standardized Testing

Whenever it came time to take our annual delay from real teaching to focus on standardized test-time—a spring ritual consisting of your ACT, your PSAT, your ISAT, your SAT, your LMNOP, your whatever—I always told the kids, "If you don't do well on these tests, you could lose your bedroom."

"*Whaaat?*" they would cry, and I told them again, "If you want to save your bedroom, don't blow these tests off."

So I would tell the kids: "Look, these tests are basically worthless in measuring anything except creating a perception of the educational strength of a school or district. Now the key word there is *perception* because what follows from that perception drives the system, drives the economics of a community, and sets in motion an exercise in power that is crucial to the people who run the world—the people with a lot of money.

"No other teacher is going to tell you what I will tell you about these tests. The main reason they exist is not to evaluate what you know, or how good a teacher I am, or to make it easier to get into a good college. These tests do make it easy for colleges to say who is in and who is out, and it does make their job easier, but that is all a sham—and it has nothing to do about how smart you are, what kind of person you are, who knows what, or anything like that. All these tests are, yet again, one more snapshot in time of how good you are at taking these standardized tests at some random point in your lives. And the only way you can do well on these tests is to do something experienced teachers find a real blasphemy—'teaching to the test.' Now, what does that mean?

"It means, to prepare students for these tests, you must look at past tests and go over and over them so everybody knows how to take the test. This is not studying American Literature. This is studying the 'art' of test taking. The problem is that you are not learning anything except how to take a multiple-choice test. And you have to be aware that the people making up these tests try to trick you.

"Oh yes, they do, they do! Let's trick the students! It's criminal in a way. That's one problem. The other problem is that I have seen tests where the questions and answers are just wrong. When I run across these babies, I will announce before the test, 'The correct answer to number 44 is *B*, but everyone fill in *C* right now because that's what the people who wrote the test think is the right answer, and that answer is just plain wrong. So fill in C, but let me tell you why *C* is the wrong answer."

You know what sparked this reaction? I remember one question that pisses me off to this day: it was on an American Literature final and had to do with *"Civil Disobedience,"* which is an essay by Henry David Thoreau about how he went to jail in 1845 because he was protesting the country's involvement in the Mexican War and refused to pay his taxes. Howard Zinn relates a supposed exchange between Thoreau and his mentor, Ralph Waldo Emerson, where Emerson asks, "Henry, what are you doing *in* there?" And the author of *Walden* retorts, "What are you doing *out* there?"

At any rate, I took issue with this question:

> **Of the following, who would be the *most unlikely to agree* with Thoreau's philosophy reflected in the essay "Civil Disobedience?"**
>
> a) Mahatma Gandhi
> b) Franklin D. Roosevelt
> c) Adolf Hitler
> d) Martin Luther King

For openers, the phrasing "most unlikely to agree" borders on a double negative, but even if you change the wording, the question is doomed. The answer the test writer wants is Hitler because he was a fascist dictator who oppressed people, even though everything he did after he took power was technically legal under German law. I surmise the test writer reasoned that because Hitler locked up massive amounts of people and murdered them, he was not a crusader for some unpopular cause, and he would never be considered a Civil Disobedient. Gandhi and King are obvious choices of people who broke the law to prove a point. But what the test writer did not take into consideration is that before he took power, Hitler was a rabble-rouser, attempting a minirevolution in 1923 in Munich and Bavaria and was eventually jailed for treason. He actually wrote *Mein Kampf* ("My Struggle") while in prison, dictating portions to fellow Nazi Rudolf Hess. That, my friends, is a man practicing civil disobedience.

And what of FDR? Well, I'm assuming that the test writer is assuming that because Roosevelt championed extensive change in his four terms to correct economic woes, he was in the Thoreau-Gandhi-King team photo. Wrong. Roosevelt was a rich white man who never spent a day in jail, and if you analyze the way the question is set up, the answer is *B*. However, FDR is such a wacky choice. It makes this whole attempt at measuring a student's understanding of Thoreau's philosophy a terrible exercise in multiple choice whack-a-mole.

Okay, this is, at best, a horseshit question on an American Lit. final. It's a social studies question for God's sake, and it is just not correct. I even went to Conrad and his buddies in the Social Studies department and to a person they agreed (1) Hitler was a terrible, wrong, totally incorrect answer and (2) the question is a perfect example of bad test writing—a really bad question. I tried for three years to get this question changed, but to no avail. Leaffler wouldn't change it. So I talked the students through this before they even took the test. They had never had a teacher tell them the answers before. But one must do what one believes is true and right.

This is how these tests work. Notice the setup; to guarantee a good score requires teaching to the test. In analyzing your basic multiple-choice question, you can usually discard two answers right away assuming the student has any working knowledge of the question being posed. The other two answers are very close; one is right, and one is wrong—but the reason one is wrong is due to some tricky wording or technicality that the test taker has to figure out.

This is not educating anybody. This is teaching to the test, or better yet, teaching *how* to take the test. And teachers know this is not a good way to educate our youth—thus the heresy of "teaching to the test." Teachers have to do it anyway to keep the scores high.

This is what these tests are measuring—how well you can figure out the trick. This is teaching? This is a good way to evaluate how good a teacher you are? These tests serve no purpose unless you're going to be a professional test taker the rest of your life; well then, sure, there may be some value in this, but—my God!—the amount of importance these tests have been given in the world of education is criminal.

Furthermore, I have had brilliant kids write wonderful essays who tank these tests. And I have had kids who haven't done a thing all year get near perfect scores on these tests. Why? Because some kids are good at figuring out the psychology of the test *writer* and some are not. It's the truth. The only way to guarantee good scores on these tests is to teach the test takers how to figure out what test creators are thinking. And as teachers, if we can't do that, we suck. Because we are supposedly to be evaluated on how well these kids do on these stupid tests.

That's why this whole test-taking system has become an industry. Students in affluent communities take test-taking classes outside of school because parents realize how much society places on the importance of these tests, and they will spend the money to ensure Dick and Jane and Spot and Puff all receive a good test score! Yay! Put me in, coach, I can do it! Rah-rah!

There must be a better way to evaluate student performance. Why not just rank everybody based on how they do grade-wise compared to their peers? Wait, we tried that, and that's been pushed out the door.

Have you noticed that more and more schools and more and more colleges are not interested in class rank? Why do you suppose that is? Well, if the kid says, "I was number 2 in my senior class," the college says, "Yeah? How many kids were in your senior class?" See, it could be twelve kids if you go to Ruralville High School, so class rank doesn't really tell us much, does it?

Oh, but these tests, they tell us what we need to know, which is how good are you at figuring out tricky tests. Hell, I am as guilty as anybody having written a number of these tests because with a Scantron machine, they are easy to grade. Particularly at the end of the year when everybody is looking to get the hell out of Dodge and onto summer, summer, summer.

So what's the big deal here? It isn't about the student, that's for damn sure; it's about the country, the state, the school district, the town. These people need to get the scores up, up, up. One lesser reason is how we fare as a country. How often have you heard, "The US is thirty-seventh in math and twenty-fourth in science, behind every other country blah blah blah." We can't have that, so we figure out how to do better on these tests. Ever see the Jeff Daniels clip on YouTube where he is playing the head honcho on the television show *The Newsroom* and the college student asks why America is the best country in the world? The first two experts on the dais go "freedom" or "diversity," but Daniels's character forcefully says, "We are not number one." He then goes on this rant about where the US ranks in a bunch of categories ending with something like "The US is number one in three things"—pause for effect—"the percentage of our people we incarcerate in prisons, the number of adults who believe angels are real, and defense spending, where we spend more than the next twenty-six countries combined, all of whom are allies. That is what we are number one in." And he concludes by saying something like "We are not the best, freest country in the world. Far from it. We used to be." Man, it's powerful. You still may be able to see it at https://www.youtube.com/watch?v=73_ds1xQmD4. Being the best, being first, our kids must score the highest; we must beat the Russians to the moon, rah-rah-rah. The whole fabric of our lives is built on philosophies like these.

And the test scores, what is the real big deal? The big deal is the "saving the bedroom" analogy, and here is how that works. The Boeing Corporation moves their home office from Seattle to Chicago with three thousand employees coming along (these numbers are probably off, but you get the gist), and the first thing they ask after they're told they are all moving to Chicago is, "Where are the best schools?" This question goes hand in hand with "What are the best towns to move to?" And what do they do? They go to the test-score rankings of the average student in a school or district and want to move there!

That is why these scores are so important—because schools with the highest test scores attract a higher clientele, and people want to move to towns where these scores are high. The higher, the better. Can't afford Town X with an average 28.6 ACT score? Well, how about Town Y with a 27.9? Or this town with 26.8? These people will go to the most affluent school districts/schools based on these tests that they can afford. If your school drops a point or two from one year to the next, they are going to bring out the brooms and clean house. Why? School boards who hire and fire superintendents and principals are usually made up of the leaders of those towns, in most cases. And if the school scores drop, fewer and fewer Boeing employees are going to want to move to your town with your shittier test scores. And then what happens?

Prices of homes drop. Your house is not worth as much anymore. This is a major economic problem.

And kids, if the worth of your home drops and your parents can no longer afford to move to a "higher" district, you might have to move to a smaller house and share your bedroom with your brother or sister. You want that? I didn't think so.

So don't blow off these tests. Keep our school number high. These test scores are not about you, the students.

They are about property value. Money. Status. Making the rich richer and the poor poorer. The American Dream is about moving from districts with shitty test scores to those with really good ones. So if your school scores drop, someone has to be blamed, and it can't be the parents who probably never read to their kids, who send these kids off to school unprepared, or there's trauma in the home—whatever the case, it is not the parents' fault.

Gotta be the teachers. They are responsible if our test scores plunge.

CHAPTER 15

The Platonic Conception of Self

This is out of order, but I was observed once more by Storm—which was to be the last time, that turned out to be a wonderful teaching moment for me and, I think, for him.

As a student back at Rich East High School in Park Forest, I began falling in love with literature and literary criticism, a world that often holds the keys to unlock the secret passages behind an author's words. Sometimes in a splendiferous way, these revelations leap out at you, hitting you right between the eyes after the words have been staring you in the face as you gloss over these penned crumbs without thought or introspection. Suddenly, you shift your vision a bit and wham!—right between the eyes, man—you see what is going on with the text.

Right between the eyes like the Zen experience of satori, or sudden enlightenment, often described metaphorically as an opening of a third eye, the *ananda* (source for the brain study of anandamide), unveiling the truth behind the wilderness of mirrors. Salinger's stories often incorporate this concept, and the experience is often compared to answering a Zen koan, or puzzle. Probably the most famous koan is "What is the sound of one hand clapping?" which is prominently displayed on an otherwise blank page beginning Salinger's *Nine Stories*. I'm pretty convinced the popularity of that Zen puzzler worked its way into our culture because of Salinger's use of the phrase as a dedication of sorts to the preface of his story collection. Sadly, the phrase has almost become trite.

Dealey Plaza, Dallas, Texas

November 22, 1963, 12:31 P.M.

Seen through the limousine's windshield as it proceeds along Elm Street past the Texas School Book Depository, President John F. Kennedy appears to raise his hand toward his head within seconds of being fatally shot in Dallas, Nov 22, 1963. Mrs. Jacqueline Kennedy holds the President's forearm in an effort to aid him. Gov. John Connally of Texas, who was in the front seat, was also shot. (AP Photo/James W. (Ike) Altgens)

LEE HARVEY
OSWALD?

PRESIDENT HAS BEEN SHOT
IN THE NECK AT THIS POINT

OPEN WINDOW

LBJ SECURITY DETAIL
REACTING TO SHOTS

I have a passion for puzzle-solving which explains my ongoing fascination for things like the JFK assassination—keep looking, keep digging, and eventually you'll find the true picture. There is a photo of President Kennedy being shot, taken by a photographer named James Altgens—this particular photo is known as Altgens 6 to assassination truth-seekers—which is taken from in front of the President's car. The photo shows, albeit unclearly, Kennedy hit, his arms beginning the strange akimbo motion as he reaches for his throat, two Secret Service agents standing, looking back at the Texas School Book Depository, with a man in the background by the front of that building who looks eerily like Lee Harvey Oswald. Others say it is a coworker of Oswald's named Billy Lovelady. What's the reality?

But if it is Oswald, it means he is not on the sixth floor. He didn't shoot JFK; somebody else did.

The photo shows a myriad of confusing images. One witness reported seeing Vice President Lyndon Johnson's supposedly ducking down in his limousine as the first shots are heard, as if he knew what was coming and the photo shows his protection detail reacting quite quickly. Perusing the picture, one finds a fire escape on the Dal-Tex building—behind the Book Depository—near an open window that supposedly leads to a broom closet of sorts. Some claim to see a rifle pointing out that window, which better explains the placement of the bullet holes in JFK's body than if they had come from the School Book Depository. Images are hidden (it seems) in many films and pictures taken in Dealey Plaza that November Dallas afternoon in 1963; some are believed to be doctored to disguise various things, and you can go mad trying to Look and See, and Blow Up images searching for elusive hidden snipers. This kind of stuff has always appealed to me. Most recently I was introduced to "Prayer Man", who also looks like LHO Search it.

In retrospect, I understand why, as a youngster, I had a passion for the seek-and-find page in *Highlights for Children*, referred to earlier—a booklet we received in the mail or at school, discovering the objects hidden in the pictures, the upside-down bunny lurking in the bush, the hat in the tree, the hammer in the tulips—and so on. Search "Prayer Man and Oswald" on the internet to see him. (https://www.google.com/?gws_rd=ssl#q=prayer+man+oswald).

WHEN MONGREL DOGS TEACH

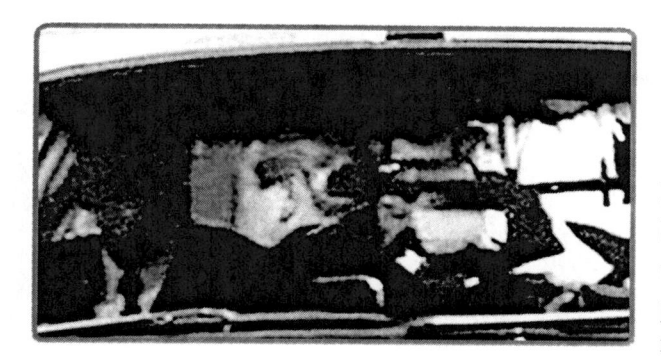

President has been shot in the neck at this point, most likely from the front.

Is it Lee Harvey Oswald or Billy Lovelady?

Open window in Dal-Tex building. Wounds in JFK's body line up more closely from a shot from here.

Is LBJ's security detail reacting a bit early to the shots? Some see a voodoo mask.

I remember Hugh Downs hosting a TV quiz show called *Camouflage* in 1961, where contestants searched for hidden objects in a large drawing on a screen. These objects became more and more apparent as, magically, layer after layer of the camouflage was removed after contestants answered questions correctly. To win, you had to trace the hidden object. At the show's close, one contestant was given the opportunity to have one crack at finding the hidden object in a totally camouflaged drawing, and if that person did it, the reward was a four-door Chevrolet station wagon. Pretty cool.

I view interpreting literature the same way. And so it was that as a teenager, after I read *Gatsby*, I began a habit of reading additional works if an author hit a chord with me. These criticisms about Fitzgerald and his work served as a beacon to find the hidden messages in my quest to fully understand this writer.

Fitzgerald published *Gatsby* in 1925; prior to that, he had published the warm-up for the book, a short story entitled "Winter Dreams" in 1922. These works are well known, but I discovered that Fitzgerald also published in 1924 "Absolution," set in 1885 Minnesota, which is the story of twelve-year-old Rudolf Miller (son of a passionate Catholic railroad man), who is convinced he is going to hell because he lied to a psychotic priest named Schwartz during confession by stating that he, Rudolf, never lies (shades of Nick Carraway).

Only academics and Fitzgerald fanatics probably know of "Absolution." My curiosity was piqued because I read in a criticism that at one time, this story was part of *The Great Gatsby,* but Fitzgerald discarded it. One critic wrote that it was believed to be a section of the book about Gatsby as a young man.

I tracked "Absolution" down because that work preceded *Gatsby*, and Fitzgerald excised it from the novel. Conditions being what they were for aspiring writers in the 1920s, Fitzgerald was able to take that chunk and turn it into a story that could be published. It also explains why the story is awful. You can't just rip something out of another work and successfully let it stand on its own, but Fitzgerald was able to polish it enough, bad as it was, to convince someone to publish it. He was known; he had a hit novel with *This Side of*

Paradise, and a magazine could sell the work on his name alone, even if the story was awful. Or so I surmised.

It took me a while in 1970s Park Forest with the resources available, but I eventually found "Absolution," read it, and remember thinking, "God, this is dark," and kind of forgot about it until I went back to teaching American Literature in 1998 at the age of forty-five. I remember reading some criticism on it, but which ones escape me.

In "Absolution," Rudolf Miller tells the priest during his confession—before he tells him that he doesn't lie—of believing that "I was not the son of my parents." What a bizarre statement from out of left field, jumping out of the page. Bizarre! During the lesson when I teach "Absolution," I instruct the kids to underline that statement, without telling them why. I emphasize the fact that the line does seem to come from out of nowhere. I tell them to make sure that section is marked on their copy. (I had discovered a subtle way to make tons of copies without raising eyebrows in the office.)

I read "Absolution" out loud, as fast as is educationally possible, with a let's-just-get-through-this kind of flippant air, without really pausing for much emphasis. Every student has a copy to make it easy to follow along, and reading the story fast keeps even the disinterested more interested.

I also comment on one more bizarre statement from Rudolf Miller. After lying in confession and believing he is destined to go to hell, Miller begins chanting the name "Blatchford Sarnemington, Blatchford Sarnemington," over and over in a singsongy voice. Fitzgerald goes on to inform us that Miller believes he can become Blatchford when he wants to escape from reality. Blatchford is his alter-ego, one of many weird names Fitzgerald is known for sticking in his works (I was told the actress Sigourney Weaver took her name from a minor character in *Gatsby*). We then discover that Miller can become Blatchford, who is so powerful in Rudolf's imagination that he can "trick God." It's a very brief section in the story—I believe Blatchford is only discussed twice, but I tell the kids to mark that section. Again, I don't tell them why, but I actually check each kid's story to see that the proper sections are, in fact, marked.

We finish the story quickly with Father Schwartz freaking out at the end and Rudolf Miller escaping unpunished for his heresy. He gets away with lying in confession. He isn't struck down by a lightning bolt. God doesn't kill him.

I usually end this with a brief discussion on 1885 Catholicism, how I was raised a Catholic and, being born in 1953, attended Catholic Sunday School (or catechism) every Sunday beginning in 1959. Pope John XXIII changed the severity of the Catholic experience around 1963, but I could tell the kids what it was like to go into that confessional, which I described as a casket upturned on one end, and fear the wrath of Father Lynch, who often verbally accosted me by ordering, "Quit your goddam swearing."

I wanted to give them the sense of fear Rudolf felt by lying in confession and that there was a real fear among my buddies at the time that "God was gonna get ya," if you didn't toe the line the penguin-draped nuns demanded with their rulers and corporal punishment. Hell, I went to public school and only had to go *one hour a week* to this madhouse, unlike my friends who had to go to Catholic school every day. At the same time, I was convinced that those nuns, with their Coke-bottle rimless glasses and their militaristic ways tried to teach us—the public school children, the pagans, if you will—they wanted to teach us in *one hour* what they had hammered into the skulls of the church school kids in *one week*.

I make sure the Catholic kids understand I'm not knocking the Catholic faith, and even ask them how they do confession today, which is a lot less stringent and a lot less severe and a lot less scary. I did everything I could, like Rudolf, to avoid the horrors of that confessional with the sliding window where you can only see the priest's shadow, and could often hear other people's confessions from the other side of the "casket." It is not a pleasant memory.

After "Absolution" is finish, I tell them "the story sucks," and they always whine, "Why did we read it?" I say, "You'll find out." And we move on to "Winter Dreams" before we tackle *Gatsby*. I keep it quick like a mystery, point out some other things we can discover later, such as Father Schwartz's fascination with an amusement park, which is reminiscent of an image on the *Gatsby* cover.

There is a lot of fun stuff for the kids to discover in *Gatsby*. It's a wise and wonderful book. I always treasure the fact that Holden Caulfield in *Catcher* says it is his favorite book. Like in chapter 4 when Fitzgerald describes the first of Gatsby's lavish parties, the tense of the writing suddenly shifts from past to present tense. I ask the kids, "What's different in the writing here?" and wait for someone to raise their hand. This can take seconds or five minutes depending on the class. Someone finally raises their hand, but I say, "Okay, don't say anything yet," and then I get four, five, six, seven hands up, and I say, "Okay, and where does the change in writing end?" And they search the text, figure it out, and we talk about how shifting the writing to present tense makes the party "come alive," as if you are there, experiencing the fun at the same time as the people in the book. It's a literary scavenger hunt. I love it, and my students can easily see it. That's the passion of teaching.

The whole novel revolves around time and the concept of time. Gatsby wants to repeat the past, and when Nick tells him he can't do that, he says, "Of course you can." This belief is part of the scope of Gatsby's imagination that even allows him to consider such a thing. This ability is one reason Fitzgerald calls him "Great" in the book's title. And this theme is effectively dramatized for us when Gatsby first reconnects with Daisy at Nick's small house, and is so undone by the intensity of the experience that he knocks a clock over and then catches it before it falls—he is literally catching time in his hands. Nice.

One challenging passage for my students is several pages into chapter 6. Rumors abound if Jay Gatsby is a bootlegger bringing in hooch from Canada or has killed a man or is a spy. No one seems to know this wealthy man who throws lavish parties for free and invites everyone and everybody; no one seems to know who this man really is. It is in this chapter where our narrator, Nick Carraway, lets the reader in on the truth. Fitzgerald's skillful writing allows Nick to hold on to this information until we are well into the book; after all, Carraway tells us on the second page that he is looking back at events about two years ago from his present time as narrator. Yet at just the right time, he tells us who Jay Gatsby really is.

I begin my lesson for Storm by writing "Platonic Conception of Self" on the board, and remind them they were to have read the first five pages of chapter 6. I eventually read this passage out loud:

> **Contemporary legends such as the "underground pipe-line to Canada" attached themselves to him, and there was one persistent story that he didn't live in a house at all, but in a boat that looked like a house and was moved secretly up and down the Long Island shore. Just why these inventions were a source of satisfaction to James Gatz of North Dakota, isn't easy to say.**
>
> **James Gatz—that was really, or at least legally, his name. He had changed it at the age of seventeen and at the specific moment that witnessed the beginning of his career—when he saw Dan Cody's yacht drop anchor over the most insidious flat on Lake Superior. It was James Gatz who had been loafing along the beach that afternoon in a torn green jersey and a pair of canvas pants, but it was already Jay Gatsby who borrowed a rowboat, pulled out to the Tuolomee, and informed Cody that a wind might catch him and break him up in half an hour.**
>
> **I suppose he'd had the name ready for a long time, even then. His parents were shiftless and unsuccessful farm people—his imagination had never really accepted them as his parents at all.**

And there I stop and ask the kids, cryptically, "Where have we heard this before in this class, this 'not accepting your parents' bit? Hands only please." It's been about two weeks since we read "Absolution," and you can hear their minds grind. They know it, they know they know it, but they can't quite find the connection. For a while, nothing, and then they start—two, five, six, nine hands in the air. "Okay," I say, "where have we heard this before?" and call on the first kid who raised a hand.

"It's from that short story you made us read that you said sucked," says the student.

"Right," I say. "'Absolution.' Take it out please." Rumble, grumble, noise of papers being searched, handing out new copies for those who don't have it.

"Okay, now what did I tell you to mark?"

"The part where the kid tells the priest he is guilty of not believing he is the son of his parents."

Reactions and so on, and I say, "Okay, let's read that section again. What did I say about Rudolf Miller saying that parents bit in the story?"

"You said it was weird and bizarre."

"See the connection? Let's go on." I continue.

> **The truth was that Jay Gatsby of West Egg, Long Island, sprang from his Platonic conception of himself. He was a son of God—a phrase which, if it means anything, means just that—and he must be about His Father's business, the service of a vast, vulgar, and meretricious beauty. So he invented just the sort of Jay Gatsby that a seventeen-year-old boy would be likely to invent, and to this conception he was faithful to the end.**

"Okay," I say, tapping the board where the phrase is written, "let's look at these words—'Platonic conception of himself'. What does this phrase mean?" We knock it around, someone looks up who Plato is, and we get into a conversation about "platonic relationships"—this they have heard of. I ask, "So what is a platonic relationship? What makes it platonic?"

"Friends with benefits!" one kid shouts out.

"Wrong," I say. "Why does that explanation not work?" More discussion. We decide platonic is "nonphysical" and, eventually, "of the mind, an idea."

"Okay, so another way to describe 'platonic conception of self' would be what? Take one minute, talk among yourselves, tell me what you come up with."

Noise, discussion, smarter kids lead the way, and hands go up in the air.

"So what does it mean?"

"It's your idea of who you are." "It's your idea of who you should be." Answers are like that.

"So who does James Gatz think he should be? Who is the 'platonic conception' of James Gatz?"

"Jay Gatsby."

"Bingo. Now take out the 'Absolution' story again. Who is the platonic conception of Rudolf Miller?" This takes a while and I have to remind them what I told them to mark and someone eventually says, "Blatchford Sarnemington."

"Yes" I say. "Now I am going to tell you what you wanted to know three weeks ago—why we had to read this awful short story. Ready?" Boy, I had everyone glued to their seats.

I read the passage from an introduction to *Gatsby* from another version they do not have, explaining that "Absolution" was once part of *Gatsby* and was about Jay Gatsby as a young man, but for some reason, Fitzgerald cut it from the book.

"Okay, so Rudolf Miller is like a young James Gatz, with an alter ego, Blatchford Sarnemington. Let me ask you this—and take a minute to talk among yourselves—look again at the Blatchford section and answer me this, what kind of an adult would Rudolf Miller likely grow up to be?"

It comes almost right away. "If he's Blatchford," one kid decides, "then he would think he's immortal, that he can trick God."

"Would he be an ethical person?"

The class decides not necessarily, but it would be a man who might lie, cut corners, not to be trusted, and so on. If you're the 'platonic conception of yourself,' then you can get away with anything pretty much. You're hiding behind your alter ego.

Now I write on the board Robert Allen Zimmerman, born 1940. This is always risky, but I usually have someone who knows, and today, it's Amy. It takes less than a minute, and Storm is really focused now.

"Isn't that Bob Dylan's real name?"

"Yes." Some from this generation knows him from "Hurricane," the song that made it into the movie of the same name, the story of Ruben "Hurricane" Carter, who "was falsely tried for something that he never done."

I calmly switch on the video projector and show the first few moments of *No Direction Home,* the Dylan documentary by director Martin Scorsese. Within the first few minutes, Bob says this:

"Sometimes people are born to the wrong parents."

I turn off the projector. The lesson reaches the intended objective.

"'Platonic Conception of Self,'" I say, pointing at the blackboard. I then write out as I calmly say, "Blatchford Sarnemington is the platonic conception of Rudolf Miller. Jay Gatsby is the platonic conception of James Gatz. And Bob Dylan is the platonic conception of Robert Allen Zimmerman."

I end the lesson by playing the Dylan song "Summer Days" from his 2002 album *"Love and Theft."* I make sure they hear him sing

> Wedding bells ringin', the choir is beginning to sing
> Yes, the wedding bells are ringing, and the choir is beginning to sing
> What looks good in the day, at night is another thing
> She's looking into my eyes, she's holding my hand
> She's looking into my eyes, she's holding my hand
> She says, "You can't repeat the past." I say, "You can't? What do you mean you can't? Of course you can."

I continue, "You can't repeat the past, of course you can." A brief pause and then, "This song is from Dylan's 2001 album *"Love and Theft,"* which, incidentally, was released on September 11 of that year, the day the Twin Towers fell. This is the only Bob Dylan album ever produced with quote marks around it, and a lot of the words interspersed throughout the whole album he basically intentionally lifted. That line—'can't repeat the past, of course you can'—comes from F. Scott Fitzgerald, *The Great Gatsby*, chapter 6."

The lesson is over.

CHAPTER 16

Amy Knows about Zimmerman in Real Time

"Whaddya mean I can't sue these assholes? They rake me over the coals, and I lose my fucking eye. I'm blind in one eye, Rick. They did it."

"You can't sue them," Rick pronounces, stressing each word.

"It's an obvious one-to-one correlation," I pronounce back. "Stress. Letter from doctor. Stress. Observation. Stress. Meeting. Blind in the eye. Hell, a blind man could see it."

"Now that's funny. You can't do it."

"Why?"

"'Cause you'll lose if it even gets that far. Look, I'm no expert in Worker's Comp. cases or whatever category this falls in. But I did my job. I've called a number of people and macular degeneration is what you got and nobody has any idea, at this point in time, why that happens. It just happens. You say stress and the meeting. Another lawyer will say you had five glasses of wine, and that caused it. Or you had a fight with your wife, and that caused it."

"I didn't have any fight—"

"Or you missed your favorite *Star Trek* rerun. It was scheduled. It was in the TV listings. You turn on the TV, *Star Trek* is not on. It's been beamed to Scotty, and you get upset, and that caused it."

I study his legal diplomas neatly framed on the bright blue wall. I walk around his office. I say "fuck" about six times.

"What is your union telling you?"

"Nothing. No help. Contractually, those pricks can observe me all they want, as often as they want. They don't have to say why. I can't prove anything. They say don't do anything."

"Well, don't do anything. Mother of God, haven't you done enough?"

"They put needles in my eye, Rick. I've had needles in my eye twice, injected with some drug that was meant for horses for some fucking reason."

"What?"

"I don't know. They find this particular drug freezes the bleeding in the retina. They found it by accident. It was used on horses for cramps or stiffness or some equestrian malady, but the state of the art for macular right now is this horse medicine. Used on horse scrotums. They inject it right into your eye."

"Sounds charming."

"You know, all I could think about while they're doing this? That old childhood chant, 'Cross my heart, hope to die, stick a needle in my eye. Or your eye.' However it goes."

Rick makes a sound, not quite a laugh, more like a whinny.

"Why'd we say that? It's like when we said to somebody, 'I won't tell anyone. I promise,' and the person you're talking to doubts you and then you say that chant. That was it, eh? Right? Well, the truth is having a needle stuck in your eye did not hurt as much as I thought. They numb it. You can hardly feel it, and the aftereffect is nothing."

"How long you have to get injected with this Secretariat scrotum juice?"

"Every four to six weeks. Then they take more pictures. I tell you, it's quite a light show they give you."

Rick is a friend of a friend who specializes in legal issues in the education field. He's taken on school boards. He's a teacher's advocate. But he costs. And I have use of the union people for free. I mentioned Rick to them, and they said, "No. You use him, we go away. And we are free." But Rick is my adviser, and the investment appears to be worthwhile. I've known him about a month. I regularly beat him at computer Scrabble. He doesn't mind it. I can tell he likes me. We think alike. He's semiretired, I think, and he has a modest office in a basement of some building and does court work with mortgages and shit.

We are having this discussion about a month after the eye incident but before Storm observes me for the second time.

"So what's next?"

"Well, they say they're going to observe me three more times, and I can't stop it."

"So?"

"Well, I can get creative and do something."

"Why don't you let them observe you, suck it up? Take whatever they say, and let it go. By my count, you have two pretty good observations to one negative one no one understands. Say it comes out four to two. Who is going to look out of touch? Leaffler will, right? You win."

"No. If Leaffler observes me one more time, she wins."

"I don't get that. How does she win?"

"She just does. She wins. I want to stop this shit now because it never should have started."

Rick stares at me. "Are you okay?"

"I'm fine."

"You sure?"

"No."

There is a period of silence. Rick writes some shit down, looking at me, half smiling, half concerned.

"Leaffler will not observe me again. Ever. Count on it."

Rick just stares. "Okay. You're the client. Keep me posted."

I don't hear anything for a while. I tell them about my eye, but they don't say much that I remember. The union head, Barnum, says he has talked to Storm about easing off the observations, but he is noncommittal. Leaffler steers clear for a while. I'm pretty sure she thinks I'm dangerous. I receive another treatment of a needle in my eye.

And then one day, I was told that Storm would observe me again in two weeks. Conrad, like Rick, tells me to bite the bullet and just suck it up, so I do. Storm watches *The Great Gatsby* "Absolution" lesson and then leaves. A few days later, we have the post-observation.

Overall, Storm is effusive. "Man, you were on a roll," he says. I said I didn't think it was a very student-oriented lesson and more of a teacher-oriented lesson, which is the hot thing in education circles—get everyone involved, make sure every student is involved every minute of the teaching moment. As usual, it's more bullshit and totally impossible.

"Yeah, maybe," he says, "but I believe if you have a well-prepared kick-ass lecture in your bag of tricks, you bring it out and just do it. The students were making connections all over the place, and the way you presented the material was captivating, complex. I have a question."

"Shoot."

"What would you do if no one knew Bob Dylan was born Robert Zimmerman?"

I laugh. "It's funny you say that. When I first started doing this in 1999, half the class knew. The movie *Hurricane* about Rubin Carter had been recently released, and Dylan had a hit with the title song, which he wrote in 1975. The kids knew all about that, and some, like Amy, still do, I guess. Also, believe it or not, I had a few kids who were familiar with John Lennon's song "God" off the first Plastic Ono Band album, and he runs through this litany of things he doesn't believe in, 'I don't believe in magic, I don't believe in I-Ching,' and right before the end, he says 'I don't believe in Elvis, I don't believe in Zimmerman,' and then he finishes with 'I don't believe in Beatles.' Well, I tell you I was floored when I heard a young woman named Lithinia say 'I have a John Lennon album where he sings "I don't believe in Zimmerman" but I never knew what it meant.' And others were asking. 'Yeah, I got that record, who's Zimmerman, what's that mean.'" Lennon was asked in a *Rolling Stone* magazine article why he used that phrase, and he replied, 'Because Dylan is bullshit. Zimmerman is the man's name.' And some kids knew that. I was stunned. But since then, every year, the number of students who know that connection is fewer and fewer. But I always had someone.

"You know what," I continued rambling, "that is a reminder of what we assume kids know and what they do not know. When I started teaching, my students were eleven years old when the

Challenger spaceship blew up. The Vietnam War is the Civil War to these kids. As of today, they were like in kindergarten when the Twin Towers fell. Next year, there may be kids who have no memory of it at all. Two years, for sure. What will their memories hold then? First black president? Death of Michael Jackson? Older siblings have an effect on what kids remember *in real time*. Time. It's about time, literally. So in answer to your question, I would have to transition to it in some other way. But on Dylan, today I had Amy."

As the days pass, I notice Storm sees Amy walking the high school halls, and I see him say, "Hi, Amy," calling her by name. She's stunned, but I know why. Storm sees her as the young lady who knows about the Dylan-Zimmerman connection.

CHAPTER 17

"So You're the Kind Who Likes to Be Beat First" / "The Pros from Dover"

Teaching American Studies with Conrad is a major highlight of my educational excusrions. There was a time if someone had asked me if I had a best friend, I would have said Conrad. I think even Conrad would have been shocked by this. I was kind of shocked when I first thought of it myself. Throughout my life, I did not have a lot of people I considered to be my best friend. Offhand, I could name three (I'm not counting my wife because that is galaxies beyond the term friendship), but I have always understood that I am not the kind of person who is easy to be best friends with because I don't warm up quickly to people and have a tendency to keep my distance a long time before I let down my guard.

I had a really good best friend in college, a fellow writer, a real charismatic, popular, top-quality guitar player whose wit meshed magically with mine. I feel I have to mention that Tom was wheelchair-bound since he was seventeen after a bout with Hodgkin's disease and massive doses of Cobalt-60, which ate portions of his spinal cord and left him with lifeless legs. I met him in a dorm cafeteria my freshman year at the University of Illinois in Urbana-Champaign, where one afternoon, we locked eyes and preceded to give each other the patented hard-guy stare for about ninety seconds, with Tom actually wheeling into an aisle of this cafeteria as if he and I, total strangers, were going outside. This lasted until we both broke out laughing, and from that day on, we were friends. It was Tom who convinced me to drop my business major and go into Rhetoric and Composition (U of I may be the only school I know that offers a Rhetoric Major). We had many great times together, but I need to focus on one series of a highly revisited joke as an aside of sorts—moments that are so key to this story I need to reproduce them here.

Like many young men who were in high school bridging the decades of the 1960s and the 1970s, I was introduced to a fantastic world of lust through the works of Harold Robbins. A master of smut and arousal fiction, Robbins penned such books as *The Carpetbaggers, The Adventurers, The Inheritors, A Stone for Danny Fisher, The Betsy*, and tons more and, over his career, sold more books than anyone including J. K. Rowling's Harry Potter books. All contained fascinating and vividly lurid sex scenes that people in libraries and book stores page through "looking for the good parts." I used to read them out loud to a group of guys in high school, who were amazed that someone was writing stuff that was so erotic.

I got a hold of a Robbins book one day (the title escapes me) where some guy was trying to close the deal with a woman who had lured him into a cabana of sorts, but suddenly switched signals on him and started playing hard to get. Robbins, never one to treat female characters as anything more than sexual creatures, carries the scene out a bit, and then after a little while, the male protagonist, taking off his belt, announces threateningly, "So you're the kind who likes to be beat first."

Tom first experienced the phrase one night at some dorm party where we were joking around in a mixed group, and I was talking to some young lady and trying to be suave. At any rate, I'm at this party, and people are high. Tom is watching me from across the room, and since I know I have his attention, I suddenly stand up and, taking off my belt, yell at the top of my lungs to this girl, "So you're the kind who likes to be beat first!"

Now I do this out of nowhere to the girl who goes "Oh my God!" and bolts away, but Tom just clasps his hands together, looks skyward with eyes closed, mouth open, and no sound escapes his person. He is just paralyzed with hilarity. It was a perfectly executed stunt, and Tom loved it. He later inserted the phrase into a short story he wrote called "The Army, the War, and the Women." Tom was a Hemingway-inspired kind of guy.

I'd like to say that was the end of the phrase, but Tom and I would often throw it around. "She looks like the kind who wants to be beat first, doesn't she?" Or just casually over a table in the cafeteria, very incidental: "So are you trying to tell me that you're the kind who likes to be beat first?" It became like our private bond-phrase. When in crowds, he'd encourage me to begin to take off the belt and use the line.

When we graduated, I moved on. Tom stayed at the University of Illinois on his social security insurance checks, the flat curbed world of Illini-land, named the most wheelchair-friendly campus in the country. They even had a bus the wheelchair bound could ride for free, a bus with an automatic ramp and few seats, tastefully referred to as the gimp bus; and I pushed Tom all over the campus, ice and snow, for four years. He was my best friend.

One night in 1986, he called me. I was now married and had a baby girl. We relived everything we could remember we did and laughed so hard through the entire call we had the really good tears flowing. And yes, we relived "So you're the kind who likes to be beat first." It was one of the most memorable and glorious phone calls I ever had.

The very next night, Tom's mother, who was a long-time registered nurse, called me and told me Tom had died. She said he was in a lot of pain. She told me he wanted to give me a message, "Tell him I'm sorry." His health had really deteriorated, and he didn't tell me. I thank God for the call the night before. I thank God his mother was a nurse. Tom was my best friend.

And for a while, Conrad was, in my mind, my best friend, in an osmosis kind of way. We didn't socialize, but I spent a ton of time with him every day at school, and we agreed on so many things and laughed together about stuff just like I had with Tom. When Holden Caulfield asks his former schoolmate Carl Luce at the Wicker Bar what Luce's father, a psychoanalyst, would tell Caulfield to solve his myriad of problems, his ongoing experience of being sickened by human behavior, as Mr. Antolini explains to Holden a few chapters later, Luce tells him that his father would help him understand "the patterns of his mind."

Well, whatever that means to anybody else, to me, it means that for a while, several years in fact, I always felt that Conrad and I had very similar "patterns of mind." As I said before, we used to complete each other's sentences. We laughed at the same stuff and saw the world through the same lens. We were so effective as co-teachers we used to joke about a line from the movie *M*A*S*H** when doctors Hawkeye and Trapper John are dressed in golf attire and flown to Japan in an emergency to operate on the son of a US congressman and basically take over the hospital. An irate female officer, Captain Peterson, was not clued in as to who these knicker-clad men in golf shoes, practicing putting for a post-surgical tee time on the local links, actually were and demands to know what-in-the-hell-is-going-on-here. The script from this scene reads as follows:

> **Capt. Peterson** (*hostile tone of voice*). What are you two hoodlums doing in this hospital?
> **Hawkeye Pierce.** Ma'am, we are surgeons, and we are here to operate. We are just waiting for a starting time. That's all.
> **Capt. Peterson.** You can't even go near a patient until Col. Merrill says it's okay, and he's still out to lunch.
> **Trapper John.** Look, mother, I want to go to work in one hour. We are the Pros from Dover and we figure to crack this kid's chest and get out to the golf course before it gets dark. So you go find the gas-passer, and you have him premedicate this patient. Then bring me the latest pictures on him. The ones we saw must be forty-eight hours old by now. Then call the kitchen and have them rustle us up some lunch. (*Turns to Hakweye.*)
> **Trapper John.** Ham and eggs will be all right. (*Turns back to Capt. Peterson.*)

> **Trapper John.** Steak would be even better. And then give me at least one nurse who knows how to work in close without getting her tits in my way.
> **Capt. Peterson** (*outraged*). Oh! (*Turns to leave and bumps into Nurse.*)
> **Capt. Peterson.** Oh! Fool! (*Stomps out of ward.*)
> **Nurse.** How do you want your steak cooked?

We used to refer to ourselves just that way, Conrad and I, the "Pros from Dover", because we worked so well together. Another bond between us was my interest in the JFK assassination, but more importantly, how my interest turned into Conrad's interest. After showing him the book *Killing of a President* by famed assassination researcher Robert Groden, Conrad became convinced that President Kennedy was killed as a result of a conspiracy. For some reason, he had a trip scheduled to some conference in Dallas, and I strongly encouraged him to go to Dealey Plaza and the Sixth Floor Museum, which is on the sixth floor of the Texas School Book Depository, where the government told us Lee Harvey Oswald fired a broken rifle at a moving target and had two hits in about eight seconds.

I was in class that day, and my cell phone rang. It was Conrad speaking in a semi-spooky voice, and he said, "I'm on the Grassy Knoll." The Knoll is where a lot of people think the shot came from that blew JFK's head off and caused it to move "back and to the left". Anyone viewing the Zapruder film can see that movement, even though those who claim Lee Harvey Oswald was the sole assassin explain that head movement with a preponderance of crap, like jet-propulsion effect or massive head spasms. But here's Conrad, reporting in as if he was calling from the moon.

"I just talked to my wife," he said in that same spooky voice. "I told her I'm on the Grassy Knoll. She called me a nerd."

Now at some time, we had lost or misplaced Groden's book, but I knew that Groden occasionally sold his books in Dealey Plaza by the Knoll, even though the city of Dallas has tried to get him out of there because they view him as a threat—when I consider him to be a patriot. I told Conrad, "Hey, look around for Robert Groden. Maybe we can get a new copy of *The Killing of a President*."

Two minutes later, my phone rings. "I'm here with Robert Groden," Conrad reports, "and he's selling books."

"That's fantastic. Buy one."

He has to call me back, which he does in one minute. "He only has hardcover, but they are two hundred bucks." Holy shit. But I knew they were out of print—I think the CIA made that happen—but I hadn't realized that the price was that steep.

"I'll split it with you."

"Done."

Conrad returned with this beautiful coffee-table sized color book with an inscription from Groden on the inside. "To the Pros from Dover," it read. "Maybe one day the truth will come out, and we will solve this important case. Bob Groden."

Signed and personalized; how cool was that?

Soon after that, I was to lose another best friend.

CHAPTER 18

A Sticker on a Briefcase

This is out of order again, and I only know this because some of it happened before Storm arrived, so I'm putting this around 2007 because Obama was running for President and a plethora of teachers were excited about this, particularly Conrad and me. Also, the teachers were in the middle of settling a new contract, which was an absolute pressure-cooker situation that dragged on for months. There was a bloc on the school board who negotiated with the teachers unions; this bloc was a fervent-at-times-vigilante-esque mob, people who believed in the ways of big business and hated unions, especially teachers unions, who represented people who "took nearly four months of vacation every year" and only worked six hours a day. According to these assholes, educators were paid way more than the workers these fascists had under their thumb at Corporation Cutthroat, where portraits of Ayn Rand decorated their posh board rooms and those not allowed in these hallowed, dark oak paneled sanctuaries were treated as peons and serfs.

This time was particularly stressful for Conrad as he served as one of the leaders of the teachers union and knew the history of such negotiation battles backward and forward. He was a formidable verbal adversary for these Milton Friedman protégés. These guys were heartless. They would send anonymous messages on Internet blogs not naming Conrad but leaving vague initials and nicknames for him, coming close to threats and implied things that he deserved or might happen to him if he didn't get off his pedagogical high horse. Conrad had two kids under four and with his wife (also employed at the school), his tendency to pick up paranoia like mine escalated, and issues came to a boiling point over some specific nitpick that has faded in its insignificance over time.

One incident I do remember is how Conrad fell on his sword over a major fuck up the board itself had created, or rather the board's lawyer, a man named Pointdexter, who we will hear more about later. There was a new law enacted by the state that forbade any school district employees from using schooltime to perform any labors, duties, whatever in conjunction with tasks related to the teachers union. All that stuff had to be done at home, and district property (computers, copying machines, paper supplies) were not to be used in support of such endeavors. One day, they caught Conrad by monitoring his district-supplied laptop. The fascists on the school board pounced, and it looked like he was in for something really bad as they investigated this impropriety.

Conrad was totally freaked out by this Inquisition, and I believe it was at this time, at least in my eyes, he changed slowly, but eventually rather drastically. The first noticeable break was over the use of the rubrics. We had kept this ridiculous evaluation incursion out of the classroom of the Pros from Dover, and when I first voiced my objection to this policy of putting students in boxes as if we were punishing kindergartners from coloring outside the lines, Conrad was right there with me. As I stated earlier, Conrad asked Leaffler why he had never heard of rubrics during his years of studying to be a teacher and who determined they were some godsend to the educational arena. Man, he was right with me.

But then he suddenly changed, and it was right around this time. He flipped. He hadn't talked to me about his new attitude on the rubric. Unfortunately, as I remember it, it happened in front of the American Studies class. I wish I could remember the specifics, but all I know is Conrad was handing out something that looked like a rubric, and I said something to the effect that "rubrics are for people who don't know how to grade papers, or who are afraid of parents and need a crutch to defend their professional judgment in assessing

A blank rubric used

INFORMATIVE/EXPL

Writing Feature	Unscorable (Score Point 0)	Lacking (Score Point 1)	Limited (Score Point 2)
FOCUS	The writing is illegible, written in a language other than English, or there is not enough information to score the response.	The response lacks a clear topic and fails to maintain the topic or idea throughout.	The response includes a clear topic but the writer is unsuccessful in efforts to maintain the topic or idea throughout.
ORGANIZATION	The writing is illegible, written in a language other than English, or there is not enough information to score the response.	The response does not represent an organization of ideas, concepts, and information.	The response reflects an unsuccessful attempt to organize ideas, concepts, and information.
DEVELOPMENT	The writing is illegible, written in a language other than English, or there is not enough information to score the response.	The response fails to demonstrate proper development of ideas, concepts, and information and/or does not make the connections and distinctions between them; the response lacks transitions which serve to link ideas and create cohesion.	The response attempts to demonstrate the development of ideas, concepts, and information but rarely raises the important connections and distinctions between them; few transitions are included and/or transitions do not link ideas or create cohesion.
SUPPORT	The writing is illegible, written in a language other than English, or there is not enough information to score the response.	The response fails to include relevant and sufficient facts, definitions, concrete details, or other important information and examples.	The response includes a mixture of relevant and irrelevant facts, clear and unclear definitions, some concrete details, or other information and examples which may or may not strengthen the response.
LANGUAGE	The writing is illegible, written in a language other than English, or there is not enough information to score the response.	The response includes vague and/or confusing language and lacks purposeful vocabulary; a formal style and/or objective tone are not maintained; there are blatant errors in grammar and conventions.	The response lacks precise language and domain-specific vocabulary; a formal style and/or objective tone are not maintained; there are errors in grammar and conventions that may detract from the overall quality of the writing.

cess student work

ORY WRITING RUBRIC

(Point 3)	Proficient (Score Point 4)	Above Average (Score Point 5)	Exemplary (Score Point 6)
nse a clear the kes an maintain or idea ut.	The response includes a clear topic and the topic or central idea is maintained throughout.	The response includes a well chosen topic and the writer successfully maintains complex idea(s) throughout.	The response includes an advanced, well chosen topic and the writer successfully maintains complex ideas throughout.
nse reflects zation of cepts, mation.	The response reflects an organization of complex ideas, concepts, and information; and provides a concluding statement or section that follows from and supports information or explanation.	The response reflects a purposeful organization of complex ideas, concepts, and information; and provides a concluding statement or section that follows from and supports information or explanation.	The response reflects a purposeful organization of complex ideas, concepts, and information that clearly contributes to the reader's understanding of the topic; and provides a concluding statement or section that follows from and supports information or explanation.
nse ates ent of cepts, mation uately ns and them; sitions nt.	The response demonstrates consistent development of complex ideas, concepts, and information and makes clear the important connections and distinctions between them; transitions are appropriate and varied.	The response demonstrates consistent development of complex ideas, concepts, and information so that each new element builds upon that which precedes it; the writer also makes clear the important connections and distinctions between them; transitions are appropriate and varied.	The response clearly demonstrates consistent development of complex ideas, concepts, and information so that each new element builds upon that which precedes it to create a unified whole; the writer also makes clear the important connections and distinctions between them; transitions are appropriate and varied.
nse includes nd facts, s, details, n and	The response includes relevant and sufficient facts, extended definitions, concrete details, or other information and examples appropriate to the audience's knowledge of the topic.	The response includes well chosen, relevant and sufficient facts, extended definitions, concrete details, or other information and examples appropriate to the audience's knowledge of the topic.	The response includes well chosen, the most significant and relevant facts, extended definitions, concrete details, or other information and examples appropriate to the audience's knowledge of the topic.
nse me guage in y; formal bjective d; the nerally norms ntions.	The response includes precise language and domain-specific vocabulary to manage the complexity of the topic; formal style and objective tone are maintained; the writing attends to the norms and conventions of the discipline.	The response includes precise language and techniques such as metaphor and simile as well as domain-specific vocabulary to manage the complexity of the topic; formal style and objective tone are maintained; the writing attends to the norms and conventions of the discipline.	The response includes precise language and techniques such as metaphor, simile, and effective analogy as well as domain-specific vocabulary to manage the complexity of the topic; formal style and objective tone are maintained; the writing attends to the norms and conventions of the discipline.

How a typical rubr[ic]

INFORMATIVE/EXPL[ANATORY]

Writing Feature	Unscorable (Score Point 0)	Lacking (Score Point 1)	Limited (Score Point 2)
FOCUS	The writing is illegible, written in a language other than English, or there is not enough information to score the response.	The response lacks a clear topic and fails to maintain the topic or idea throughout.	The response includes a clear topic but the writer is unsuccessful in efforts to maintain the topic or idea throughout.
ORGANIZATION	The writing is illegible, written in a language other than English, or there is not enough information to score the response.	The response does not represent an organization of ideas, concepts, and information.	The response reflects an unsuccessful attempt to organize ideas, concepts, and information.
DEVELOPMENT	The writing is illegible, written in a language other than English, or there is not enough information to score the response.	The response fails to demonstrate proper development of ideas, concepts, and information and/or does not make the connections and distinctions between them; the response lacks transitions which serve to link ideas and create cohesion.	The response attempts to demonstrate the development of ideas, concepts, and information but rarely raises the important connections and distinctions between them; few transitions are included and/or transitions do not link ideas or create cohesion.
SUPPORT	The writing is illegible, written in a language other than English, or there is not enough information to score the response.	The response fails to include relevant and sufficient facts, definitions, concrete details, or other important information and examples.	The response includes a mixture of relevant and irrelevant facts, clear and unclear definitions, some concrete details, or other information and examples which may or may not strengthen the response.
LANGUAGE	The writing is illegible, written in a language other than English, or there is not enough information to score the response.	The response includes vague and/or confusing language and lacks purposeful vocabulary; a formal style and/or objective tone are not maintained; there are blatant errors in grammar and conventions.	The response lacks precise language and domain specific vocabulary; a formal style and/or objective tone are not maintained; there are errors in grammar and conventions that may detract from the overall quality of the writing.

might be filled out

ORY WRITING RUBRIC

oaching (Point 3)	Proficient (Score Point 4)	Above Average (Score Point 5)	Exemplary (Score Point 6)
onse a clear d the akes an maintain or idea but.	The response includes a clear topic and the topic or central idea is maintained throughout.	The response includes a well chosen topic and the writer successfully maintains complex idea(s) throughout.	The response includes an advanced, well chosen topic and the writer successfully maintains complex ideas throughout
onse y reflects zation of ncepts, mation.	The response reflects an organization of complex ideas, concepts, and information; and provides a concluding statement or section that follows from and supports information or explanation.	The response reflects a purposeful organization of complex ideas, concepts, and information; and provides a concluding statement or section that follows from and supports information or explanation.	The response reflects a purposeful organization of complex ideas, concepts, and information that clearly contributes to the reader's understanding of the topic; and provides a concluding statement or section that follows from and supports information or explanation.
onse rates ment of ncepts, mation quate e ons and ns them; ctions nt.	The response demonstrates consistent development of complex ideas, concepts, and information and makes clear the important connections and distinctions between them; transitions are appropriate and varied.	The response demonstrates consistent development of complex ideas, concepts, and information so that each new element builds upon that which precedes it; the writer also makes clear the important connections and distinctions between them; transitions are appropriate and varied	The response clearly demonstrates consistent development of complex ideas, concepts, and information so that each new element builds upon that which precedes it to create a unified whole; the writer also makes clear the important connections and distinctions between them; transitions are appropriate and varied.
onse includes and facts, s, details, on and	The response includes relevant and sufficient facts, extended definitions, concrete details, or other information and examples appropriate to the audience's knowledge of the topic.	The response includes well chosen, relevant and sufficient facts, extended definitions, concrete details, or other information and examples appropriate to the audience's knowledge of the topic.	The response includes well chosen, the most significant and relevant facts, extended definitions, concrete details, or other information and examples appropriate to the audience's knowledge of the topic.
onse some anguage an y; formal objective d; the nerally norms ntions.	The response includes precise language and domain specific vocabulary to manage the complexity of the topic; formal style and objective tone are maintained; the writing attends to the norms and conventions of the discipline.	The response includes precise language and techniques such as metaphor and simile as well as domain specific vocabulary to manage the complexity of the topic; formal style and objective tone are maintained; the writing attends to the norms and conventions of the discipline.	The response includes precise language and techniques such as metaphor, simile, and effective analogy as well as domain specific vocabulary to manage the complexity of the topic; formal style and objective tone are maintained; the writing attends to the norms and conventions of the discipline.

Draft created 08/01/2012 (revised 08/20/12)

My rubric

INFORMATIVE/EXPLA...

Writing Feature	Unscorable (Score Point 0)	Lacking (Score Point 1)	Limited (Score Point 2)
FOCUS	The writing is illegible, written in a language other than English, or there is not enough information to score the response.	The response lacks a clear topic and fails to maintain the topic or idea throughout.	The response includes a clear topic but the writer is unsuccessful in efforts to maintain the topic or idea throughout.
ORGANIZATION	The writing is illegible, written in a language other than English, or there is not enough information to score the response.	The response does not represent an organization of ideas, concepts, and information.	The response reflects an unsuccessful attempt to organize ideas, concepts, and information.
DEVELOPMENT	The writing is illegible, written in a language other than English, or there is not enough information to score the response.	The response fails to demonstrate proper development of ideas, concepts, and information and/or does not make the connections and distinctions between them; the response lacks transitions which serve to link ideas and create cohesion.	The response attempts to demonstrate the development of ideas, concepts, and information but rarely raises the important connections and distinctions between them; few transitions are included and/or transitions do not link ideas or create cohesion.
SUPPORT	The writing is illegible, written in a language other than English, or there is not enough information to score the response.	The response fails to include relevant and sufficient facts, definitions, concrete details, or other important information and examples.	The response includes a mixture of relevant and irrelevant facts, clear and unclear definitions, some concrete details, or other information and examples which may or may not strengthen the response.
LANGUAGE	The writing is illegible, written in a language other than English, or there is not enough information to score the response.	The response includes vague and/or confusing language and lacks purposeful vocabulary; a formal style and/or objective tone are not maintained; there are blatant errors in grammar and conventions.	The response lacks precise language and doesn't use specific vocabulary; a formal style and/or objective tone are not maintained; there are errors in grammar and conventions that may detract from the overall quality of the writing.

oked like this.

RY WRITING RUBRIC

ching (oint 3)	Proficient (Score Point 4)	Above Average (Score Point 5)	Exemplary (Score Point 6)
rse clear the es an aintain	The response includes a clear topic and the topic or central idea is maintained	The response includes a clear topic and the topic and the carefully maintains complex idea(s) throughout	The response includes an advanced, well-chosen topic and the writer successfully maintains complex ideas throughout
jects on of epts, ation	The response reflects an organization of complex ideas, concepts, and information; and provides a concluding statement or section that follows from and supports information or explanation	The response reflects a purposeful organization of complex ideas, concepts, and information that provides a concluding section that follows from and supports information or explanation	The response reflects a purposeful organization of complex ideas, concepts, and information that clearly contributes to the reader's understanding of the topic; and provides a concluding statement or section that follows from and supports information or explanation
ise tes nt of epts, ation ately s and nem itions	The response demonstrates consistent development of complex ideas, concepts, and information and makes clear the important connections and distinctions between them; transitions are appropriate and varied	The response demonstrates consistent development of complex ideas, concepts, and information so that each new element builds upon that which precedes it; the writer also makes clear the important connections and distinctions between them; transitions are appropriate and varied	The response clearly demonstrates consistent development of complex ideas, concepts, and information so that each new element builds upon that which precedes it to create a unified whole; the writer also makes clear the important connections and distinctions between them; transitions are appropriate and varied
ise ncludes id acts, tails, and	The response includes relevant and sufficient facts, extended definitions, concrete details, and other information and examples appropriate to the audience's knowledge of the topic	The response includes well-chosen, relevant and sufficient facts, extended definitions, concrete details, or other information and examples appropriate to the audience's knowledge of the topic	The response includes well-chosen, the most significant and relevant facts, extended definitions, concrete details, or other information and examples appropriate to the audience's knowledge of the topic
se me uage formal bjective the erally norms tions	The response includes precise language and domain specific vocabulary to manage the complexity of the topic; formal style and objective tone are maintained; the writing attends to the norms and conventions of the discipline	The response includes precise language and techniques such as metaphor and simile as well as domain specific vocabulary to manage the complexity of the topic; formal style and objective tone are maintained; the writing attends to the norms and conventions of the discipline	The response includes precise language and techniques such as metaphor, simile, and effective analogy as well as domain specific vocabulary to manage the complexity of the topic; formal style and objective tone are maintained; the writing attends to the norms and conventions of the discipline

student work." Conrad replied something like "that's not necessarily so," and we argued briefly. I thought he was joking or trying to make some point, but no, he was dead fucking serious.

After class, he said, "I don't like the way that went down."

"When did you change your mind about rubrics? I don't remember that conversation."

"It's the way things are going. Everyone is using them. They make grading easier and clearer."

I was astounded and took my medication immediately or I am sure I would have had a meltdown. We actually started using rubrics in class. We never talked anymore about it. I used them as little as possible and when forced, like when we were both grading the presentation of student projects in front of the class. I would not circle boxes, but instead I would color them in with my felt purple pen, going between the lines to show where I thought the student "was" in a more specific way. Graphically, it was similar to those audience-control devices used to rate the President's State of the Union address, with meters going up and down as different highs and lows are recorded as audiences react to what they like or don't like. I'm not sure if they actually use these things, but I saw it on *The West Wing*.

Around this time, as Conrad seemed to change, he began demonstrating something he had admitted to me earlier in our relationship in a moment of candor. He admitted he had been challenged by the man he student-taught-for—a man, incidentally, still employed at our very school—he admitted he had been accused in the past of waffling on certain causes, and he asked me to point it out to him if I ever witnessed him doing that. This was not the time.

A second incident further drove home this point and put a definite, probably irreversible gouge in our relationship. Barack Obama and Joe Biden were running for office, and I had an Obama/Biden sticker on my car. I put another one on a filing cabinet behind my desk in a corner of the American Studies room. We were having parent-teacher conferences, so this must have been mid-October.

Conrad was in the middle of his stressful negotiations, and we shared our room for conferences so we could move between

Studies parents (which we did together) and American Lit. or Drama students (which I did), or International Relations kids (which Conrad did). Parents came on Thursday evening and Friday morning. This happened Friday. That morning, out of the blue, Conrad looked around and said, "What's that Obama sticker doing there?"

"I put it there. It's been there about three weeks."

"I never noticed it before. You'll have to take it down."

"Why?"

"Because as teachers, we have to be impartial on issues like politics. Parents can't see that. You could get in trouble."

"I'll take my chances." There were other teachers in the room watching this, and one was Leaffler.

"Well, I could get in trouble, and I don't need any more people thinking whatever it is they think about me, so you'll have to take it down."

"I'm *not* going to take it down. I don't check my constitutional right of expression when I enter this building. Read *Tinker vs. Iowa*." This was a famous Supreme Court case that said students could wear black armbands protesting the Vietnam War, and the school could not stop them from expressing themselves.

"That was for students. Teachers don't get the same protection. You can put things on your car, you can wear a button on your coat, but you can't display it like that. Now take it down or I'll take it down."

"You take it down, and I take you down."

Man, things were heated, and the water started running down my face. *Ticktock, ticktock*. He just stared at me.

I asked him, "Why the fuck are you doing this? That sticker has been up for three fucking weeks, and you never said a fucking word! Now you're threatening me."

Someone said to me, "What's the big deal, why don't you just take it down."

"Okay, fine!" I yell as I rip it off and slap it on the side of my briefcase. Which is on the desk.

"Put the briefcase under your desk."

I put it on the floor with the sticker still visible. "Happy?"

"Turn the briefcase so we can't see the sticker."

I turn it twenty degrees. Then twenty-five. Then twenty-seven. Then thirty. Every time I turn it, I'm screaming, "Happy? Happy now? Happier? Don't you see what an ass you're being?"

Finally, I turn it all the way around and storm out. I take the medicine, wait ten minutes. And return.

"Okay," I say. "I'm calm. But I want to say you would never have done this if the school board was not putting pressure on you or if you were not getting hate mail on the Internet. I understand that. Had you asked me three weeks ago when I first put the sticker up, I would have seen your point. But you never noticed that sticker until now? This problem is in your head, Conrad, not mine."

Nobody said anything for a while. Finally he says, "I should have noticed the sticker three weeks ago."

Ironically, regarding Conrad's use of schooltime to do union business, someone found out that Pointdexter, the attorney for the school district, had been told by the state to disseminate this *new* information about use of schooltime to all district employees, but Pointdexter had not done so. If Conrad wanted to pursue that, he could have made a lot of trouble for Pointdexter and the board. The incident reached a compromise when Conrad signed a memo saying he had used *seventeen seconds* of personal time at school, and they put it in his file. That's how he fell on his sword.

"I took one for the team," he explained later. "This will make the union negotiations go smoother."

"Yeah? Well, I wouldn't have signed shit. Why should you? They fucked up. Pointdexter fucked up."

"I did what I had to do."

Things were never the same after that. Storm came the next year.

But this was my first indication that my best friend Conrad did indeed need a weatherman to know which way the wind blows.

CHAPTER 19

Captain Canary Sings

It was much later I began sensing I would be moved out of American Studies, and the Pros from Dover would no longer be. At that point, I didn't know where Conrad's head was. This was after Leaffler had become my full-time boss and Storm completed his observation-evaluation plan. I believed Conrad knew the breakup was coming, which meant he was in the mix. This was after the meeting where I exploded at Leaffler, Storm, and Mrs. Sad, and after Storm's observation of the *Gatsby* lesson.

After Storm's observation, things calmed, but I still couldn't shake this premonition that something was up, that they would move me out of Studies or something. Things were too quiet. I even asked Conrad directly, "When are they going to move me out of Studies?" He swore he knew nothing about it, that he hadn't heard anything about it, and that no one had even hinted about it, but all his protestations rang hollow.

Conrad had a new boss as well, a woman who used a foreign-sounding accented first name that escapes me, but I recall it contained either an accent *grave* or an accent *aigu*, and that should tell you how affected she was. I was not at all surprised that this woman and Leaffler soon became best friends. Strictly a climber, all the way.

The Humanities Department was responsible for half of our teaching team and the other half by the Communication Arts Department. My connect-the-dots conspiracy mind saw this one coming like a high-speed train with a powerful laser light streaking through a long, dark tunnel.

I had not heard a word from Storm about the next observation, which, if they held to the previous semester lineup, would be Mrs. Sad, so I thought maybe I had cleared this road block. But things were hanging in the air, and I could sense the impending doom like a bad smell coming from a dead rat—some pungent rotting rodent no one could locate. The smell is there; no one knows where it is coming from. I was sensing all this through another source, and after a period of contemplation, I realized the source was Caitlyn.

My awareness of Caitlyn's presence always made me feel safe. I knew whatever was going to happen, I would be okay. During this time, I would often visit her grave and talk to her, something people often do at grave sites, and these little spiritual chats always made me feel better. I have a strong faith and believe there is help for the confused and disillusioned beyond our standard senses. It's the same thing that led to my anxiety attack hospital incident two weeks before she died, and as a kind of guardian angel, I felt and still feel that she is near when I need her.

Conrad is a terrible actor. We had both been drafted to play roles in the school's production of *West Side Story* a while back. I was Lieutenant Schrank, and he played the goofball organizer of the dance trying to pair up the Jets' girls with the Shark guys and vice versa; it's a real cornball character, but he never nailed the part, and I could tell. So when the day came, I knew it because he pretty much telegraphed the entire situation.

Ironically, it was another parent-teacher Friday, and late in the day, I knew it was coming. Conrad was avoiding my eyes and jumping around like Mr. Heebie-Jeebies. The conferences were about over, traffic was light, and I was loudly announcing it was coming and even predicted my friend Rocket would replace me. The real tip-off came when one of Leaffler's stooges said, "Why do you keep saying that? He's not the only person who could do it!" How dumb is that? Conrad suddenly announced that he had been summoned to a meeting in the Humanities Department. Not fifteen seconds later, Leaffler strolled in—the Conrad exit and the Leaffler entrance obviously and horribly choreographed.

Then Leaffler says to me, "I need to see you in my office."

I smile at her and say, "Nonsense. Let's do this right here."

She sits. She is nervous. "I'm announcing teaching assignments for next year, and here's yours."

Slipping a piece of paper across the desk, I see two Theatre classes and three American Literature classes.

"I don't see American Studies on here."

"We're making a change."

"Why?"

"We want to go with a more student-centered approach."

Now this was a real hoot, the old raft of horseshit coming down the river with the dead rat aboard. The only time I'd heard this criticism was after she observed me because they were concerned about classroom management.

I stare at her. She has that scared-penguin-in-the-harpoonists-eye look on her face. I think she believes I have a .357 Magnum under my desk, and I am about to blow her brains all over my new teaching assignments. She knows this is all crap.

"Okay," I say. "That's fine."

And she leaves. Ten minutes later, Conrad comes back in and, with this "oh gee-whiz" look on his face, says, "Guess what? I just heard I'm getting another partner for American Studies next year. Talk about a shocker!"

Not that it matters, but I find out later that Storm had tipped Conrad off about the change about two months before.

"We're going to make that change in Studies," Storm reportedly said as if this whole thing had been a subject of previous conversations.

I found it deliciously ironic that Conrad received this message while the two of them were pissing in adjoining white urinals in the plush restroom outside Storm's office.

Right after the removal from Studies for the next year, I received notice that Leaffler would observe me in my one American Literature class in about two weeks. This pissed me off royally as I had visions that this part of this plan had been ditched, but *no*. So I wrote e-mail after e-mail to Storm, reminding him of the letter from my doctor and how my health and my anxiety condition were being endangered, that I had been observed four times, and further observations was the height of professional indignity.

I was not only losing my battle with Storm, I was losing a grip on everything due to the fact that this entire situation was unfair, unexplained, unnecessary, and un-fucking-believable.

I began sharing my perception of the Communication Arts Department, which I nicknamed the Vagina Mafia. Horrible, I know, but that was the appearance with Leaffler's known male bias and her comrades in heels.

I was directing Steve Martin's *Picasso at the Lapin Agile* for the spring play, and the set, which was under the technical supervision of a long-haired uncooperative Hippie who never did anything on time or in a spirit of cooperation; every time I asked him to do something, like add a window to a set wall, he always had some convoluted reason why it was akin to scaling Mount Everest. With three weeks left before opening, the set hadn't even been started. I openly commented to the cast that the set would probably never be built unless someone went to the auditorium and had sex with him, but I didn't know which gender to send or, for that matter, if the Hippie even had a gender.

There was a kid called Captain Canary who I had in a special class for those interested in producing for the stage, and part of his semester project was to design the set for *Picasso* and supervise the building of it with the Hippie. The Captain was a royal suck-up, a rumor monger, and was known for taking something one teacher said and repeating it in a slimy version to another teacher, all with the intent of ingratiating himself to gossip fanatics in the Vagina Mafia, attempting to stir any pot he could find. He was a real asshole.

Things came to a head with Canary when I went to see Mrs. Sad, who was the Hippie's boss, regarding a special lighting effect for the play. Martin's witty script has Einstein and Picasso meeting in a 1904 Paris bar called the Lapin Agile (translated "rapid rabbit"), and at the play's climax, a special visitor from the future (Elvis!) appears with much fanfare in a cosmic atmosphere. This is a critical moment in the play. The effect has to be perfect and was going to cost some money. Captain Canary and I met with Mrs. Sad, and we three agreed that the Hippie would be responsible for buying, building, and executing the effect.

Fine. This was as it should be as the project was way over Canary's skills. Mrs. Sad then met with me and the Hippie and told us both that Canary would build the effect under the Hippie's supervision. This was a bit odd, but okay, fine. The next day, Captain Canary told me he had met with Mrs. Sad and that I was to build the effect (this was an obvious lie and an excuse to get the Canary out of the responsibility). I then went to see Mrs. Sad and asked her one more time to clarify who was responsible for the effect, and she said the Hippie alone, which was the right decision. Then Captain Canary ran into me at a rehearsal and said Mrs. Sad had told him that he, Canary, would build the effect, and I would supervise. I lost it.

"When did you talk to her?"

"A few hours ago."

"What did she say?"

"I don't remember exactly."

"C'mon, Canary. What did the woman say?"

"Several things."

"Look, Canary, don't fuck with me. Tell me what Sad told you."

"That I'd do it."

I immediately went down the stairs to see Sad, really fuming, and said that it's not cool to go behind my back with a student, which she denied she did. The Hippie would do the effect.

I went back up to kick Canary's ass, but he was gone.

The next day, I was summoned to Storm's office and was encouraged to bring a union representative with me. Conrad was conveniently unavailable, so I contacted the math teacher who was on the union team and met her briefly outside Storm's office, filling her in about what I thought this might be about (I wasn't sure but knew it wouldn't be good). Leaffler walked by boring her harpoon eyes back at my macular-degenerated eye. When I went in, there was Storm, Sad, Leaffler, and a heavyset woman with saggy panty hose who was introduced as Ms. Blister, the Director of Personnel for the entire school district. Technically, she had more clout than Storm.

Once things quieted, Storm began the meeting by asking me if I said "Don't Fuck With Me" to Captain Canary, and we were off to the races.

CHAPTER 20

The Lessons No One Observed: Great Chain of Being

I later concluded that it was my upcoming observation by Leaffler, scheduled two days after the latest meeting in Storm's office, that skewed my emotions. I never did teach that lesson for anyone, and it's probably a good thing. But I don't know. I do know this—it would have been quite memorable. I had two options, I felt.

The philosophy I needed to steer toward was Transcendentalism, which, as I mentioned, I had done in part for Mrs. Sad the previous semester. This subject is often hard for high school students to fully grasp but is a lesson that I feel is the most important one to teach in American Literature. It falls after the Realism Unit, near the end of the Romanticism unit.

But to really get into this topic, you really need to go all the way back to the Europeans who settled in this country—what they believed and what was, to them, incontrovertible truth. I didn't have the time to teach all this, but I did lay out an outline for both, which follows. Parenthetical remarks are prompts to be used with the students to help them grasp these lessons.

The people who settled in this land, and their ancestors, believed in "The Great Chain of Being." This phantasmagorical interpretation of life and everything it touches stands as one of the greatest human errors in all eternity. A lot of this I learned when I took a British Literature class as part of my preparation to teach.

WILLIAM J. BURGHARDT

Writing on the board the words hierarchy and order, the class and I ponder what these words really mean. Hierarchy is putting things in order from top to bottom in a very specific sequence. For example, the succession of office in the United States: if the President dies, then the Vice President, then the Speaker of the House, and so on. Order is a bigger part of that picture because human beings need, require cannot exist without order. The opposite is chaos, and we discuss why people cannot function in a world without order. Presented with chaos, the first thing a human being does is proceed to look at the chaos and proceed to put it in order. Once done, the "ordered chaos" can be dealt with, can be adjusted, can be talked about, can be understood.

Think about the constellations. They are just a group of stars human beings put in some kind of order to make them understandable. This is how the Great Chain of Being comes into existence.

Now you can find pictures of this Chain of Being online, but I'll just draw it for you on the board. At the top is God, and the chain comes off the left side of his throne and connects to Earth, which is in the center of the solar system. This concept is by Ptolemy, but when putting things in order, you can see how it makes sense to these people. Now watch the order here. Under God, you have angels, and there are nine levels in groups of three: Seraphim, seraph is the primary, or superior, type of angel, Cherubim, Thrones. Then next is Dominations, Virtues, and Powers. And finally, Principalities, Archangels, and Angels.

I'll go through this quickly. The planets are ordered and so are the stars the latter in twelve groups called the Zodiac. Pisces, Aries, Leo, Taurus, where do we see this every day, usually in the newspaper?

Answer: the horoscope.

Romeo and Juliet are what kind of lovers? (Star-crossed, someone usually knows this.) You may not know the musical *Hair*, a 1968 Broadway production that mostly made news because people took their clothes off at the end of Act I, but you may know the song "Aquarius" from that musical and the opening lyrics (play a brief section). Hear that? "When the moon is in the seventh house and Jupiter aligns with Mars, then peace will guide the planets, and love will steer the stars. This is the dawning of the age of Aquarius."

Now I don't know what any of that means, but it's all Chain of Being stuff, and they go on from there to the atmosphere and the elements. Everything is in order, and that's the key. Order! And when the planets and the stars are in a certain alignment, everyone's life is affected.

The elements—where do we see this represented today? It's painted on the wall downstairs in the science hall. Right, the periodic table, and do we have any chemist scholars in here who can tell us about how organized this table is, because for me, it is the height of human anal-ness, excuse me, analysis.

(Find some kid to talk about electrons, protons, neutrons, noble gases, how this thing is organized.)

Well, back then, they had alchemists—from which we get the word chemistry—and these guys, who were like amateur pharmacists, thought they could turn rocks into gold if they could just find the right way to do it, crack the code, so to speak. And today, we are more educated and sophisticated and have the periodic table. But it took years to iron all these things out: research, microscopes, and other things scientific.

Any biologists in here? Good. Can you tell me about the plants and the animals? Again, human beings feel the need to put everything in order. How do we do that here?

(Find some biology kid to talk Kingdom, Phyla, Order, Class, Species, the whole nine yards, and focus on the classification of birds and insects, how many species, how many new species, and so on.)

And how about us? How do we organize our own selves? We're not all the same—we're all different—but why? There must be some reason. There's more here, and Shakespeare's *Romeo and Juliet* again helps us. The Humours (British spelling), ever hear of them? There are four humours, and all four words are in our dictionary today and mean the same for us as it did for them.

The four humours are described as Melancholic, Choleric, Phlegmatic, and Sanguine. If you were a Melancholic type, like Romeo, you had too much black bile and were dreamy, head in the clouds, easily depressed, you think too much, like Hamlet. Today we have Prozac. If you were choleric, you had too much choler, so you were a hothead like Tybalt. You know the type; fire first, kick ass, and ask questions later. You talking to me? Bada bing bada boom. One example, Sonny, a character in the film *The Godfather* (directed by Coppola, written by Mario Puzo, mention). Choleric types need help with anger management, but you want them on your side in a fight. If you were Phlegmatic, you had too much phlegm—yes, gross—and you were uncaring, laid-back, didn't give a crap about anything, uninvolved, like Benvolio. Blow with the wind, change your mind depending on which way the wind blows. Phlegmatics are "whatever." Don't get excited about anything. And if you were Sanguine, you were goofy, had too much blood, bawdy, wild, a bit like the Nurse and Falstaff. Think Jim Carrey, Robin Williams, funny-but-crazy, you can take them in short time intervals but don't want them in your house. The class clowns, perhaps people who need drugs to survive. John Belushi, Chris Farley; folks who may need to go into rehab. You get the idea.

Now the people who settled America and their ancestors believed this stuff passionately. It was taken for granted. And, say, if lightning struck your house, everyone in town would come over and check—"What the hell is going on in there?"—because God fired the bolt right down the chain. Women particularly got the shaft; if you were unmarried by, I don't know, say thirty, people began to wonder what's wrong with you. Like it or not, ladies, we still have this today in a more subtle form—"Why can't Susie find a nice man to settle down with?" Of course, back then, if you got on in years and were single, you were labeled as a witch.

No better example is the Salem Witch Trials of 1692, and you know what happened there. Everyone was suspected eventually. But something else happened first in Italy, in about 1608, just about the time people were coming to America.

You see, the key to making this work is the "truth" of the Earth being in the center of the solar system. That's why everything else was "in order." But a guy named Galileo had a telescope and was familiar with the writings of a guy named Copernicus, who had written in about 1514 about the sun being the center. His friends told him to publish his work, but he kept it somewhat secret. Wrote very technically. Showed some scientists. But he didn't want the hullabaloo that would result from stating such a controversial view.

You have to understand, people spouting theories like this were not just floating ideas, they were committing heresy. What's heresy? (If necessary, have someone look it up).

People were reluctant to talk about such things because they were attacking an entire belief system, a tradition that had been handed down for who knows how long. You don't talk about this stuff openly.

Not so Galileo. He proudly announced to one and all that the sun was the center of the solar system, and Copernicus's theory, aided by some further thought from Johannes Kepler, was right on and he could prove it. See, he didn't just have one telescope; he had several, the next one better than the one before. Oh look, there are shadows on the moon and on Venus. Why. Hmmm. And he knew how to communicate this stuff so people could understand it.

But what he really was doing was announcing that the Earth was not the center of things, Plato was wrong, Aristotle was wrong, Ptolemy was wrong, and—guess what else boys and girls?—that the Great Chain of Being was basically a load of crap. Which meant what else was crap? Everything! Think about that. Everything they believed was el wrongo.

Now when you publicly attack a belief system that huge, you're not just saying man's view of the sky and the planets is wrong; you're saying everything is wrong. Result: no order. Chaos. And we humans do not like chaos. So it's no wonder they threw Galileo in jail and threatened to kill him until he recanted, which he did in 1633. But as they say, the cat was out of the bag. And the Catholic Church, not quick to welcome change, finally admitted Galileo was right—in 1992.

The Age of Enlightenment, which runs around 1650 to 1780, changed things and helped move us out of this morass. The Salem Witch Trials served as a catalyst to keep religion out of the law enforcement business. It ended "theocracy." It ended "spectral evidence" ("I see the devil right now cavorting with Goody Nurse"—you do? I don't see squat, but I can't say anything because you'll think I'm possessed).

The Age of Enlightenment embraced a more balanced view of God through Deism. The common metaphor to describe this tangent is "God as watchmaker"; he winds the clock and lets it run. He doesn't interfere. Ben Franklin proves lightning is, well, lightning.

Hurricanes are hurricanes. Oh, by the way, this "Chain of Being" nonsense still rears its head even today; many TV evangelists blamed Hurricane Katrina in 2005, which leveled New Orleans, on that city's sinful lifestyle, ditto the massive earthquake in Haiti in 2010 a natural catastrophe (which a minister in this very town blamed on the island's Voodoo Lifestyle). When the Twin Towers fell on 9/11, the word in the "Chain of Being" school was that America had embraced homosexuality and women's rights and God was *really* pissed! All this is based on man's innate desire to explain every event that happens as some "Ordered Command." Otherwise, we have chaos and no one to blame our tragedies on. I mean, even today in insurance policies, we lump all these devastating events as "Acts of God," and quite frankly, I believe He is pissed about that.

Now what does all this have to do with American Literature, I hear you ask. Well, our beliefs affect our writings and ideas; it's that simple. During the Age of Enlightenment, while we were deep sixing the Chain and the witches, we began getting analytical, scientific, more thoughtful. There is little or no fiction written in America at this time. Poetry becomes stuff like Phillis Wheatley's "To His Excellency George Washington," really patriotic stuff. Your textbook highlights this as the Age of Reason or Realism and highlights such works as "Patrick Henry's Address to the Virginia Assembly," featuring the famous line "Give Me Liberty or Give Me Death" as well as Thomas Paine's *Common Sense,* a pamphlet that in today's marketing had a penetration percentage of 99.9—in other words, everyone had it or had read it. Thomas Jefferson writes "The Declaration of Independence"—basically plagiarizing the ideas of philosophers John Locke and Jean-Jacques Rousseau on natural rights—writing that gives vivid use of parallelism, and your textbook highlights a literary letter from Abigail Adams, who contributes to the literature by writing hubby John "to not forget the ladies" while he's overthrowing the government.

The Puritans landed in great numbers around and after 1630. The Age of Enlightenment began around 1650. After the Salem Witch Trials, or by about 1700, the Chain of Being had been snapped and scrapped.

One last thought about the Puritans and the Anglicans. The Puritans did not believe in hierarchy. They had no use for the Pope, Archbishop, Bishop, Priest order of who represents God on earth. They believed in "inner light," that you could reach God directly yourself. They also didn't like extravagance. They didn't like fancy clothes, elaborate costumes, buttons—in many ways, they were very Amish. Keep it basic, and everybody is pretty equal. They believe in Congregations and town meetings and ironing things out. After the Chain is gone, they evolve into Abolitionists—they hate slavery.

The Anglicans and the Catholics, on the other hand, love hierarchy. It clarifies who's who and what's what. For Anglicans, the King is God's representative on earth; for the Catholics, it is the Pope. We talked about Catholic hierarchy—Pope, Archbishop, Bishop, Priest. Well, for the Anglicans, it's like King, Queen, Duke, Earl, Lord, and Serf. These are terms I think you are familiar with. The Anglican/Catholic guys like fancy clothes—robes and jewels, women with huge loopy dresses, and men in uniform with a lot of buttons and medals on their shirts. They like to live in huge castles and homes and want the "lower class" to serve the "upper class;" hence your maids, hand-servants, messenger, court jesters, and so on.

To understand America and American Literature, you must understand the people who founded the nation and, more importantly, how they thought and what they believed.

Okay, now follow me here. (Draw map on the board of the East Coast of the United States.) The Puritans settle here, in Massachusetts, the largest colony up north. The Catholics settle here, in Maryland, and the Anglicans here, in Virginia. These colonies represent the largest ones during the lead up to the American Revolution.

The Puritans go north and become the antislavery abolitionists, plainly dressed, democratic.

The Anglican/Catholic bunch go south with their plantations, hierarchy, fancy clothes, servants, and everybody has a title like Colonel or General.

And one hundred years later, they fight the Civil War. Think about it.

In many ways, they are still at it today.

CHAPTER 21

The Lessons No One Observed: Transcendentalism

As in all literary cycles, there is a pushback of sorts against the previous popular genre, and right after the American Revolution, we witness a movement away from the Realist style of writing (just the facts please), and this leads us to Romanticism. Allow me to present a handy graphic organizer about Romanticism.

Romanticism
Intuition over Fact
Imagination over Reason
Individualism over Society

Transcendentalism ◄— Good ◄—NATURE —► Bad —► **Gothic**
Emphasis on the Individual   *Emphasis on dark side*
Emphasis on the Supernatural

Briefly, you can see that Romanticism and Realism are opposites in many ways. Romanticism's first novelist—the first purely American novelist with little or no European influences—is James Fenimore Cooper. He gives us Natty Bumppo—my guy—who is vividly portrayed by Daniel Day Lewis in the film version of Cooper's *Last of the Mohicans*, directed by Michael Mann. This is the first Batman. This is the first Clint Eastwood-like guy. Bumppo is an archetype—means what? Yes, the template, or model of the American hero, personified as we move west as a country. This is a gunslinger, always gets the girl, does impossible things, leaps tall buildings in a single bound. Ironically, this is the first James Bond even though he is not British. Ever wonder why the James Bond franchise has such a bigger following in America than Europe? Because of Natty Bumppo. Americans love guys like this; they never miss. They are cool.

Romanticism's biggest marker is NATURE—all those Hudson River School paintings. And nature can be good or bad in Romanticism. Bad nature is scary—dark woods, the devil or "Old Scratch," talking birds like Edgar Allan Poe's "The Raven"—this is Gothic literature where you see the supernatural all over the place. This comes over from Europe with Frankenstein and the like and later moves on to the grotesque in Southern Gothic, as evidenced in the later works of two of my favorites, Flannery O'Connor and William Faulkner.

Now Transcendentalism is all us, all American, all about the self and the individual. Our representatives are Ralph Waldo Emerson and Henry David Thoreau with a little Walt Whitman thrown in for poetic effect. If you've seen Peter Weir's film *Dead Poets Society*, you've seen Robin Williams hammer this theme over and over again. "Gather ye rosebuds while ye may," and the anthem *Carpe Diem*, which means make the most of the present with no thought for the future. Seize the day! Today! Act now! Rise above, or transcend, the ordinary.

Thoreau you may have heard of because you know he spent some time living at Walden Pond (he actually left his "hut" to go to the store quite often, visited friends in the village and such, so it's not that "romantic," but still), and you may also know him for the phrase "If a man does not keep pace with his companions, perhaps it is because he hears a different drummer. Let him step to the music which he hears, however measured or far away." Yes, walk to the beat of a different drummer if that is what you hear.

Emerson you may not know a lot about because he is more of a philosopher than a writer, but he did contribute some powerful essays to the American canon, such as "On Nature" and "Self-Reliance," the latter of which we will focus on as we wrap up this introduction. Emerson wrote in aphorisms, which are witty little sayings that pack a lot of punch. Ben Franklin wrote aphorisms too, but his weren't as powerful as Emerson's. Franklin wrote, "A penny saved is a penny earned" and "Early to bed, early to rise, makes a man healthy, wealthy and wise." Good enough, but as we turn to Emerson's "Self-Reliance," I want you to just ponder the meanings of his aphorisms.

- Envy is ignorance. (If you want something that someone else has, you're denying your own passions.)
- Imitation is suicide. (If you try to be someone else, you are "killing" you, who you are.)
- Trust thyself.
- Every heart vibrates to that iron string. (The "iron" is permanent; it's yours.)
- Accept the place the divine providence has found for you. (There is a map for you alone, and you must do everything to find it!)
- Who would be a man must be a nonconformist. (Don't follow the crowd.)
- Nothing is as sacred as the integrity of your own mind. (Don't kid yourself.)
- Absolve you to yourself and you will have the suffrage of the world. (Stand up for what you believe in, and people will sense that and approve.)
- No law can be sacred to that of my own nature. (When would *you* break the law for a principle?)
- The only right is after my constitution and the only wrong is what is against it (i.e., "to thine own self be true," Polonius to Laertes, allude to *Hamlet*.)
- I must do all that concerns me and not what the people think. (Bob Dylan: "Don't follow leaders, watch your parking meters.")

- The great man is he who in the midst of the crowds keeps with perfect sweetness the independence of solitude. (Don't back down to what you know is true, even if you are alone.)
- The sour faces of the solitude, like their sweet faces, have no deep cause, but are put on and off as the wind blows and a newspaper directs. (Don't believe everything you read or the silly opinions of others. Dylan again, "You don't need a weatherman to know which way the wind blows.")
- A foolish consistency is the hobgoblin of many minds. (Don't get trapped in doing the same thing every day, like a job you hate; tons of people do that and ruin their lives. Note: hobgoblin—source of fear and dread.)
- With consistency a great soul has nothing to do. (What are you doing with your life? Every day?)
- Speak what you think now in hard words and tomorrow speak what tomorrow thinks in hard words again though it contradicts everything you said today. (It's okay to change your mind, or "evolve" on an issue, gay attitude shift in the world.)
- Jesus, Galileo, Copernicus, and Newton were all misunderstood. To be great is to be misunderstood.

Break into groups. Have two or three kids ruminate on each aphorism and what it may mean to *you*.

And one more, if you look at your text, you can see the section highlights this quote to begin this chapter on Transcendentalism: "Good men must not obey the laws too well."

What this means is that to be true to yourself, you sometimes have to buck the law and buck society. Thoreau went to jail rather than pay taxes in support of what he saw as an immoral cause—the Mexican-American war. Kids drafted into the Vietnam War broke the law by burning their draft cards; that's how powerfully they believed in what their hearts told them to do. You all know about Martin Luther King Jr. standing up for the immoral laws forced upon African Americans, and he changed the world without throwing one stone. We read that in "Letter from Birmingham Jail." Is there anything you believe in so much that you would break the law or break the rules to take a stand against it? (See where discussion goes.)

I'm sure you noticed Ms. Leaffler in the back of our classroom today, observing me. This is something I have fought against Principal Storm and Mrs. Sad and others because I don't believe it is fair or warranted. How much do I believe this? I believe this enough to put on a black armband and walk down to Storm's office and sit there—for days if necessary—until they stop these unnecessary infringements on my sanity, my professionalism, my integrity. If you—or any other students in the school—would like to join my protest, please follow me, grab a black armband, and head down to Storm's office.

And I leave. The lesson is over.

CHAPTER 22

Surrounded by Morons Making Millions

I lock eyes with Storm.
"Did I tell a student 'Don't Fuck With Me?'" All eyes are on me. I look around: Storm, Leaffler, Sad, Blister, the union lady. I calculate I'm surrounded roughly by people making a million dollars of tax payer's money. I'm making five percent of that.

"Yes. Yes, I did." It's Storm's meeting.

"Can you explain that?"

"Well, sure. I was frustrated. I thought I was being lied to. You, Mrs. Sad, know about the confusion about getting the special effect for the Steve Martin play. The student—Captain Canary—had given me contradictory explanations about who was responsible, The Hippie was doing his usual routine, washing his hands of all responsibility in a New York nanosecond, and you, Mrs. Sad, seemed to be giving me mixed messages. So I was confused, frustrated, you all know about my anxiety disorder"—I made sure I lock my macular-degenerated eye on Ms. Blister to see if she has been let in on that fact—"and all these things led to my uttering those words."

"So you think the remark was justified?"

I pause. Suddenly, I'm seeing other people in the room. I see my father dressed in a green suit and bow tie, with arms folded, stern look on his face, seemingly standing behind Storm. He's not happy; I've seen the look. In the corner, I see Tom in his wheelchair, huge

153

grin on his face; he's digging the shit out of this. Next to him, silent and showing no emotion, I see Caitlyn. My eyes start watering—all these people are people I love, and they are all dead. Storm pulls me out of the vision.

"So you think the remark was justified?" He's louder now. It dawns on me that in a sense, Ms. Blister kind of outranks him, so in a sense, I'm watching Storm being observed.

"Well. No. No, I don't. Well, yes and no. I mean, it is technically inappropriate language in a school setting, but I was with a special group of students, if you will, and it was not in a classroom, per se, I was with 'my kids,' if you will after school. They've been in plays with me before, and not that, that justifies what I said, but it does, in a sense, explain it."

Tom is making the fish hook sign. We used that when someone was telling someone else a story that was a crock, but sounded real, and you were trying to get the listener to bite on the story. When you were done setting them up, someone, usually Tom, would slowly make a hook out of his finger and slowly move it past his mouth. This was a sign to the one being duped that he was being conned, that he had swallowed the bait. I look at my father and remember watching him coach high school football at Rich East when I was little. Storm again.

"I'm not sure we understand. Explains it how?"

I love it when people shift into the royal we. It's like they need to be not alone. As Bob says, they just want to be on the side that's winning.

"Well, okay, it's like sports in a way. My son plays football, and he told me once he wished he had a nickel for every time this one coach called him or the team, and I quote, "a whole bunch of fucking pussies," or one player a "fucking pussy." I've heard this. I'm sure all of us, if we observed a football practice"—I really punch we observed—"we would hear stuff like that all the time. You know, sometimes these coaches whip kids with whistles or shove them, you know, really get in their faces to motivate them. And I'm betting that these coaches are rarely called into an office like this one to explain what they were doing. There's an implied bond, between the coach and his team, and the team knows if someone 'ratted' out the coach, no one would accept that, and that person would be seen as a traitor of sorts and ostracized by the whole team in an unofficial way. I mean no one would be blatant about it, but it is unspoken and known. The team is the team, right? There is no 'I' in team, right? Everyone supports the concept of team, rah rah rah, all that kind of bond building."

And, I'm thinking, Captain Canary will be ostracized the same way, the little suck-up. My father is not mad at this, but he is not amused either. Tom is grinning, his eyes sparkling. Caitlyn is stoic.

Storm doesn't know what to say to all that, so he passes the baton to Mrs. Sad with kind of a disgusted wave of his hand. She clears her throat before she speaks.

"Did you announce at a play rehearsal that someone in the cast—one of the teenagers on your team—that one of them would have to perform a sexual act on the auditorium manager, or the set for the spring play would not be finished on time?"

This sets Tom off on one of his hands-clasped, shut-eyes-at-the-ceiling, voiceless laughs. This is like "So you're the type who likes to be beat first." And Caitlyn laughs because she knows exactly what I'm talking about. I don't look at my dad.

"Well, uh, yeah, it was a joke, a bad joke perhaps, but I meant in a humorous way."

"That does it," says Storm. I don't know what *it* is.

My eyes explode with warm water, and I stand up.

"Wait a minute, wait a minute, wait a goddam minute here. It was a joke. At the time, I thought it was funny, and the kids did laugh, but is it funny now? Not so much. Yes, it was inappropriate, and yes, I've been a little off these past weeks, but whose fault is that? Not mine. These people—in this very room!—have conspired with a series of unexplained, unwarranted, unwanted observations that my doctor told you"—pointing at Storm—"at least twice that this inhumane practice was detrimental to my health, my psyche, hell, my entire being (*ticktock*) and yet you go ahead and keep this shit up, and now I'm scheduled once again to be observed by *that* person"—pointing at Leaffler—"in two fucking days, and I have lost (*ticktock*) total vision in my right eye because of these, these methods, strategies, whatever the fuck you want to call them, and the last time she observed me, the write-up was so unbelievably filled with 'teacherese' bullshit (*ticktock*) that nobody in their goddam right mind would understand it, let alone implement the fucking thing because it has nothing to do with changing students' lives if you don't know, so why else are we here in this building? What is our purpose? It's about the future of these kids, and if you think"—pointing at Sad—"that whatever this charade you played with Captain Canary— did you really think you could fool a Corleone with that (*ticktock*), and why, oh why I had to endure this treatment from the likes of Leaffler and Drake—oh, don't think I don't know she's behind this as well in that department, your department—"

I stop, and I am losing my breath, but Leaffler speaks up suddenly. "The department you referred to as the Vagina Militia?"

"*That's a goddam lie!* I never said that. I never said that. You"—pointing at the union rep—"write that down, I want that on the record. I *never ever used the term 'Vagina Militia.'*"

This was technically true. I called them the Vagina *Mafia*. But I wasn't going to explain to them at this point that a militia is a good thing, it protected people during the Revolutionary War or whatever, but the Mafia was a bad thing with bad people, and the comparison was much more accurate, and I stop.

Tom is gone. Caitlyn is gone. My father is gone.

I look around the room, and everyone is stunned with these frozen expressions of, well, not concern, but something similar. Finally, Blister speaks.

"I think you should take some time off with paid leave. We have a psychiatrist our district uses, and I want an independent analysis from him to see if you're fit to teach. His classes will have to be covered and his theater responsibilities as well."

"Biff can take over the play," I say calmly. "But do you see what you've done? This woman"—pointing at Blister—"is the only person here who is concerned about my health, and I don't even know her."

More silence. "Can you drive yourself home?"

"Yes."

More silence. "Does this mean I won't be observed by Leaffler?"

"Oh no," says Storm. "I'm sure this will only take a day or two, and you'll be back good as new and—"

Blister cuts him off. "We don't know how long it will or won't take. Can you inform the union as to these events," she says to the union rep who says she'll tell Conrad.

I'm thinking there's about three weeks left in school. Conrad can handle American Studies. Anybody can handle the two acting classes. American Literature could be a problem, but I think Mrs. Tanks could handle that. I look at Leaffler, and she's freaking scared.

"I will send you detailed lesson plans for my classes for the next week or so," I tell her.

"I would appreciate that," she says.

Storm escorts me to my room where I pick up my briefcase and other papers that need grading. He walks me out the back to the parking lot.

"It was just a stupid joke," I tell him. "I didn't mean anything by it. I was just trying to be funny with my kids."

"I didn't want it to go this way," he says. "I thought you'd get through the last observation, and I'd put it to rest."

"I'm sorry," I say, still tearing. "It was just a stupid joke."

"Don't worry about that," says Storm. He puts his arm around me. "Take care of yourself."

And I leave. I call Conrad from the road and fill him in. I have to stop about halfway home and pull over and just sob—for quite a while. And I take more pills, which work quickly.

I never went back that year. They filled in for me, and my union guy, Barnum, told me not to worry, that everybody wanted to see me better in the fall. He also said not to contact anyone unless he knew about it—visions of future serious, approaching waters flashed.

It was at this time I got the call from the former district teacher whose son I had in American Lit. and how he hadn't read a book since fourth grade. But now he couldn't stop reading, and when she asked him why, he said that "his teacher made *Gatsby* come alive, and he really wanted to become a writer." She had heard I was taking a leave and didn't press for details, but as a teacher, she wanted me to know I had changed her son's life. Best medicine in the world. See, she knew what teaching was about.

Think about that. This kid's mother was a teacher, and she could not motivate him for whatever reasons, and fortunately, I found a way to do so. This is a kid who didn't like to read, raised in a home with a concerned parent. Now he wants to be a writer.

Now think of all the kids who did not have the advantage of having a concerned parent. All these kids are mixed together, and the current thinking is that a teacher's evaluation will rest on test scores from whoever makes their way into that teacher's classroom.

Even if a kid is raised in an educationally centered home, there's no guarantee on that child's performance. Throw in the kids from non-educationally concerned homes and then give them all a test written by a committee of morons.

Now grade the teacher on the test results. It's ridiculous.

I eventually met with the district psychiatrist who had no clue as to why I was there, but his report said that I was one of the most nervous people he had ever met. Regardless, there was no reason I could not teach. I assume Blister met with the union, and they found a way to keep me paid while on leave. I didn't return until the following August.

And the observation from Leaffler? Never happened.

I was never observed again.

CHAPTER 23

Lights Fade, Curtain Drops

The next few weeks were a jumbled mix of emotions and confusion boats—I literally felt adrift. On one of my recent visits to have that needle stuck in my eye, the doctor noticed a bump on my cheek that turned out to be cancer. It was benign but I still, I had to have surgery. This occurred before my appointment with the district shrink Blister insisted I see, and I asked her if I could delay the shrink until after my cancer surgery. She flat-out refused. "We are paying you, and we are doing enough for you," she e-mailed me. "You will meet with the psychiatrist as required." (So much for measuring her temperature—another hostile factor to deal with.)

After talking with Conrad, who was, I believe, genuinely sympathetic with my situation, I began to see the head union attorney Barnum and his hands-on professional backup, a woman I liked named Kelly. The decision was made that I should communicate only with Conrad and Storm. Leaffler would communicate through Storm, and Blister would communicate through Barnum. The whole thing became very military, very stringent, very much don't-talk-to-anybody and just sit. Barnum and Kelly were also sympathetic to my plight, especially the health issues, and we built a strong bond at that particular time.

For the remainder of the semester, I had American Studies with Conrad, the two acting classes, and one American Lit. class. I had already lost American Studies for the following year and assumed they would put Rocket in that spot. In fact, that's exactly what Leaffler planned until Conrad lobbied Leaffler to put another new teacher in Comm. Arts there, who was buddies with Conrad's boss. Without me there, and with Conrad gone for some reason, (he was conveniently away a lot for athletic events or sick kids) the class made the new teacher cry on her first day. Why? Because she was not part of the class culture the Pros from Dover had created. She came in like a commandant, and they turned on her, revolted—I don't blame them—but I cannot believe Conrad threw her in there alone to face over fifty students. These kids were, as Robin Williams character says in *Dead Poets,* "freethinkers." Would it surprise anyone that these students might think, "Something is happening here, what it is ain't exactly clear." The next day, Conrad, Conrad's boss, Leaffler—they all had to come in and read the kids the riot act and explain why things had changed. The kids were pissed because I was gone, but their teachers were vague about why. I was told via e-mail from Amy that there was a petition going around to reinstate me.

I have no idea why Conrad lobbied so hard for this teacher, but she was a disaster from day one and basically created a class of students who unanimously hated her guts—in just two days. She was a typical Leaffler hire. Forgive me for assuming that the reason for the students' reaction to her was the same reason why students from Conrad and my American Studies class, who were moved at semester over the years to the other section that was then co-taught by Leaffler, tried to beg their way back into ours. The reason? The Pros from Dover were the superior teachers so the students related to us, and they knew our priority was them. Period. There is no doubt in my mind that's the way it went down.

That decision by Conrad, convincing Leaffler to bring in this new incompetent and remove me from the American Studies class— eventually destroyed the existence of American Studies at that school. Why? No one signed up for it. Why? Whatever Conrad and I had created was gone. Much later on, when I saw him and mentioned the "Pros from Dover," he smiled with his gee-whiz smile and said, "I don't know, the new teacher is pretty good." When he said *that,* I couldn't fucking believe anything else he said. He had destroyed everything we ever had as a unit with that one snotty remark. It was the second-to-last sincerely approached conversation I ever had with him. From then on, it was a surface relationship. There was nothing left between us. And this from a guy whose mother hugged me the first time I met her because the previous teacher he worked with was causing him to lose sleep; she was so bad she gave him nightmares. His mother saw me as the antidote to his nightmares. Because now, he had found the perfect partner for American Studies, and his sound sleep returned. His mom hugged me ironically at a cross-country sectional meet at Rich East. I'm still pissed that he deserted me, pissed at myself as well, and it's not what anyone did to anyone. It's that it happened to us. And he never came clean with me about what happened. And he denied what we were. He acted as if we never happened. I have trouble forgiving him for that.

Barnum, my union man, was a key voice of support at this time, as was Duke and my counselor Canella. We talked about what I had been through, how far I had come, the difference between the man who had walked into Canella's door and the person she was looking at now. One thing about Canella, as I've said, when I felt like giving up, she inspired me to continue to fight, to refuse to let up, to "finish the job," an ironic phrase on many levels.

I also met with Rick again, my lawyer buddy, who thought I had won the lottery.

"Look, you're getting paid. The district is probably pissed at Storm and Leaffler for letting this shit go so far. They're not mad at you. I'm guessing, they're secretly admitting you're the victim. I'm betting they are afraid of some kind of legal action, so they just want this to go away. They've taken off the boxing gloves. Rest up over the summer, come back in the fall, and I'm betting things will go back to normal. Leaffler won't observe you, right? You won. I'd just stay clear of Conrad. I don't trust him."

I nodded. "Yeah, maybe. Maybe, yeah—"

"What about your retirement status?"

I haven't mentioned that yet, as the timing on all of this—and all the rest of the mess that was to follow—I'm still having chronological issues with, particularly the final years.

I had received a notice from Personnel—Blister's department sends it to everyone every year, and I had always ignored it because it talked about retirement, which I had never thought about. Most teachers who start right after college usually stay thirty or thirty-five years and really clean up on pension. I, on the other hand, had started at forty-five, but it dawned on me one day, after receiving the memo, that I could retire at age sixty with fifteen years of teaching. I hadn't really thought about it before.

At the same time, teachers can accumulate sick days and personal leave days, and it's a much better deal than you could ever find in the corporate arena. There, if you don't use your sick days, you're likely to lose them. In education, you can accumulate them, and they are comparatively generous. I checked, and at age fifty-seven, my age when this possibility hit me, I had nearly one entire year of accrued sick time. Anyway, I figured when I turned sixty, I would have put in fourteen years. However, you add in these sick days, and I could count that as year fifteen and begin receiving retirement with health insurance (you pay for it, but it's cheap), and you get a 3 percent cost of living bump every year. The State of Illinois was going through major problems with their fund, but the state constitution clearly states that this pension money for state employees is sacrosanct and cannot be touched. Courts recently confirmed that fact.

Part of the attraction here was the pay I was receiving as a stipend for directing the school plays. There are four levels of rating for these stipends based on education and experience, and when I gave Mrs. Sad my resume, with acting in over forty-five plays since 1978 and directing another fifteen, I started at the top of the pay scale. My experience was at a community theater—a very good one—but I didn't emphasize that; and for all she knew, I had all this experience at the Goodman Theatre or at Steppenwolf, both prestigious Chicago theatres. Maybe it didn't matter. But to secure this, as I believe I mentioned before, I immediately set out to get my master's in a special fast-track program at Roosevelt University over three summers. This secured my position. Prior to that I had no "theatrical educational training"—no endorsement in drama, which they lumped in with Speech. Adding my master's degree made this retirement option look golden.

Other teachers with more service would hold on for extra years because there was a substantial difference between twenty-five or thirty or thirty-five years of service, but at fifteen, there was no real incentive to keep going. I think the next bump was at twenty years, and it wouldn't be worth waiting for. So when all this crap hit the wind tunnel, things looked pretty good as far as my financial future. I could teach two more years—by August, I'd be fifty-eight—and retire.

"You survived this observation shit," he said.

"Barely."

"Oh fuck you, suck it up. It's all there laid out for you. Just lay low, be cool, make peace, and you're done. You see that, right?"

"Yes, yes I do."

But then, just before school ended, the call came from Storm.

"I'm in my office with Ms. Leaffler and Mrs. Sad," he said, a little tersely. "You're on speakerphone."

"Are you taping me?"

There was a pause, and although Storm tried to cover the receiver, I could hear him laughing. One thing about our relationship, somehow I could always make the guy laugh.

"No," he said. "No. We're not taping the call."

"Okay."

"But I'm calling to inform you of a change we're making. We feel the timing is right on many levels. This change will be good for you and good for the school. We're going in a different direction, and one of the areas affected is the school's theater program."

I thank God I just took a pill. Boy, long pause. I spoke.

"Are you asking my opinion on this?"

"No," said Storm. "This is a done deal. We are extending you the courtesy of informing you that we are going in a different direction with that program."

"What direction is that?"

"We've hired a new musical director. And we are anxious to put a strong emphasis to develop a show choir. Like the television show *Glee*. Parents have been asking for it, and while Mr. Pitts was never a big fan of the show-choir concept, he has retired, as I'm sure you know, and we have found a new, young person who has a ton of experience with this type of musical, and we won't be seeing a need for as much stage time, auditorium time, we have used in the past to create the quality dramas you've directed. Also, these musical performances will dominate students' time after school and will take a huge chunk of the calendar. Now we won't be abandoning the plays. So you see, that's why we're making the change we're making, and as a courtesy, I'm informing you of that decision."

Pause again. Man, my mind was racing like the speed of light.

"Well, so what happens to the plays."

"Two things. We'll be reducing the number. And considering recent events, we're asking another teacher to direct those as part of this new direction."

"Who's that?"

Leaffler spoke. "Mr. Hose."

I knew the guy. He did have a background in theatre, but he was new to teaching and the extent of his educational theatre experience was chaperoning a bus on a trip downstate. But that means I'd lose the stipend. I didn't think they could do that. I was trying to remember the exact wording of the contract, but Storm was way ahead of me.

"I want to be clear"—his voice rose—"that we are not making this change for cause. We are going in a new direction. This has nothing to do with your performance as a director or the quality of work you have done for our school. You should be proud of that. I know you have taken our students downstate four times. Before you arrived, that had never happened. So again, I want to be clear"—that voice again, rising, where had I heard that?—"and again, I repeat, we are not doing this for cause. We are not firing you from this responsibility. Do you understand that?"

Boy, Storm was a smart guy if I was hearing him right. It was like he was talking in code. If I had been fired from that position, I would receive no stipend money. But I believe the contract read something like if there was a change in the stipend position, or more precisely, if it was not for "cause," it would be the school's responsibility to find me another stipend position that paid the same. If they couldn't find one, I would be paid anyway. I wasn't sure, though, I didn't think I could speak knowledgeably to the group on the speakerphone about this. But I couldn't just leave it hanging either.

"I think I understand. And I would frankly admit that the additional responsibilities may have been adding to my stress and anxiety, particularly through the observation process. But I need you to clarify something."

I paused.

"It is my understanding of the current teacher's contract that if a change is made in a stipend position, and it is nor for *cause*"—I let my voice rise—"then it is the district's responsibility to find me another responsibility, another after-school responsibility as close to the level of the previous responsibility as far as money goes, but failing that, I would be due the original stipend dollars, even if there was no new responsibility. Is that your understanding?"

He came right in and a little louder.

"I'm not sure about that! I think you're right. But I am not an expert on what the contract says or does not say or what it means. The teachers' contract is between the teachers and the school board. This is a union matter. I'm sure the union will guide you through this. But I repeat, and you tell Mr. Barnum this—we are making this change because we are going in a new direction, and we are not making this change for *cause*. Are we clear? *Are we clear?*"

It hits me. He's doing Jack Nicholson from *A Few Good Men*. Got the voice down pretty good too. I know my line.

"Crystal."

Storm was throwing me a bone but kind of disguising it. He could have just dumped me, I think, but he made sure it was not for cause.

"I would like to speak to Ms. Leaffler," I said.

"I'm here."

"What happened to us? We used to be friends."

Pause. "We still are."

"Okay. Fresh start, okay?"

"Okay."

"Then I'll see you all in August," I said.

Storm spoke, "That's what I wanted to hear."

And then all three spoke over each other with "Take care of yourself, rest up, have a great summer," and so on, and we hung up.

I was sweating. I had to find the wording in the contract. I had to get to Barnum. And Rick. And maybe Conrad. He was still the main teacher representative with the union.

I thought Storm was doing me a favor. It sounded like he was. Or maybe I'd been had. Surely the district and Blister had to okay this. Or maybe not.

I needed to know what was going down.

CHAPTER 24

Contracts, Stipends, and the Art of Ultimate Frisbee

My return in August for the first few days of teacher information and announcements of the newest improved curricular bullshit were uneventful, save for Leaffler coming up to me in the crowded cafeteria where we were all seated, greeting me warmly, and stating—sincerely, I felt then, and I still do—that she was glad last year was over, that she was happy to see me and happy I was back. You never know, but I felt she really wanted this crap to end.

Storm kept his distance (a growing trend, I was to discover), except for a brief encounter about a week after the semester I returned when he and Mr. Fainero, who, you might recall, was the temporary Student Activities Director when Mrs. Sad was on maternity leave. Fainero was the guy who said "We must do" *The Laramie Project*, and had subsequently been promoted to Head Director of Counseling Services. This meant he was the boss of all four deans, including Mazona Drake, and was, for all intents and purposes, the second most powerful person in the building after Storm himself. Storm walked to my room with Fainero the evening of "meet the parents" night—about a week after school started—and Storm informed me that if I had any problems, situations, anxieties, and so on, I should contact Fainero. Directly. No one else. I was stunned because this basically usurped Leaffler's authority to supervise, criticize, observe or have any other impact on my career.

This was huge and had several possible meanings. Maybe the district was pissed at Storm and Leaffler and wanted my situation turned over to someone else. It had to piss off Leaffler. In fact, that night, I had gone downstairs to give a book to Conrad's boss (the lady with the affected foreign-sounding name) about a woman raised in a very conservative church who had left when they were gay-bashing from the pulpit. It was a book I thought she would like because she had lived a very similar life. I had the book, her door was closed, and I was just going to leave it when I heard her shout "Come in!" and there, behind closed doors, were Conrad's boss and Leaffler. It was very apparent to me by the awkward vibes that they had been talking about me, and I'm sure it was about Storm yanking the rug out from under Leaffler. I liked Fainero and had always gotten along well with him, but this whole thing looked a little weird from the get-go and proceeded to evolve into something even weirder.

My first stop after I returned was to connect with Mrs. Sad, who was also warm and welcoming, to confirm that I would receive my stipend dollars as play director for the performance of *Picasso at the Lapin Agile* last spring. The confusion resulted because Biff finished directing the play, and they paid him part of my stipend. This was okay with me because I was going to give Biff some of it anyway, so Sad and I figured out the hours I worked, more or less, and she processed my check, which was deposited within a week or so. That was one problem solved.

The union contract said I was due future stipends, as a result of Storm's benevolent "change not for cause" but it did say that the school was responsible for finding me a comparable duty. But when I talked with Storm, he said "he hadn't had the time to do anything about it," and then said, off the record to me, "You know, you read the language here and it says find a comparable stipend, but if there is no comparable duty found, the employee gets the money anyway. Well, there is no comparable stipend. Let's let this sit. If the district asks, which I don't think they will, I'll tell them there is nothing available. We'll just pay you. You're retiring, when, after next school year? Let's not do anything right now. Let's test the district on this. I checked with Barnum, and the union will support this. Just chill out for a while."

"But I'm not against doing something," I said. "I thought I could help. Maybe supervise the weight room after school, something like that." Man, he laughed out loud about that. He tried to be witty and said, "Do you really want to walk in to that sweat-filled, humid environment with young men and women pumping iron, and work out and shower afterwards with no clothes on in front of these athletes?" He was poking fun at me, a confessed man of size; and as I recently found out, I was two years older than Storm. I replied, "No, young man, I guess not."

More and more, I sensed that something happened between Storm and the district, specifically Blister. Storm took the position that he was not going to do anything, would claim he'd never been ordered to make me do something after school, and he would feign ignorance about anything they asked about me. He told me I should make certain the union continued to press them on the monies owed me, as the contract was clear I was due the money. The next stipend was due in November.

The convolution of all this pertained to the language in the current contract, and needs more clarification. My two stipends—for directing the fall and the spring plays—totaled $10,600 per school year. This was at the high end of the stipend scale because I was placed there by Sad when I first took the job, due to the ton of theatrical experience I amassed on my theatre resume. And this also affected my retirement because the amount of my pension would be calculated by averaging the last four years of salary. On top of that, once I signed the form, I was, under the contract, assured a 6 percent raise for the last two years of my employment.

Sweet deal, eh? Yet in my mind, this was no different from the obscene bonuses given in the corporate world to vice presidents in charge of looking out the window, or the ridiculous golden parachutes handed out to CEOs, many of whom have done a terrible job.

Teaching isn't easy—it's grueling. You have to have the gift or you won't make it. I know I'm repeating myself, but goddamit, it has always been my view that teachers should be paid like doctors and lawyers; their contributions affect the lives of millions of young people, and from a societal standpoint, what they give back to the human race is far, far greater. We've blown these other professions up to be much more than they are, and the push-back from private business is huge, particularly from people in the community, many of whom have found their ways onto school boards, who equate teachers as nothing more than unionized communists.

This issue is huge in many states right now where teacher pensions are being attacked for such factors as the 6 percent salary bump in the teacher's final year. This is standard operating procedure in my experience though it's changing. The downside, of course, is the people—like Drake—who are drawn to the profession not to help students learn, not to change lives, but to steamroll anyone who gets in their way as they climb the educational salary ladder as fast as possible. It's at the top of these pension hierarchies where you find these injustices, and it is the exception, not the rule. But those who abuse the system, the climbers; those who pretend to care about students but are only interested in their raises and summers off—these people are a major part of the educational problem in this country.

The union was hearing nothing from the district, yet Storm assured me they had told him I was covered. I became so worried about this, at the urging of the union folks, I pushed Storm to put it in writing or at least solidify the arrangement with the district. November came, and there was no stipend. I needed to have this settled.

One day, I brought this up again in Storm's office, and he said, "Do you want me to call over there so you can hear it yourself?"

"Yes."

So I watched him call Blister, and yes, she agreed I was due the stipend, but she instructed him to find something for me to do. He winked at me and said on the phone, "I'm unclear about this. You told me to find him something to do, but there was nothing comparable. I think the contract is quite clear on that." There was a pause, and then he said, "It was my understanding that this was, you know, a Sunday school suggestion. I wasn't aware this was something I had to do. I may have misunderstood that." There was a pause, and he said, "All right. I'll take care of it."

"She's insistent you do something."

He called Mrs. Sad and told her to find me something, anything, and he then told me to follow up. I met with her, and then a week later, she informed me of my new duty.

And that's how I became the first coach of the ultimate Frisbee team.

CHAPTER 25

"You're Very Well Read, It's Well Known"

I had three American Literature classes that year and two called Literary Themes, which is an interesting class that requires some explanation. The premise of the class was for students to read for fifty minutes, with no talking (except on discussion days), and the selection of the book was totally left up to the student.

The class was open to eleventh- and twelfth-grade students, and had a very strong reputation as a blow-off class only because the parameters were so loose. This was a perfect challenge for me because as the students were given less structure, the teacher was allowed at the same time to be freer to employ creativity, experimenting to see what would work. The teacher's immediate job was to find those who were in the class because they loved to read. These students moved through their books with total intrinsic motivation and averaged about one-third of the class. The other two-thirds had signed up for the supposed laxness in the structure and often had no idea what books they wanted to read, or should read. These were the students needing extrinsic motivation that I took on as my personal targets for life-changing possibilities.

The Hunger Games trilogy by Suzanne Collins was popular that year, as was Erik Larson's *Devil in the White City,* and another trilogy called the *Millenium* by Swedish writer Stieg Larsson, which included *The Girl with the Dragon Tattoo.* Before class even started, I invested in an assortment of John Grisham books because he was easier to read, wrote page-turners, and kept his chapters short. I bought multiple copies, so I would, say, have four students reading *The Pelican Brief*, and another three students reading *The Runaway Jury*, or *A Time to Kill*. This created naturally formed groups to present to the class the themes of the books as well as a visual aspect that generated some really thought-provoking student-generated artwork from all over the spectrum. For students not comfortable with group work, who preferred going solo, a straightforward literary analysis was always an option.

Occasionally, I would have the class read the same piece, usually nonfiction, usually a longer article from either *The New Yorker* or *The New York Times Magazine*, for a broad discussion because of a lack of really good, current nonfiction. From *The New Yorker*, we read Nicholas Schmidle's article on the hunt for Osama bin Laden. My thinking that this was a current event the whole class knew about, and it was written like an adventure story. It also served as the basis for the film *Zero Dark Thirty*. Part of this lesson was to analyze the writer's sources, and analyze how Schmidle knew the facts. My goal was a start a discussion about what facts were reliable and true. If I were to do this lesson today, I would include Seymour Hersh's controversial reporting rejected by the American media but printed in *The London Review of Books*, analyzing why Hersh's research was questioned and by whom? And I would also add *The New York Times Magazine* cover story of October 22, 2015 by Jonathan Mahler entitled "What do we really know about the killing of Osama bin Laden?" The truth is out there somewhere.

Classroom management issues arose again, which ultimately led to a gigantic dilemma for me. It started because the kids were supposed to read silently for fifty minutes, and they had their phones, which I refused to fight over. Some students would play Crazy Birds, or whatever it is, and some would text. I tried to keep an eye on this, but it was impossible without turning into a cop, which I refused to do. One civil compromise we reached was to allow earphones so they could listen to music as they read, and that helped both of us—students and teacher—manage this without allowing it to explode into a big deal. At least initially.

Some kids were attracted to books I loved—for all my teaching years, I had two full bookcases filled with books I had collected over time—and here I could steer the willing to read the complete works of J. D. Salinger (everything except *Catcher* which they had already read, but turning them on to *Nine Stories, Franny and Zooey,* and *Raise High the Roof Beam, Carpenters and Seymour: An Introduction*)

I had one student read all the Hunter S. Thompson collection, particularly *Fear and Loathing in Las Vegas* and *Fear and Loathing on the Campaign Trail,* a superior work in my opinion. I also had available *The Great Shark Hunt*, which includes essays that offered an introduction to Thompson's "Gonzo Journalism" approach, a relatively new genre they had not been exposed to, but, in my opinion, were great things to have under one's literary belt before heading for the Halls of Ivy or wherever their future led.

I remember I had one special kid who was a bicycle racing phenomenon. High schools didn't offer anything like bicycle racing in the standard sports official curriculum. The ultimate Frisbee thing was more a club than official, though I do believe lacrosse was added to the approved list before I left, a few years after bowling was deemed a competitive team sport. What I didn't realize was that this kid already had a full four-year bicycle-racing scholarship to the University of Montreal or somewhere up in Canada—in bicycle racing!—and he was a senior, I believe, in his last semester. This biker was doing enough to get by, but his mother approached me at a teacher-parent conference night, and pleaded with me to do something to stimulate his mind before he left high school. I was not aware of his bicycle prowess; he never said a thing, and I don't really think anyone else knew. So mom and I, who were on the same page on literature in general and liked the same kind of books, had a meeting of the minds about my collection. I grabbed Robert Pirsig's *Zen and the Art of Motorcycle Maintenance.* I didn't tell mom I had never finished the book, but mom had read it and was really excited about the choice. I talked to the kid for a while the following Monday, talked about bicycle racing for a while, and brought out this book. He gave me a look as if to say, "Are you nuts?" But he did start it and, unlike me, did finish it, and mom sent me a note later that he was really enjoying it. He did a bang-up job on some motorcycle-themed sculpture and went on to pedal his way through life. I do not know what happened to him.

But I do know that without that specific class, and without mom stepping up, his reading that book—a potential life changer—would have never happened.

CHAPTER 26

The Plot to Assassinate Huckleberry Finn

I had three other American Lit. classes that last year, a curriculum I knew backward and forward, required novels being *Gatsby* and *Catcher* and one other from a list of the teacher's choosing, and it was at this time, in my final year, that there was a secret cabal who were intent on killing Mark Twain's *The Adventures of Huckleberry Finn*.

Conrad, and I continued to teach *Huck Finn* when I was still in American Studies, and it drove the climber female clones crazy. Conrad was beyond their control, as the book was considered rightly, both history and literature. They wanted to kill Huck Finn—imagine—a literal character assassination. Mrs. Tanks, who shared my passion for *Dead Poets Society*, was particularly vehement in beating the Hucktricide drum.

"These kids don't understand it. They can't deal with the N-word, and I find it out of step with modern literature," she would bellow. No shit. A novel written in 1884 and set in 1850 is not modern? I would usually reply something neutral such as "Well, you throw out the fact that it stands out as the archetype of the Great American novel and had a direct effect on every major writer since its release and, well, our kids eat it up in American Studies. Are you sure you're teaching it right or maybe you are just, well, uh—" Silence. Tanks responded, "What? I'm what? Are you calling me a bad teacher?" "Oh no," I said with a smile and just stared her down. Another friend made. But I will state unequivocally right now that if you are a teacher and can't effectively teach *Huck Finn,* then you are a shitty teacher.

I heard Leaffler at one meeting say, "Then we can finally kill *Huck Finn,*" and the other mafiosi were heard to utter the tired mantra of "dead white males dominating the curriculum" when Harper Lee and Amy Tan were required at the freshman and sophomore levels.

They eventually offered an option to replace *Huck Finn* with a more modern book called *Into the Wild* by Jon Krakauer, an overblown tale about some dumb kid who idolized Thoreau and went off on an odyssey looking for, I don't know, America or "the meaning of life," and he ends up in an abandoned bus in Alaska where he starves to death. It was awful. The proponents of teaching the book as a frontier experience tried to paint this wanderer as some existential, transcendental hero when, in fact, if you examine his actions, he was some dude trying to be cool and, instead at the end of the day, was an idiot.

And the choice to replace *Huck Finn* with that was extremely stupid.

There's no doubt there are challenges teaching Twain's masterpiece—it's a very tricky novel to teach if you're lazy or don't know what you're doing. Even year to year, the teacher might have to use different methods and strategies to make the book's message resonate. But seriously, to be a teacher and say, "I can't teach *Huck Finn*"?

I'm reminded of the scene in *Mr. Holland's Opus* when the title character is asked to coach a failing kid to bang a bass drum to qualify him for wrestling—where a college scholarship awaits. When Mr. Holland is asked by the coach if the kid is going to make it, Holland replies, "I don't think so," The coach replies something to the effect that if you can't teach a kid to bang a drum, then you are a shitty teacher. Holland is taken aback, rededicates himself to the cause, the kid eventually "finds the beat" and marches, glowing, in a parade pounding the bass drum. Holland's initial comment about the kid "not making it" takes on a huge ironical effect when he returns in a body bag from Vietnam.

But the lesson remains—if you can't teach a kid to bang a drum, you are a shitty teacher; and if you can't teach *Huck Finn,* you're a shitty teacher.

The challenge, of course, *is* more difficult in the current climate, and that reason is basically because of the use of the word nigger.

Even now, typing it gives one the guilts. But I give credit to Conrad—for three or four years, he opened the book by saying, "Do I have the right to say the word nigger?" It was a fair question. Only about five of the forty-five of the students in a typical class were African-American. But Conrad's direction made the point quite clear until one year, I was grading in the back of the room when Conrad asked that question, and one African-American student went ballistic.

I didn't know what was happening at first, but Conrad, who always introduced the book because he had such a passion for it, called me by name and actually said out loud, "I need your help." Incidentally, it was the last time we incorporated that particular strategy when discussing Twain's masterpiece. I don't recall how we recovered from that, but I gave the best speech I could on the history of the word (without reusing it). It got us out of it, and I later had to ask Conrad what happened because I didn't see it. He told me that the student stood up, finger in Conrad's face, and strongly stated, "No, you do not!" We eventually came up with a new strategy, which I'll get to in a minute.

Conrad and I taught the book with passion and as much insight as we could muster. Supported by some awesome videos featuring scholars—mostly African-Americans—the key nuances in the book were made very relevant to our students, whatever race or background.

One of the unique structures in the book is use of time, particularly that Twain, writing mostly around and before 1884, after the Civil War, when the country is in the throes of Reconstruction, sets *Huck Finn* circa 1850. This takes the book "out of time" in a sense and makes a speech by a Colonel Sherburn so much more meaningful. Twain actually started writing *Huck Finn* but put it away and let it sit in his desk for years. Scholars disagree about where he stopped before picking the manuscript back up, but many believe it is right here, at Sherburn's speech, because the change in tone is so drastic.

Twain writes as Sherburn—it is Twain's voice we hear—facing a mob, wanting to lynch a white man named Boggs in Chapter XXII.

> **THEY** swarmed up towards Sherburn's house, a-whooping and raging like Injuns, and everything had to clear the way or get run over and tromped to mush, and it was awful to see. Children was heeling it ahead of the mob, screaming and trying to get out of the way; and every window along the road was full of women's heads, and there was nigger boys in every tree, and bucks and wenches looking over every fence; and as soon as the mob would get nearly to them they would break and skaddle back out of reach. Lots of the women and girls was crying and taking on, scared most to death.
>
> They swarmed up in front of Sherburn's palings as thick as they could jam together, and you couldn't hear yourself think for the noise. It was a little twenty-foot yard. Some sung out "Tear down the fence! Tear down the fence!" Then there was a racket of ripping and tearing and smashing, and down she goes, and the front wall of the crowd begins to roll in like a wave.
>
> Just then Sherburn steps out on to the roof of his little front porch, with a double-barrel gun in his hand, and takes his stand, perfectly ca'm and deliberate, not saying a word. The racket stopped, and the wave sucked back.

Sherburn never said a word—just stood there, looking down. The stillness was awful creepy and uncomfortable. Sherburn run his eye slow along the crowd; and wherever it struck the people tried a little to out-gaze him, but they couldn't; they dropped their eyes and looked sneaky. Then pretty soon Sherburn sort of laughed; not the pleasant kind, but the kind that makes you feel like when you are eating bread that's got sand in it.

Then he says, slow and scornful:

"The idea of *you* lynching anybody! It's amusing. The idea of you thinking you had pluck enough to lynch a *man*! Because you're brave enough to tar and feather poor friendless cast-out women that come along here, did that make you think you had grit enough to lay your hands on a *man*? Why, a *man's* safe in the hands of ten thousand of your kind—as long as it's daytime and you're not behind him.

"Do I know you? I know you clear through. I was born and raised in the South, and I've lived in the North; so I know the average all around. The average man's a coward. In the North he lets anybody walk over him that wants to, and goes home and prays for a humble spirit to bear it. In the South one man all by himself, has stopped a stage full of men in the daytime, and robbed the lot. Your newspapers call you a brave people so much that you think you are braver than any other people—whereas you're just *as* brave, and no braver. Why don't your juries hang murderers? Because they're afraid the man's friends will shoot them in the back, in the dark—and it's just what they *would* do.

"So they always acquit; and then a *man* goes in the night, with a hundred masked cowards at his back and lynches the rascal. Your mistake is, that you didn't bring a man with you; that's one mistake, and the other is that you didn't come in the dark and fetch your masks. You brought *part* of a man—Buck Harkness, there—and if you hadn't had him to start you, you'd a taken it out in blowing.

"You didn't want to come. The average man don't like trouble and danger. *You* don't like trouble and danger. But if only *half* a man—like Buck Harkness, there—shouts 'Lynch him! lynch him!' you're afraid to back down—afraid you'll be found out to be what you are—*cowards*—and so you raise a yell, and hang yourselves on to that half-a-man's coat-tail, and come raging up here, swearing what big things you're going to do. The pitifulest thing out is a mob; that's what an army is—a mob; they don't fight with courage that's born in them, but with courage that's borrowed from their mass, and from their officers. But a mob without any *man* at the head of it is *beneath* pitifulness. Now the thing for *you* to do is to droop your tails and go home and crawl in a hole. If any real lynching's going to be done it will be done in the dark, Southern fashion; and when they come they'll bring their masks, and fetch a *man* along. Now *leave*—and take your half-a-man with you"—tossing his gun up across his left arm and cocking it when he says this.

What you see here is Twain letting himself speak through Sherburn, a voice from the future lecturing an audience from the past at the same time he's lecturing his peers in his present time as well as us, future readers. He calls them "beneath pitifulness" and cowards and pinpoints their criminal behavior, which is America's criminal behavior.

How do we know this? Because he mentions those who ride by night disguised with masks. The obvious reference is to the Ku Klux Klan which, for the book's time, was a good fifteen years in the future. Most references and researchers cite a date circa 1865 for the Klan's birth with a rebirth around 1915.

So Twain, knowing his audience, uses this time-out-of-time technique to underscore the book's many themes, most importantly that racism is alive and well despite the Civil War, despite the thirteenth, fourteenth, and fifteenth amendments, despite Reconstruction, with any proposed nail removed from the coffin in 1877, with the removal of Northern troops from the South and subsequently the rise of Jim Crow. "Separate but equal is okay" said the Supreme Court in *Plessey v. Ferguson* (1896), which was not overturned until 1954 with the Supreme Court's decision *Brown v. Board of Education*, and still racism persists to this day despite the election of a man of color to the highest office in our land in 2008. Twain envisioned it all. *The Adventures of Huckleberry Finn* is arguably more important to today's youth than it was when first written. Particularly as we once again struggle as a country with the issue of race. Because of the past, Twain describes this issue as an American anomaly and it is still alive.

The second major achievement in the book is the character of Huck Finn. Huck is Twain's hope for the future. Huck represents what is possible against the most incredible odds. He learns the lesson that can dispel the crime of culture assassination and barbarism against the African American and any other growth of bigotry anywhere, anytime. Huck Finn represents a bright halo of hope for humanity. Huck represents Locke's tabula rasa (or "blank slate"), having all the negative aspects of the slave experience imbedded in his brain—on his personal "slate"—and these thoughts are not just carved into his soul as normal, but as holy, or divine.

Yet through his friendship with Jim, those deep slashes become uncarved as he unlearns all the crap he has been spoon-fed from his earliest days. Conrad and I used to cordially argue in front of our classes whether Twain created Huck as a "Transcendentalist"—rising above the world he knows—even though Twain is on record as hating the Romantics. For example he often mocked the works of James Fennimore Cooper and called a shipwrecked houseboat the *Sir Walter Scott*. And Transcendentalism, as you have read in a previous chapter, is included under the Romanticism umbrella.

But I don't care. Huck's change comes from inside, from his gut, what Emerson enumerates many times in his essay "Self-Reliance," shown strongest and most vividly as the iron string that vibrates in one's heart. And this is depicted most convincingly in two key scenes from Chapter XXIII and Chapter XXXII.

> **I went to sleep, and Jim didn't call me when it was my turn. He often done that. When I waked up just at daybreak he was sitting there with his head down betwixt his knees, moaning and mourning to himself. I didn't take notice nor let on. I knowed what it was about.** *He was thinking about his wife and his children, away up yonder, and he was low and homesick; because he hadn't ever been away from home before in his life; and I do believe he cared just as much for his people as white folks does for their'n. It don't seem natural, but I reckon it's so—*(emphasis mine.) **He was often moaning and mourning that way nights, when he judged I was asleep, and saying, "Po' little 'Lizabeth! po' little Johnny! it's mighty hard; I spec' I ain't ever gwyne to see you no mo', no mo'!" He was a mighty good nigger, Jim was.**

As one of the scholars says on one of the many supporting recordings we used, "Huck begins to see Jim as a human being, as a person with a family, as a man—not a piece of property. He's a dad with children."

Then in Chapter XXXII, Huck convinces himself to turn Jim in as an escaped slave and actually writes down where to find Jim with the intent of turning him over to the proper authorities.

> I felt good and all washed clean of sin for the first time I had ever felt so in my life, and I knowed I could pray now. But I didn't do it straight off, but laid the paper down and set there thinking—thinking how good it was all this happened so, and how near I come to being lost and going to hell. And went on thinking. And got to thinking over our trip down the river; and I see Jim before me all the time: in the day and in the night-time, sometimes moonlight, sometimes storms, and we a-floating along, talking and singing and laughing. But somehow I couldn't seem to strike no places to harden me against him, but only the other kind. I'd see him standing my watch on top of his'n, 'stead of calling me, so I could go on sleeping; and see him how glad he was when I come back out of the fog; and when I come to him again in the swamp, up there where the feud was; and such-like times; and would always call me honey, and pet me and do everything he could think of for me, and how good he always was; and at last I struck the time I saved him by telling the men we had small-pox aboard, and he was so grateful, and said I was the best friend old Jim ever had in the world, and the *only* one he's got now; and then I happened to look around and see that paper.
>
> It was a close place. I took it up, and held it in my hand. I was a-trembling, because I'd got to decide, forever, betwixt two things, and I knowed it. I studied a minute, sort of holding my breath, and then says to myself:

> "All right, then, I'll *go* to hell"—and tore it up.
>
> It was awful thoughts and awful words, but they was said. And I let them stay said; and never thought no more about reforming. I shoved the whole thing out of my head, and said I would take up wickedness again, which was in my line, being brung up to it, and the other warn't. And for a starter I would go to work and steal Jim out of slavery again; and if I could think up anything worse, I would do that, too; because as long as I was in, and in for good, I might as well go the whole hog.

Twain shows us that change is possible, but it takes a total rejection of the lies learned—and Huck decides he will go to hell rather than betray his friend. It always helps to recall what horrors that phrase really paints, particularly for a young boy in 1850. But he does it anyway. Huck will go to Hell rather than turn in a friend. For Dante's nine circles of hell, the worst is for people who do just that, and it is where he places Brutus, who orchestrated the death of his friend Julius Caesar by stabbing him in the back.

Even though Huck has been taught that is exactly what he should do, he cannot. That's the message of the book.

Twain's revelatory message is aimed right where it belongs—at the United States of America after the Civil War and after the slaves were freed, albeit only on paper from his view.

The book is under fire from several sides. Among them, I believe is Common Core, the controversial new educational standards being set nationwide. Knowing our education system, they're probably changing all that as you read this. The most common objection is the over two hundred mentions of the word nigger in the book, especially difficult for African American students, and others who are rightfully sensitive about the word's use, and they should be.

One way I used to handle this is to meet it head on, not as boldly as Conrad used to, but I find it helps to quote Atticus Finch from Harper Lee's masterpiece *To Kill a Mockingbird*, which almost all students at the high school level have read by the time they are introduced to *Huck Finn*. Lee's book is set in the early 1930s, and when young Scout asks her father, Atticus, a literary moralistic hero of heroes, defender of Tom Robinson, and arguably the wisest and most-liked character in the American Literature canon, it is interesting to note his comment on the word's use in *his* time.

> **"Do you defend niggers, Atticus?" I asked him that evening.**
> **"Of course I do. Don't say nigger, Scout. That's common."**
> **"'s what everybody at school says."**
> **"From now on it'll be everybody less one—"**
> **"Well if you don't want me to grow up talkin' that way, why do you send me to school?"**

Note Atticus does not say the word is racist or inflammatory or a major sin. No, he says it's common, or used by uneducated people or nasty slang. At one time, he says it's like saying "snot nose," and it's hard to explain. This gives the word some perspective in its use over time.

In class, I avoid the word unless reading directly from the text; and even then, I skillfully rush by it, not giving it any emphasis or attention. Students often wonder why African Americans use the word among themselves and in their music, but otherwise usage is not cool and totally inappropriate.

I tell them that from my perspective—in my time—that African Americans, because of our country's history, own that word. They earned control of it through lynchings and the worst condition of human life imaginable, as so accurately documented by Mark Twain; a lifestyle that included the entire destruction of their culture.

They can bring the word up, but others cannot.

My explanation may not convince young minds, but it's effective in making the class aware of the power of that word—in their time.

CHAPTER 27

Biff, Max, *Deathtrap*, and *Oswald*: The Actual Interrogation

Biff and I kept in touch as he finished his two-year degree at the College of DuPage where he won the John Belushi Scholarship, and the completion of his degree at the University of Southern California, majoring in theater, film, and anything else related to both disciplines. While still in high school, Biff landed a professional gig at an off-Loop Chicago theatre in his senior year, portraying the kid Kenny in David Lindsay-Abaire's *Fuddy Meers*, collecting strong reviews. He played a ton of stuff at the local college.

After graduation, Biff returned to the area for a while, trying to do commercial and voice-over work, low-budget films that were somehow never completed, and he was all set to "go West, young man" to follow the American Dream to L.A. when—quite suddenly—he was offered the chance to join the professional theatre ensemble in residence at the junior college. A dead end as far as I was concerned, this troupe was very insular, cast the same people over and over again, and I felt the performances at the local community theater where I regularly performed and directed were comparable, if not superior. Nobody ever came out of there to do anything major that I could think of except Tracy Letts, who paraded around naked on that local stage in a version of *Lady Chatterley's Lover*. Years later, he won the Pulitzer for writing *August Osage County*, and a Tony Award for playing George in Edward Albee's *Who's Afraid of*

Virginia Woolf that originated at Chicago's Steppenwolf Theatre. As I recall, his *Lady Chatterley* experience had long vanished from his professional resume.

Typical young man turn-of-the road decision on life's map for Biff—be the big fish in the small pond or take your chance and go for the gold on the West Coast. We both experienced a spiritual moment in the high school parking lot, and I advised him to trust his gut, which in my spirit meant listen for that Transcendental inner voice from life's Commander in Chief, and follow it. So he headed west where, as of this writing, he is making a solid living doing commercials and voice-overs and has at least three agents. When I speak to him, when he calls about his latest success, I remind him of our parking-lot chat. Incidentally, the local professional troupe no longer exists.

But Biff did something crucial for me before that chat, which leads me to Max, the kid who wrote "I'm not participating in this stupid exercise" when given those asinine achievement tests; the student I rewarded with the highest rating of "six" for his candor and balls to stand up for what he believed, earning me a reprimand from Leaffler and friends. Max lacked motivation, but was a bright kid wrestling with his own demons. Conrad and I taught him in American Studies, and he sporadically finished his assignments. When he did, his creativity and whacked-out view of the world resulted in some significant pieces, but at the end of the day, at this point in his personal odyssey, he really did not care.

So I got him in the drama program where he excelled. His first major role was as religious fanatic Brady in *Inherit the Wind* and which was based on the Scopes "monkey trial". Penned by Jerome Lawrence and Robert Edwin Lee. Max's Brady was paired with another outstanding actor named Victor playing Clarence Darrow. The chemistry between the two helped execute one of the better plays I ever directed.

I also cast Max in the lead in our summer production of Ira Levin's *Deathtrap,* as playwright Sidney Bruhl. These summer productions, would begin the Friday after Labor Day. The cast would be comprised of juniors and underclass students from the previous spring, giving the actors all summer to learn lines and periodically rehearse before school began mid-August. The summer play provided opportunities for smaller casts, featuring the best kids, and we'd often enter these in the downstate competition. Actors usually came in ready to go, off book, but Max didn't. Something happened.

He was hanging in Chicago a lot. He would stay overnight with a group of kids at some warehouse. His parents, apparently saw no harm in this. I lost touch with him for weeks. When we talked, he assured me he'd do the part. His mother, who was a counselor at a neighboring high school, seemed unconcerned, as did his father.

He blew off rehearsals, telling me all summer everything was cool. It wasn't.

I let Mrs. Sad know my concerns, and sure enough, two weeks before opening night, Max walked into the school with his father to talk to her. Not only did Max drop out of the play, he dropped out of school. A girl he had met over the summer was pregnant with his child. Eventually, he did something I can't remember, and he was banned from the building. He later went to an alternative class offered by the district for wayward youth, and eventually graduated. And became a father.

While Max and his dad were talking to Mrs. Sad, I sat outside and called Biff, who had not yet left for LA. He was sitting with me when Mrs. Sad came out and I presented her with Plan B, whereupon she offered Biff one thousand dollars to learn the lead role in six days. And to perform the play for three nights with kids about six years younger—great educational experience all the way around.

Problem solved, and it comes back to me that all this was pre-Storm, which means it must have been around 2009. It was also post-Caitlyn's death. It really doesn't matter, does it?

Three years later, I ecstatically grabbed at the chance to direct at the community theater a special studio version (small sets, limited tech) of a play-in-work by Dennis Richard called *Oswald: The Actual Interrogation*. The play was based as accurately as could be determined from available sources—on everything Lee Harvey Oswald did and said and heard from the time of his arrest around 2:15 p.m. on Friday, November 22, 1963, to the time he was fatally shot by Jack

Ruby in the basement of the Dallas County jail on national television on Sunday, November 24, 1963, at about 11:20 a.m. Oswald died less than two hours later.

I really liked the script even though it had no real arc as some local hotshot high school grad told me (after he turned down the part of Oswald), but it didn't really matter. The point of the script was to show what happened because, unbelievably, no one had taped the interrogation of Oswald under his some thirty-six hours in the hands of Dallas's finest. And while I didn't agree with everything in the script, it was close enough, as well as interesting and thought-provoking. Plus, I needed an Oswald.

Few people recall that Oswald was only twenty-four years old when he was accused of shooting President Kennedy and Officer Tippit. Biff, on a stretch, could have played it, but he was in LA by then I began querying other alums I had taught, but in the back of my mind, the perfect person to play Oswald was Max.

He looked like him. He had the attitude; "You're the cop, you figure it out," Oswald said handcuffed in the Dallas jail. He was cocky like that. I hadn't talked to him in years, but I had connected with him on social media; and before that, as we still had each other's cell phone numbers. At least twice I received messages at 3:00 a.m. with Max's voice as Dylan singing "How does it feel" over and over again.

I checked around, and former girlfriends of his like Rose thought he might be interested. "He's much better with himself," she said. His child and her mother were friendly with him, and even though they moved to the West Coast for some reason, Max played the father role as best as he could and even carried pictures of his daughter for anyone who wanted to see.

So I called him, met him at a local pub, and pitched him the role. He was more mature, he exhumed an air of confidence, and he accepted the part. "I owe you one," he said, and he did it and was terrific.

Word of my doing Dennis Richard's play as a Midwest premiere spread and attracted intense interest in JFK assassination online forums and local Kennedy aficionados, both "lone-nutters" ("Oswald obviously did it all by himself") and conspiracy enthusiasts ("the rogue elements of the CIA plus the Mafia plus LBJ made it happen"). John McAdams, the king of the Oswald-did-it-alone-side of the issue, taught at Marquette University in Milwaukee and agreed to come see the play. A man named Phil also sought me out. He had a trove of JFK stuff and we became fast friends.

One day after a performance of the play, I mentioned Robert Groden, the patriot who gave the public the Zapruder film and numerous photographs from the autopsy of the president. (He was an adviser on the 1978 congressional reinvestigation into the crime and the top adviser on Oliver Stone's film *JFK*) and was the guy who had signed his book for Conrad and me after Conrad visited the Grassy Knoll at my urging. When I mentioned Groden, my new friend Phil placed a call, and two seconds later, I was talking to him. How cool.

We tried to get him to come up from Dallas to debate McAdams, but he couldn't. In the end, we taped a post-show debate between Phil and McAdams. It was, well, a thrilling moment for me.

I won't say the show itself went off without a hitch. I added some film of the assassination the playwright found intrusive, and there were some other cast headaches, but overall, I was very pleased with the results.

Right before, closing night, Max had an anxiety attack at the intermission. Came out of nowhere. Reminded me of when I had mine two weeks before Caitlyn's death. He took the same medicine I did—Klonopin—to ward off the anxiety, and I had some on me. Luckily, though, the guy who played Jack Ruby was a nurse and was able to get Max calm without it. Max asked to see his present girlfriend, who was in the audience that night. I allowed her to come downstairs to the actors area after Max asked to see her because I wanted Max calm. Between Nurse Ruby and this attractive young lady, Max finished that performance and the run.

He was terrific. He stole the show. I received all the feedback; he had the toughest role by far and more than pulled it off. He captured every nuance of the man, even though every nuance of Lee Harvey Oswald remains a mystery.

And another benefit later on, I met Robert Groden through Phil at a dinner, and he signed the two other books I had in hardcover.

I was three for three, and he had a fourth one coming out in about a year.

How this all ended made no sense.

A few weeks after the play concluded, Max walked over to see his girlfriend—the young lady who had helped calm him during his anxiety episode—at her home around 11:00 a.m.

He found her. She put a handgun to her face.

No one knew why.

I lost touch with Max for a while.

CHAPTER 28

In the Heat of the Storm

Let's call them Mika, Layla, and Evergreen. They sat front row, right in front of my desk and were former students of mine from American Studies. They were extremely bright and took total advantage of my laid-back classroom environment. When I left American Studies for the last time the previous year, it was this trio that caused the woman appointed to replace me to burst into tears. They were very likeable as students, and blonde, blue-eyed Suzy Creamcheese types with meticulous perfect tans and perfectly polished nails on both fingers and toes. Things were tolerable until the final two weeks of the last semester of the year. In my opinion seniors should be allowed go home anytime they want the second semester of senior year. They want out, they hate being there, and in the most extreme cases, as evidenced by this trio of wealthy suburban snits, they don't have any regard for anything outside the loop of their personal queendoms. But it had started earlier, and I didn't see it evolving.

The year was smooth until then. Few panic issues, and everything seemed all cool with Storm, Leaffler, and the rest. I happily agreed to teach five American Lit. classes next year—which was to be my last—to help Leaffler resolve some teacher assignment headaches. But with about two weeks to go, the Lit. Themes kids had finished all the class requirements. The American Lit. kids, had been assigned their final paper and were reviewing for the standardized multiple-choice final. Translation: my classes did not have anything concrete to do for the rest of the year. Worse was that the Lit. Themes gang, for the most part, who were scheduled to leave school early anyway for graduation practice and the like, were antsy and mentally out of the building, which left me to invent a brief final unit to cover the time without shortchanging my responsibilities.

The issues that slowly surfaced with the cream cheese trio started way before those last two weeks, and these issues were totally—I mean like totally—my fault. Happening so slowly I failed to fix it, the experience gnawed at me on several levels. Later on, as Storm listened to my explanation, I said the entire situation was out of control, and the only adult in the room was yours truly. End of discussion.

Crystallizing here was my specific weakness for becoming too attached to my students (Mr. Holland experienced a similar quandary) and subconsciously reliving the pains of my own high school dramas. In addition, I cemented my feelings that my teaching peers were a quart low, and the kids were the people to whom I related. One kid in my acting class heard me talking openly about this one day and loudly said, "My God, he is Holden Caulfield." I could not disagree.

I did it to Biff, I did it to Caitlyn, I did it to another actor, a thirteen year old freshman, who was outshining the seniors; and in four years, I became way too attached to that person because I forgot I was there to teach, which I did do, but I also loved being "part of the gang." The acting kids were my kids.

Mika, Layla, and Evergreen sought me out as a teacher of an elective class they were required to fill because I was the "cool" teacher to have. They didn't realize I was still their teacher. My problem was that their collective foxiness raised memories of my own failed high school attempted romances. Young women like these were untouchable in my social sphere back then though I was bold. I even recall asking the soon-to-be-crowned prom queen out, knowing I'd get turned down, but I asked her anyway. I was Don Quixote chasing windmills back then, and that trait surfaces at times, even now. I even asked this gorgeous green-eyed beauty to run away with me to Vermont in 1971, a la Holden and Sally Hayes at the skating rink, and she said, "Sure, let's go." "I'm serious," I said. "So am I," she said. We didn't, of course; I probably chickened out, but I remember receiving a somewhat brief kiss from her at our twentieth high school reunion.

Rereading this, I'm thinking, Who gives a shit about all this teenage bullshit? Somehow, it's relatable to something.

So this trio—particularly Layla—started to push my buttons. They were all smart, all accepted at decent universities, and as I assigned group work, papers, other assignments on books they were supposed to be reading, whatever, they collectively blew me off. Came in late every day. Talked all through class. Then prom was coming up, and I must have had flashbacks from the whole drama, and somehow from my deepest psyche, I decided to start giving these spoiled brats some shit. Rather adult of me, yes?

This involved listening and querying subtly about their conversations. Mika described the boy Layla was waiting to ask her as a right wing Nazi lacrosse player, so I started to speak to "Layyyy-la" in a very strong German accent about everything, including her missing work.

"Layyy-la vere is de homework, ja? Ve have vays, you know of getting to da truth, ja?"

"Layyy-la it appears you are spending *too much* time *vith* Nazi boyfriend, *no?*"

"Layyyy-la, vat is dis I hear about Swastika invite for your Nazi, ja?"

You get the drift.

Mika pissed me off one Friday when she casually informed me she would be absent the next ten days because she was going to a resort in the Dominican Republic with her mother. Reminded of upcoming work, including her group presentation next week, her tart reply was "Whatever, I'll do something when I'm back."

When I asked Layla about her work, I'd get this sarcastic "Not feeling it."

Evergreen walked in fifteen minutes late every day, appearing stoned, with a huge pile of leafy lunches from Taco Bell or Subway and stuffed her face all period, saying to me "It's the only time I have to eat lunch!"

This shit was maddening. Toward the semester's end, I'd see visions of Tom in his wheelchair laughing his ass off. I must have occasionally said something to him, I learned later. Caitlyn would appear looking sad. My father appeared, lips pursed, arms crossed, silently staring, expressions exuding disappointment.

I once gave Layla the Nazi treatment in the school cafeteria in front of the guy supposedly asking her to prom, very loudly. "Is dis lacrosse player from Deutschland I hear about. Oh Layyyy-la, can do so much better, no?" She was extremely embarrassed, and I did it.

Prom came and went. The educationally checked-out trio made the papers—part of a large group of kids arrested for intoxication. Someone had knocked over a mailbox. Police were called. Most of the names of those involved were not printed in the paper because of their age, but word reached me that these young ladies were part of the group.

Several things happened all at once, so the order of events may be off, but pay attention please.

I had planned a lesson focusing on racism for all five classes—the three American Lit. and the two Lit. Themes. My lesson centered on several sources, but included in all classes was the 1967 Norman Jewison film *In the Heat of the Night* starring Rod Steiger as Chief Gillespie, and Sidney Poitier as Virgil Tibbs. Now the American Lit. kids had all read *Huck Finn*, so the assignment was to contrast and compare Twain's view of race from 1884 to the film, about one hundred years apart and some thirty years before any of these students were born.

It's actually a very stark comparison, and Twain's message, that nothing changed after the Civil War and Reconstruction—is hammered home again by the film. Things still haven't changed much. Poitier, who is African American, recounted in an interview he was uncomfortable filming this stuff south of the Mason-Dixon line due to threats, which is why in the film, Sparta, Illinois, substitutes for Sparta, Mississippi. For the Lit. Themes kids, I came up with a similar assignment, individualized for each student based on whether they had read Twain or not.

This is how I remember these events. During the week after prom, I introduced the film and started it. The kids who were arrested for being drunk at the prom or as minors in somebody's home must have been suspended for a day or two.

I had heard about the prom events the following Monday. I subtly asked Layla and Mika, before I started the film, if they felt like talking about what happened.

"Like what?" Mika asked.

"Well, I was wondering if you guys received any, you know, consequences because of the prom thing."

"Yeah," said Layla. "All the kids got three-hundred-dollar fines. No sweat though, my parents paid it."

"So did mine."

Tom is rolling toward the front, laughing at me.

"Well, what about the parents in the house you were all at, did they get a fine or anything? Because legally, I believe, they're responsible."

"Yeah, they got—what was it?"

"A twelve-thousand dollar fine."

"Really?"

"Yeah," said Layla, "but no sweat again. They paid it and then had a bunch of kids over the next night for drinks."

I could not believe it. "You are kidding."

"No," they said in unison. "Why?"

"Why? Here's why—you're learning no lesson here. Your parents don't care."

"No, not really. We're off for college. They don't care."

Unbelievable. I said, "You know what? You guys are spoiled rotten."

Then I said to Mika, "You know, if I was your parent and you were my kid, I'd spank you. Unbelievable."

The whole class heard it.

Ray Charles opens *In the Heat of the Night* with a tremendous title song written just for the film, and I karaoked along with it, playing air piano at my desk, rocking my head back and forth, throwing out semidecipherable lyrics I made up about Layla and the Nazi and the prom and the fines. The volume was up pretty high on Ray Charles, so I was confident that no one but the trio would hear my version. What I didn't know was Layla was recording me full-frame on her phone.

Very early on in the film, which, incidentally, came out before the motion picture industry slapped letters on films to guide audiences for appropriateness, there is a scene where a character named Delores Purdy walks around the kitchen of her home naked while the local cop Sam Wood looks on lasciviously. It dawns on me, technically, I should have sent a letter home to all parents of all five classes advising them I was showing what might be considered an R-rated film. But there's no rating on the film, so I stop the film before the scene and say,

"Okay, guys, listen up. There's a scene coming up where, for about twelve seconds, a girl walks around her kitchen naked while drinking a Coke. Now trust me on this, you really can't see anything—the bars of the window block her, and they probably airbrushed it or however they handled that in 1967. Now this young lady named Delores Purdy, who is key to the plot, is described a bit later in the film by another guy named Harvey Oberst that, and I quote, 'she is very proud of what mother nature has done for her,' if you get my drift. So if you think you might be offended by this or don't want to watch it, just close your eyes. There is no dialogue. Again, it's only twelve seconds. Many of you are eighteen anyway or close to it, and I was probably supposed to send home a permission letter, but I did not. So here's your warning—again, twelve seconds, no dialogue, and you can't really see anything anyway. Are we cool here?"

Classes are cool, all five of them.

After school ended for the day, word spread quite quickly that I threatened to spank the Lovely Mika Meter Maid, though I didn't know the word was spreading at the time.

Later that afternoon, I'm having a pedicure of all things when my cell phone rings, and it's Storm.

"I need to see you at 7:00 a.m. in my office."

"Oh c'mon, man. Can't we just do this on the phone?"

"No, we can't, and I need you here at seven sharp and please bring lesson plans for your classes because I may have to send you home."

"I want the union there," I said.

"Conrad will be here as your union rep."

"Okay, fine."

Call over. My brain starts running (*ticktock*), and I don't really think (*ticktock*) that they can fire me for anything I said or did (*ticktock*) that I remember because to fire a tenured teacher takes time (*ticktock, ticktock, ticktock*), but all night, I get mentally ready to face the upcoming Storm.

CHAPTER 29

"Paranoia Strikes Deep, Into Your Life It Will Creep"

Mind racing all night, I think of recent events with my massive memory and talent to turn irrelevant thoughts into cataclysms of fear, searching for the catalyst that might be the trigger for Storm's morning summons.

Drake has, over the past week or so, sent e-mails to me that she wants to see me, but won't say why, and says she wants to clarify something. She makes a big deal about the fact that she does not need me to come to her office. (This is reaction, no doubt, to her ordering me to her classroom when we were both teachers, and I technically had seniority, but she ordered me around anyway like a lackey).

I tell her I have a study hall supervision in the large cafeteria right outside her office the first half of third period, and she can drop by *anytime,* but she can't meet me because she has all these conflicts I don't care about. This eats at me for days, and one day after school, I have a bad attack. I approach the newest teacher secured to secretly serve as my trusted friend when I have the attacks—and I really did trust her—so I let everything out to her, and she calms me quite effectively. I had previously shared with her my departmental description of the Vagina Mafia, and she wholeheartedly agreed at that time. When I had told her that just before that disastrous meeting last year, she had said, "Look, at least it's out there. Everyone knows where you stand. I'm a woman, and I see the bias going on around here. And if Drake is upset about anything, trust me, it's because she has a deep-down, seemingly irreversible hatred for men."

After talking to her, I said to myself, What the hell am I doing? And so I go see Fainero, the guy Storm himself told me to see whenever I felt things were amiss. Fainero just happened to be Drake's boss, so that's what I did. I told him I was getting upset because Drake plays fucking games, and he listened and left for a while and came back and said, "Look, are you hassling some kids you think are breaking the dress code?"

I paused for a few seconds, and then I told him that over the past semester, the only kids I "hassled" were female cheerleaders and a soccer player who did break the dress code each time they wore their uniforms to school. I did it, I said, to prove a point that even Storm was aware of. In fact, I had pointed out to Drake in the hallway one day and told her, "You're a dean. There's a kid breaking the dress code. Do your job."

A little pimpy, yes, but my intention was to point out to the students and the school that there was a rule on the books the school itself was breaking—that is, shorts and skirts must cover all areas that are above the student's fingers as they stand straight with their arms at their sides.

I actually didn't care about the dress code one way or another, but my lesson to *all* the students was if cheerleaders and soccer players were getting away with breaking that rule, then everybody should.

Whenever I did this, I never sent anyone to the dean's office; my favorite response from the students to me was, "I'm not going anywhere. Report me if you want."

"Good for you," I'd say, and I would talk to them about the hypocrisy of the issue; and as I told Storm, more than a year earlier, when asked how to solve this conundrum, I replied, "Either enforce the rule or change the uniforms or, better yet, get rid of the damn dress code."

Kids complained to me the last few years that they couldn't buy any shorts at the trendy local stores because all they sold were clothes that were, according to the school, too short. I knew this; I had raised two teenage daughters. I was instructed at that time to just report anything really inappropriate, and I told Storm, "Unless they walk in stark naked, nothing is inappropriate as far as I'm concerned. I'm not a fashion cop!" "Well, we all are," he said and ended that discussion.

I used to tell the students, "When I was in high school, we had a dress code that said 'no jeans, shirts tucked in, socks worn at all times, as well as belts.'" Can you imagine their response to that? Ridiculous, they all agreed, and I told them how we got rid of the dress code in one day.

The student leaders in our high school knew that most of the parents didn't give a shit about the dress code, and I was pretty sure their parents didn't either. I told them, one day, a strict coach stopped me in the hall for not wearing socks and lectured me on the indisputable fact that "socks were made to be worn."

"That's right, coach, and so were neckties. Why aren't you wearing one now?"

When they begged me to tell them the story of how we got rid of the dress code in one day, I said, "Very easily.

"You always underestimate the power you all have. This building was constructed for you. I was hired for you. There are three thousand of you and, what, about 250 teachers and administrators, give or take. You have the numbers on your side. So one day, everyone—and I mean every student in the high school—came to school in jeans with no belt and no socks and their shirttails out. The next day, they banished the dress code. They couldn't enforce it. School would become a full-time fashion lesson.

"The same kind of group organizing ended the support for the Vietnam War. If you're right and you know you're right and enough people agree with you, well then, you can change the world. Even yours."

Okay, a bit simplistic, I admit, but I wanted to show them they could unite, they could get things changed, which to me is one of the greatest lessons a teacher can give a student.

Anyway, I gave Fainero a shortened version of all this, what I was trying to do, and he said, "Look. You have an issue with the dress code, don't say anything. Just send them down to us. Okay? I hear what you're saying, but you're confusing the kids."

"Okay, done," I said. "And that's what Drake wanted to see me about?"

He paused and said, "Yeah. That's it." He saw the stress literally leave my face. As I left Fainero's office, I saw my secret confidante leave Drake's office. Our eyes locked for a moment, but there was no discussion, nothing. All this happened about three days before my call from Storm.

This was but one issue I ruminated on that night. There was the spanking comment. There was the film approval form. There was Layla's Nazi boyfriend.

My imagination ran wild, as it is prone to do. I remember Mika once told me, after a brief discussion on the JFK assassination, that her father had a very high-security clearance and worked for the government, and she could ask him if he knew anything about Dallas, 1963, when he got back from Afghanistan. "Knock yourself out," I said, but a few days later, she said she mentioned it and her father said, "Don't ever mention that to me again. Whatever happened in Dallas, no one knows and no will probably ever know." I had found her dad's name and discovered he worked for a kind of mercenary company, one of those "private armies" used in the Iraq war, and his Facebook page looked to me as if he had worked in military intelligence.

But I doubt that's why Storm wanted to see me. If it were, I'd be dead already.

CHAPTER 30

"Clickety-Clack, Clickety-Clack. If You Go, You Can't Come Back"

Surprise, Surprise! When I walk into the meeting, who is there seated next to Storm but Leaffler and Drake, each wearing their high-heeled skirty uniforms (probably damn near breaking the dress code), and set before them like Mannlicher-Carcanos are two laptop computers from which they never look up during the course of the meeting.

Conrad is late as usual. And after his arrival, Storm begins.

"The only people I expect to talk are you and me, unless your union rep has a question. Now do you know why you are here?"

Oh my God. So this is how it's going to be.

"My union rep, you mean Conrad, right? I mean the man has a name. We all know one another, right? Or do we need name tags?"

Storm nods. I detect a smirk, but I can't be sure. I'm glad I took extra meds.

First, Tom appears, then Caitlyn, then my father. The two ladies seated behind their weapons are emotionless, robotic, unfeeling masses of flesh whose fingers fly throughout. *Clickety-clack, clickety-clack, clickety-clack*, Tom bouncing his knee, snapping his fingers, having a good old time. What he's doing is the old Bill Bailey bit, picks up one of his useless legs and drops it just right, and the minispasms cause it to bounce rhythmically, beyond his control, but still cadenced as if the leg had a mind of its own. We called it the

Bill Bailey bit because he looks like he was going to start swinging into, "Won't you come home, Bill Bailey, won't you come home, you've been away so long." He's looking at me, he's singing to me. It goes perfectly with the *clickety-clack, clickety-clack* of the typing duos playing their melodic keyboards.

"I'm not sure," I said, "but my first guess was Thomas Colonise."

This freezes the room a bit, and Storm, using his witty style, smirks and says, "Oh, please do tell us about Mr. Colonise."

"I have him fifth hour for American Lit. He seems to be continually high on drugs, and he told me he was going to sneak into the huge senior photo because, while a junior, he was going to graduate early next year, so he would miss that opportunity. Young Thomas told me what he was going to do and he did it and I understand he got caught, but I never told anyone he was going to do it—in fact, I told him it sounded like something I might do when I was his age."

Which was true, and I personally thought it was hilarious. They have the entire senior class in the football stadium seats to shoot this slow, time-developed photo, no-one-can-move sort of thing, and Colonise had indeed snuck into the shot, but a dean collared him—not Drake, I think it was Ms. Regnis—and then Colonise told me they were going to airbrush him out of the shot, which I also thought was hilarious. Nice use of public tax dollars, that.

Storm just looks (*clickety-clack, clickety clack*), and I'm not sure he believes that I believe that is why I was called in (I don't). Brief stare-off (*clickety-clack*), Tom's doing Bill Bailey, my father has his arms crossed and his lips pursed, and Caitlyn is just there. Occasionally, she dances. I think she's wearing ballet shoes.

"Well, no, but thanks for telling me that," said Storm. "I hadn't heard that. Why else did you think I called this meeting?"

I let it fly, confidentially. "I thought it might be about the senior girls in Lit. Themes."

"Yes," said Storm. "Let's talk about that. From your perspective, what is going on in that class?"

"Totally my fault," I blurt immediately. "It's a class that got out of hand. It happened slowly, and I didn't stop it. They began to push my buttons, and I stupidly pushed back. While nothing ominous occurred, it was senioritis on steroids and I didn't stop it. I thought I could just ride it out."

There is an old song my dad used to play. What was it? No, it was not The Lettermen, too high-schooly; it was The Kingston Trio, folkies. "Freight Train," something like that. I was six or seven. I'm remembering that song because of the typing. Something about a hobo, "Be a bum, be a bum. Clickety-clack, clickety-clack, the wheels are saying to the railroad track, well if you go you can't come back, if you go you can't come back, clickety-clack, clickety-clack." It goes perfect with the typing. My father is mouthing the words "The wheels are saying to the railroad track, if you go, you can't come back. Clickety-clack." I'm thinking journeys, I'm thinking maps. Tom doing Bill Bailey, Caitlyn dancing.

Storm asks, "Did you threaten to spank a student?"

"It wasn't a threat. Far from it. But that's how this shit gets started."

I repeat the whole drinking-at-prom particulars and express my total incredulity that these kids went over to have cocktails the night after getting busted, and their parents apparently did not care.

"The teacher in me briefly turned parent. I felt I owed it to these kids to instruct them on why their behavior was not just incomprehensible, but just flat-out wrong. I told them they were spoiled. I told Mika or Layla if either one was my daughter, I'd spank them. That was it. And yes, it was inappropriate on my part."

Tom stops bouncing his leg and rolls his wheelchair closer as if to read what Drake and Leaffler are typing. He clasps his hands together and laughs. He's pointing at one screen, then the other, laughing and clasping his hands. I want to tell him to knock it off; it's not funny.

Storm says, "Tell me about the dress-code issue." So I repeat what I told Fainero. I remind him we had talked about this "*con-un-drum*" (I purposely emphasize each syllable, imitating the way he said it to me last year). He nods.

"Tell me, did you use—how can I say this—a *prurient* story from your college days to further illustrate a point about"—he looks down at his notes—"Stradlater in *The Catcher in the Rye*—something about your being visited by a high school friend from another school?" He has a really puzzled look on his face, and clickety-clack stops because I don't think anyone in the room knows the story.

Except Tom. He sure as hell knows it. He's giving me the two thumbs-up with that broad grin, which is always plastered across his face.

I had forgotten I used that, but I knew what he was referring to, and I didn't miss a beat.

"Oh, that. That would be in American Literature. Well, yeah, and it's a true story, by the way. You see, a lot of that novel, most of it actually, focuses on sex as part of the journey from childhood to adulthood. And specifically, it focuses on two road maps, if you will, or where you are on that map as a person, and Holden is at one point on the map, and Stradlater is at another point, but they exist in time at the same moment. Holden's attitude about sex is more of a spiritual view, and at this point in his life. Stradlater views it as a purely physical one.

"The story, all true, goes like this. My friend comes to visit me at my dorm room, which adjoins a girl's dorm, separated by a cafeteria, whatever. We weren't quite at the time where males and females shared the same floor, which my daughter did at the University of Wisconsin. Anyway, this kid, who had a reputation as a player in high school, arrives and asks me who he can call to have sex. Just like that.

"I said to him, 'Are you nuts? I just can't do that. I don't know anyone I can say that to.' So he sits down, picks up the girl's dorm phone directory, starts with the As and begins his alphabetical search, telling each girl who answers that he just arrived in town and was wondering if she, or her roommate, would be interested in having sex. I was appalled. Girls keep hanging up on him, he doesn't even know what these people look like or anything. Yet when he hits the Ds, one girl says yes, invites him over, he leaves and returns about two hours later, and nothing more was said about it. I didn't ask who, I didn't ask how it went, I was just appalled not only that he tried it, but he made it work.

"The point is, this guy's attitude toward sex mirrors Stradlater's, and I bet, some students in the room, while others totally identify with Holden and find my college visitor's behavior, as I did, well, incomprehensible and just wrong.

"They get the point. I tell them everyone's sexuality is their own business, and people will proceed in that area when they are ready. Stradlater is ready. Holden, as evidenced by his rendezvous with the young prostitute, Sunny, is not. It's that simple."

Storm asks, "So you feel this is important to understanding the book?"

"I think it is important to understanding the characters. And the book, yes."

"So you use prurient moments to incorporate into your lesson?"

I'm trying to remember the exact definition of prurient, but I let it go.

Storm continues, "Don't you think that particular facet of the lesson might be better, say, in the health curriculum when they talk about physical development?"

"No, because schools are too afraid to teach what I just told you, and it's important. That is why Salinger's book is so relevant in all time periods and all people. Maybe you should link the Comm. Arts and the Health curriculums on that topic together. The book is an excellent tool for discussing the issue. Isn't that why we're here?"

Then the hammer drops. Storm is reading off a list.

"Did you tell or ask or sing something referring to a female student, and I quote, 'So you're the kind who likes to be beat first?'"

I am stunned. Tom is going ape-shit. He's imitating the clickety-clackers. My father looks down. A tear streaks Caitlyn's face.

I say nothing. Storm senses my fear.

"I have to say, this is the first time you seem to have no answer, no explanation. Do you recall saying anything like that?" and he holds up the sheet and waves it in the air.

I regroup. *Clickety-clack, clickety-clack* is hitting warp drive—if you go, you can't go back.

"Well, I must have said it, and here's why. That is a phrase, a joke, if you will, I used in college with a friend of mine"—I may have even nodded toward Tom—"and he used it in a short story. How you know that phrase is—unexplainable, unbelievable—if I didn't say it. How else would you know? I don't remember saying it or singing it. Perhaps I said it to myself and someone heard. That's all I got."

I remember Layla taping me doing Ray Charles air piano at the beginning of *In the Heat of the Night*. I don't say anything, but figure that's got to be it. I do not remember saying it, but maybe I said it to Tom when he was in the room. I am, well, stunned. How can you explain that to anybody and have it sound normal?

Storm looks around the room, and as he rises, Tom, Caitlyn, and my father fade. "Here's what we're going to do. Today's Thursday. I want you to take a two-day unpaid leave of absence. I need to get a little more feedback on this. Come back Tuesday morning. See me when you return to school early. You have lesson plans?"

"Yes, here. All five classes are watching the film, and these are prompts for in-class writing assessments."

I hand them to Leaffler. Meeting over. Conrad says, "I'll inform the union about this."

I go home. I hear nothing over the weekend or Friday or Monday. I come back Tuesday, and Storm tells me to go to work and to behave myself.

I teach hours 1 and 2, do my 3-A study hall, return to my room, and here's Storm walking toward me, coming from Leaffler's office.

"There's been a development," he says. "I need your computer. I need you to grab whatever you need and follow me. And I'll need your keys."

Stunned again. I ask Storm what's going on, and he looks at me directly and says, "I don't know." I believe him.

On our way to some conference room Storm asks me if I want Conrad there and I say yes. We grab Conrad out of his American Studies class, and he asks, "What's going on?" I tell him I don't know, but they asked for my computer and my keys. When we get to the room, there's a guy I bumped into not five minutes before I saw Storm walking toward me in the hall, and here he is again.

The four of us—Storm, Conrad, the stranger, and I—go into the room. The stranger speaks.

"My name is Robert Strickman, and I am the interim Superintendent of Schools for the District. I am personally delivering and handing you this letter, and we are sending the same letter by registered mail to your home."

> Effective immediately, you are officially suspended with pay until you are informed you may return to school. You will have no access to the school building or any school activities. You are to contact no students and no faculty, with the exception of Mr. Storm. You may contact union representatives through Mr. Barnum. Failure to adhere to these parameters will be met with the severest consequences.

I explode.

"What is this? Who are you? I don't even know who the fuck you are. Are you familiar with my case? Do you know I'm set to retire in one year? Do you know these people cost me my vision? Who are you? I ask you again—are you familiar with my case?"

"No."

"Did you know I was set to retire after next year?"

"No."

"Great. You don't know shit. You know what, you better get caught up on my situation, and I mean *now!*"

He asks Conrad, "Can you give me his retirement numbers from the union?" Conrad nods.

He turns to me.

"Look, you're right. I don't know you and you don't know me. But I will tell you this. I'm a fair guy." And he and Storm leave and close the door.

I ask Conrad, "Can I get my pay for the last two days back?"

He laughs. "I wouldn't ask about that now. Look, I'll call the union. Then I'll call you."

One of the theater kids, Victor, his parents had given me a key ring with a turn knob. I'm shaking so bad I can't open it. Conrad goes out and comes back with some pliers. Storm returns, and I hand him the keys and an electronic pass used for weekend admittance. I walk out with him.

"This is it," I tell him.

"You can't be sure of that."

"Yes I can, and I'll tell you if you're interested—Drake is behind this. I know it."

He asks me if I'm sure and asks me about another dean and how I get along with her.

"No. It's Drake. Follow the money as Deep Throat used to say."

"You're okay to drive?"

"Oh, yeah. Feel free to e-mail me. I have a feeling there's some student work that will need my attention."

"Would you do me a favor?" he asks.

I meet his stare. "Could you write a note or something to Layla? Her father called me earlier, and she is taking it very hard and feels it's her fault this all happened."

"Sure. I told you, I was the only adult in the room. I'm responsible." I leave the building for the last time as a professional teacher.

CHAPTER 31

Tits

At home, things remain somewhat calm. I remember that I'm being paid; and Conrad says even if they think they have cause to terminate me, it will be a long haul, and union head Barnum and his colleague Kelly are working this with the district office, solely, it seems, with Blister.

I call the union, and they want to see me. I go in and tell them what I know, including the incredible use of the line "So you're the kind who likes to be beat first," which gives no one much comfort. I had to explain that again.

"Something happened between that meeting on Friday and the Superintendent showing up on Tuesday and Storm was caught by surprise. He had told me to go back to the classroom and teach, and he didn't know what happened and I believe him."

"Why?" asks Kelly.

"I just do. I could see it in his eyes. He also asked me to write a note to a student who was upset over the weekend because she is afraid she got me fired. Her father called Storm, for God's sake."

"What?," says Kelly, who is more and more taking charge of this fiasco. "Did you?"

"I have it here."

"Tear it up. I don't want anything in writing until we know what's going on."

Barnum says, "I have a call into Blister, and as soon as we find out anything, let's regroup. Who's talking to you at school?"

It dawns on me we are in *Law and Order* territory. This is now in a legal arena.

"Storm and Conrad, per Strickman's delightful hand-delivered, especially-mailed, registered letter sent to my home, as well as handed to me across the table at the Tuesday surprise meeting. All very thorough."

"Okay, keep it that way."

I leave them. At home, I'm getting e-mails from Storm.

> **There are a number of American Lit. essays from your three classes that need grading, and Leaffler says you're the only one who can grade them.**

I'm thinking, Let her grade them herself, but I have to remember I am still on the payroll and don't want to fuck that up. At the same time, I'm beginning to realize the Kafkaesque nature of this ongoing circle jerk so I blend two scenes, one from Alan Pakula's *All the President's Men*, the other from Sydney Pollack's *Three Days of the Condor*, one of the greatest CIA movies ever made, and reply to Storm in a manner reflecting the ridiculousness and absurdity of this escapade. I write back,

> Here's how this works. Put all the essays in a plain box and bring them to the third floor of the parking garage on Chicago Ave. You will carry a Wall Street Journal in your left hand. I'll see you but you won't see me. There will be an empty parking space with a flowerpot holding a red flag. Drop the box in that parking spot and take the red flag with you. This is necessary because of Strickman's May 15 memo banning me from headquarters. If you find these arrangements unsatisfactory, I may consider a riskier Plan B, though I strongly suggest

we both carry cyanide capsules in case we are caught or captured (no need to remind you in that eventuality, the secretary will disavow any knowledge of your actions). Plan B follows: At 3:13, right after school, come outside the front door of the school with the box. Students will be leaving the building at that time, but blend in; don't look conspicuous. You will wear a monocle and a paper hat, preferably of a mauve shade. I will be driving a gray Ford Escape and will pull up before 3:22. At 3:23, consider this mission aborted. I will suddenly approach, and the passenger's side window will be open. Quickly step to the curb, and drop the box on the passenger's seat. Come alone. Over and out.

Storm replies, "I'll meet you out front."

I drive to the school, park in the back row of the teacher's parking area, and when there is an opening at 3:21, I pull out and go the long way to the front of the school. I screech into the spot, and Storm steps forward.

"Hey, where's your monocle and hat?"

"Don't have one. I just got a call that there are two more essays on their way. Can you wait?"

"Are you wearing a wire? Hurry it up."

Storm's executive assistant comes out, and we add the papers to the box.

"What's going on?" I ask him. "What happened between your meeting and Strickman's delivery of the letter?"

He looks around and then sticks his head in. "Not sure. Something happened. Lots of meetings. They're meeting individually with your students. I'm collecting everything, but I have to seal it and send it directly to Blister."

I slap the steering wheel. "Are you out of the loop?"

"Maybe. I don't know. Right now, this is a Blister operation all the way. Just enter the grades on the computer." I can do this from home. He slaps the car door, and I tear out.

Storm forwards e-mails he receives from students. Some come directly. Some kids are asking for letters of recommendation; the ones I get directly are from kids like Amy, my student aide, who writes, "This sucks. What's going on? Kids are freaking out." I don't answer.

Then Storm begins to send more quizzical emails.

"I have been asked to find out what films you showed in Lit Themes this semester. Will you let me know, please?" That's at 1:08 p.m.

I reply at 1:45 p.m., "*Finding Forrester* and *In the Heat of the Night.*"

I show *Forrester*, directed by Gus Van Sant and featuring Sean Connery and Rob Brown because it's a great film about how to write, and there is subtle racism that fits the last lesson's theme. I think I used that film for any kids in Lit. Themes who had not read *Huck Finn.*

Then almost immediately, "What movie had some brief nudity in it?"

I write back, *"In The Heat of the Night."* I do not mention the warning I gave the kids or the fact that I didn't send a permission slip home. If that's what they're after, they'll find that, but I'd rather explain it in person.

Then at 3:10 p.m., "A student told us that you and the student are 'friends' on Facebook. Possible?"

"Yes, some drama kids perhaps, for rehearsal purposes, mostly alums."

I check quickly, and I find two active students; but one is Mika, and I do not remember how we became friends. This stuff was not such a big deal just six months ago. I delete them both.

That's it from Storm. After drinking several large cabernets, I start feeling bold and pissed off. So I write the union rep Kelly and copy Conrad the following at 8:09 p.m.

Why was Mazona Drake in that meeting? What happened to the notes they took? They typed

> them on their computers. Where did they go, what did they say? How do they compare with Conrad's notes? Something happened between the two-day suspension I received on Friday and what happened today. Did students go to the District? Doubtful. So what changed Blister's et al's mind?

Kelly responded at 8:21 p.m.

> **The District can have anyone they want in the meeting, just as you can have a rep of your choosing. Same thing with the notes; they can take notes by hand or by computer, just as we can. We can't stop them. We also don't have right to their notes, unless we want to give them access to our notes. I highly recommend that the Association never shares notes with the District. Barnum left a message with Blister, and hopefully after he talks to her, we'll have a better understanding of what happened between Friday and Tuesday.**
>
> **Kelly**

This drags on. I go see Rick.

"Something happened between the Friday meeting and Tuesday. I don't think Storm knows or he can't tell me. It appears they are focusing on the film."

Rick is stoically pensive.

"It's like I'm being subtly threatened."

"Threatened or threatening?" I say nothing. "What does Conrad say?"

"Not much. He's saying, like Storm, he doesn't know, but it doesn't look good. They're interviewing kids, they're holding meetings, Storm says it's all Blister."

"Here's my legal advice. Wait. Don't say or do anything. No more e-mails. You want me involved?"

"I don't think so. I'm not sure how they would react to an outside attorney. And they're free."

"Yes," says Rick. "They are. Wait."

Kelly and I exchange more late-night e-mails.

> "Kelly, right now I am on paid leave. How long can I ride this out. This is a strategy no one had broached." (Friday 5:52 p.m.)
>
> "I don't think we have time to ride the wave of paid leave. Let's talk on Monday." (7:32 p.m.)
>
> "Kelly, messages like this do not help. Where is my union? If they fire me, I'll grieve it, and that will take a year. Then I retire. WTF are you not telling me?" (8:32 p.m.)
>
> "This is why I said we need to meet in person on Monday. We need to walk through all of your possible moves. Your union is here and is willing to help guide you to a decision that will work for you. We will talk on Monday at the office. In the future, I would appreciate you not e-mailing me with profanities. It's not necessary." (8:58 p.m.)
>
> "You're right. I apologize. I am obviously stressed by this entire thing." (8:59 p.m.)
>
> "We'll get you through this in the way that's best for you. Try to relax; nothing is going to be solved over the weekend, and you need to get a break from worrying." (Saturday 7:57 a.m.)

I can't remember the exact timing, but I figured that sometime before Monday, maybe Saturday, I did have a brief meeting with Storm probably to pick up a few more essays. Saturday makes sense because I remember being in his office, and on Saturday, neither one of us would be sweating my being in the building.

He told me, "These things have a life of their own. I know they had meetings. They asked me—this was from Blister—no, they ordered me to set up the four deans to interview ten random kids from each of your classes. Then I had notes from those meetings sent over, but I wasn't allowed to read them." He told me something like that before, but I didn't believe him.

"But they must have something," he went on. "I am out of the main loop here. This is totally a district matter now. I know their lawyer is involved."

"Pointdexter?" I'm remembering the guy who screwed Conrad about the seventeen seconds of schooltime he used on union matters.

"That's the man's name. Whatever they have, they are looking for a legal precedent in past cases of tenured teacher dismissal they can apply to you. So if you said something or did something beyond what you've already discussed with me, that's what you should be thinking about. But here's the thing—as more and more people get involved, the harder this thing is to turn around. Now that's all I am going to say."

I'm not sure what he knows and doesn't know, but on my next visit to the union on Monday, I find out.

Kelly opens. "You have a problem. Did you use the word tits in describing a scene in that film?"

"No. No way." I explained what happened there and how I handled it.

"You're claiming you did not say, 'Check out these girls' tits,' or 'Look at her tits.'"

"Hell. No. I remember what I did say. I stopped the film. I said there is a brief nude scene coming up, a girl walks around naked in her kitchen for about twelve seconds, she is key to the plot, and, as you will hear in an upcoming scene, another character says, 'She is very proud of what mother nature has done for her.' That is verbatim! Kelly, you ever teach school?"

"Yes."

"Would you ever, ever say tits? It's ridiculous. It's suicide. It's a death sentence. 'Okay, everyone, it's very important we all look at this girl's mambo titties.' Who would say that or anything like that? I know I never said that in any class."

"Yeah, well, who would say, 'So you're the kind who likes to beat first?'"

Touché. Pause. "Tell me what you know?"

"I know this," says Kelly, "I was at the district office, and I ran into their lawyer Pointdexter in the hall. I asked about your case, and he said, 'Oh, he's history. He said tits to a class watching a nude scene in a film, and it's pretty solid.' Listen to me. They are going to fire you, maybe today."

"They can't. They just can't. Wait a minute. You ran into this moron Pointdexter in the hall?"

"We were between meetings."

"So based on a discussion in the *fucking hall,* you are ready to throw me to the dogs?"

I go on, "You're my union. How do we fight this?"

"It's hard. We have to get every kid in class to sign an affidavit saying you didn't say tits. A lot of these kids are already gone for the summer. That takes time we do not have." After a pause, Barnum says, "Are you sure you didn't say anything like that?"

"No. I told you that. Don't you believe me?"

Silence. They don't.

"Look, I have a year's worth of sick time. I'm taking it. Now. I'll stop this by requesting medical leave."

Barnum speaks, "Do it fast. Get the paperwork. You'll need medical letters."

"They have all that from when they were trying to observe me. Let's do it."

There is some scrambling, and someone makes a phone call to the district.

"I think they'll agree to a medical leave. I think they have to. Disability. Just get it all in ASAP before they decide to try and fire you."

"Fine. And guys? I didn't say tits, just so you know."

I do the forms. They are accepted. I have a year off with pay—a year I need to retire at sixty, which means I'll have to come back the following year. But that's a future problem.

Right now I have a lot of problems and a whole lot of unanswered questions.

I'm informed that they have packed all my books and possessions in thirty-one boxes and a bookcase that I have to pick up over the summer. The day I go over, Storm secures a big pushcart and helps me load the boxes into my car. I had to send some back because I had four boxes of Conrad's stuff.

Storm seems pissed. "Sometimes cocksuckers like us don't belong in places like this," he said as he loaded boxes.

"Maybe not," I reply. "Maybe I'll see you around campus."

CHAPTER 32

"Chasing Paper; On Our Way Back Home"

The end of May brings many e-mails from the union, from Storm, from Blister's minions at the district, all waxing the slope for my year of Disability. This was a paperwork swamp of swamps.

For example, after I mentioned Rick as part of my "unofficial outside team" and forwarded some questions he had, I received this from Kelly.

> **Who is your unofficial outside team? Our staff are not required to work with outside attorneys, and as you mentioned this morning that you had consulted one, I need to let you know this. I typically do not provide this kind of detailed information to outside counsel. We discussed the need to move quickly this morning. Once the Board receives a recommendation for termination, it will be next to impossible to do anything but resign or be terminated. Also, just as a heads up, if you work with an outside attorney on this, our attorney will not be able to represent you. You also need a quick medical note documenting anxiety.**

I reply:

> Okay, okay. I left a detailed note with my doctor today. No one is representing me. My unofficial outside team is just a guy I bounce things off of to be sure about stuff. Unofficial means just that.

Another note to Kelly:

> The district rep called and said she would need a letter from me requesting "family medical leave" with my signature, which she said I could scan in and e-mail. Subsequently, another district staff says she has the letter from Dr. Duke and I don't need another letter. I wonder if Storm and Leaffler know I won't be back? She says I have 154 sick days, plus 2 personal days and would need to request sick bank days for the remainder. I have entered all my grades for the year and informed Storm. I did not tell the District Rep that technically I should not be talking to her per the warm, cordial yet refreshingly succinct Strickman memo of 5/15. Comments? Reactions? Advice?

Trying to keep things in perspective for Storm, I sent the following:

> My good friend and fellow colleague Bruno offered me a trade today in our fantasy baseball league, and I felt like an idiot that I could not respond to him. Is there a statute of limitations on the memo of 5/15? Please advise. Yours for Peace in our Time.

And Storm's reply, "No reason you can't play fantasy baseball."

It went on like this for quite a while. The stipend issue came up again because not only had I not been paid, I wasn't even sure if I could retire if, for some reason, they wouldn't let me back. So

I keep hammering at Blister with e-mails about the stipend money since Storm and the union said they couldn't do anything, and the average salary that determined my retirement was a huge issue. So later on, these kinds of e-mails went out, summarizing the key issues. One idea for continuing the stipend was to perform a qualifying duty while I was on leave, which could be used as a stipend, even though the language of the contract was pretty clear that I deserved that money.

This note was from me to the district:

> **I signed the early retirement option in February 2011, which stated salary and stipend would be included in the annual salary calculation. So far this year, I have not received the stipend payment. I assume this is just an oversight; it happened last year and was corrected after I called the District office. I met with Storm yesterday regarding this, and we collectively recalled I was assigned an additional duty last year, which he would be happy to do again this year, if need be, though we both felt this was probably unnecessary.**
>
> **Either way, since I am strongly considering retiring this year instead of next, the stipend payment greatly affects my retirement plans to the tune of some $500 per month, which is why I need this to be rectified ASAP.**

No response. Then this from Kelly:

> **Just spoke to the attorney. As long as the district is okay with it, you can perform a stipend position from home while on Family Medical Leave.**

This from me to Storm, Conrad, and the union:

> Hello, gentlemen. Please read all of the enclosed. Basically, the union attorney has approved me for an in-home stipend if the District is okay with that, and they suggested I start with you. I have explained to both of you separately regarding the importance of this to my upcoming retirement. Storm, perhaps you would like to call me to talk about this or knock it around with Conrad, who informs me he sees you on a regular basis, specifically tomorrow. Of course I am available to come in if you prefer. This is the suggested procedure from the union. Thanks for this, guys. I appreciate whatever you can do to make this happen.
>
> **FYI: Kelly's note to me**
>
> Since you have already spoken with Storm about this, I'd say you should go ahead and talk to him. If you run into problems, get back to us.

Storm replies,

> I am not the proper starting point because I do not make decisions about what, when, or how anyone is paid. The proper starting point is Blister. She would be able to have a conversation with you about the stipend. She would then have a conversation with me. I take direction from her.

So I write directly to Blister:

> I am requesting your help and advice. As you may or may not recall, I am at home for this year

on Family Medical Leave and did not receive the stipend payment so far this year. Why this is so important to me is that it dramatically will affect my retirement income for me and my family. I have had several meetings with Steve from Teacher's Retirement Service on this very topic. The reason is because of the February 2011 early retirement option, which is structured to give me 6 % raises each year—including stipend as of that date—until I retire as long as I have 15 years and have reached age 60. I will be 60 on June 23, 2013. I was planning on having the 15 years by then, but because I am using accrued sick time this year, I will only have 14 years. I understand you have discussed this with Kelly from the union. I was also told that I would not receive the stipend this year because I was not at school. I e-mailed the appropriate person in your office last week regarding the stipend before I was told this. In discussions with Kelly, she discovered I can do work at home according to the FMLA, and the NEA attorney said it would be proper to take a stipend assignment at home this year to ensure the dollars contracted in the February 2011 Early Retirement Option agreement would remain intact, if the district agreed. I have talked with both Storm and Conrad regarding this, and we have some ideas that address these concerns. Kelly thought I should start with Storm on this. Storm responded I should talk to you. Following is the correspondence string on this. From the bottom up is my note to the District, Kelly's note to me, my correspondence with the union, Storm, and Conrad on the topic, and Storm's response. I ask that you look

> into this to see if you can help my transition to retirement go much smoother. I am aware I owe you a letter by Feb. 15 indicating my intentions for next year. I am aware Kelly and you have discussed this previously. I do not think it best for me to return to secure year 15—I'm told there is some other way—but as I am sure you understand, I must keep my options open. Thank you in advance for your prompt attention to this matter.

No response. I try again:

> I sent you a memo on Jan. 17 offering a solution to my stipend issue among other concerns. I have not heard back from you. If, for some reason, you did not receive it, that memo follows. I am very anxious for a reply. Thank you.

I write to Barnum and Kelly at the union:

> I sent Blister two memos regarding working at home for stipend, among other concerns, which I believe you have copies. A copy follows this note. I have not heard from her, and the 2/15 deadline for my letter of intention for next year approaches. Unless you instruct me otherwise, my plan is to e-mail her tomorrow to see what's up, and, if no response, I feel I should contact Strickman directly. Please advise. Thanks.

Kelly responds:

> **Neither Barnum nor I have heard anything.**

I go see Rick.
"These fuckers won't move."

Rick has a brainstorm. "What if I write Blister a letter directly and say I'm your financial adviser—not your lawyer. I'll just say I need some information to plan your post-retirement activities."

Rick writes Kelly:

> **I represent your colleague regarding his estate plan. He has shared with me the efforts undertaken to smooth his transition into retirement status, and he is very grateful for that support. He has a big decision to make. That decision has to be made by the 15th of this month. He has told me that he has not received an answer from Blister regarding his status for next year. My questions are twofold:**
>
> 1. **What can I do to assist you in getting a response from Blister?**
> 2. **As you know, your colleague has taken the early retire-ment option. Jurisdictionally, is the Early Retirement Agreement an individual contract or part of the Union contract? I ask this not to discount the help the union has provided, but to find out if he can sue to enforce the agreement on his own. If not individually enforceable, what is the union's position on grievance for enforcement?**
>
> **Thank you for the help and your work to continue to provide the highest quality education experience to the children in your district.**
>
> **Rick, Attorney-at-Law**

Kelly responds:

Hi Rick,

Unless I'm mistaken, from talking to him I've understood that he has 14 years in the District at the end of this year. He needs to have 15 years in the District in order to retire with the retirement enhancement. If he would choose to retire at the end of this school year, he would have to pay back any incentive he's received. As far as the early retirement agreement, it is an agreement between the employee and the district. I'm not sure what you mean that they would not follow through with it; again, if he does not have 15 years in the district, he does not meet the requirements for early retirement, and I would think that would void the contract. I truthfully have no idea if he could sue the District regarding that agreement or not. As far as a response from Blister, I know he has e-mailed her twice, and Barnum, the Union president, has reminded her to reply to him. At this point, perhaps an e-mail from you with the word "attorney" would get her attention. Just be sure to tell her you are representing him on his estate. If you have other questions about the retirement enhancement, please feel free to give me a call. I will be in today until 4:30 and in and out tomorrow.

Rick mails the letter to Blister and on his Attorney-at-Law letterhead. That night, after cabernet time, I say fuck it and call Strickman directly. I get his admin's voice mail. It beeps, and I say:

"I think you know who I am. The last time we talked, you said you were a 'fair guy'. Well, prove it." And I hang up.

The next day, Strickman writes to me and asks that I send him everything.

I write back and attach *everything*:

> **This is my previous correspondence with Blister. By Friday of this week, I am told by my union I must declare my intentions to return to or not. The issue of the stipend greatly affects my retirement. There is a very workable solution, which Conrad can fill you in on, but if I need to come back, which I am legally allowed to do, I will—why?—because it affects my family and my retirement earnings. Legally, I have been advised, because of the contract signed by the district, I am entitled to these monies. I ask you again to please familiarize yourself with my case.**

Then this from Blister:

> **I will be meeting with Barnum on Thursday morning at which time we will discuss your e-mails and voice mails. You will hear from the district shortly.**

The next day, Barnum calls. "You got everything. All stipends, all increases, and—wait for it—credit for year 15. You got it all, and you don't have to come back."

"Whooo! How? What'd they say?"

"They said you were an outstanding teacher and wanted to give you what you're entitled."

"Right. C'mon. What was said? You know, I don't care. You guys are the best!"

I call Rick. These e-mails follow, first Rick to Kelly.

> **You guys are great! Can you give me some kind of a memo that substantiates their offer for his**

> retirement so we can confirm with TRS? I'd like to have the numbers before we retire.

Kelly to Rick:

> I just e-mailed the District to see what we can get. The Human Resources director is in a meeting until at least 3 today, so I'm not sure I'll hear back from her until tomorrow. He seemed thrilled when we spoke earlier. I hope this will allow him to de-stress a little bit and start to enjoy his retirement. I'm glad for him. This will hopefully let him retire with some dignity as well, which he has earned after a long career. As soon as I hear from the District, I'll be in touch.

Me to Storm: "I got everything."

His response: "Congratulations."

That's it. One word. Other teachers did not respond when I selectively shared what happened. I was very much under the impression that everyone in the school—my colleagues, not the students—was convinced I said "tits."

It was a lie I could not yet disprove.

CHAPTER 33

When Rubrics Become Maps

So I'm free. Pretty much. Kelly tells me I have to go see Blister, and I flat-out refuse.
"I'm not talking to her."
"You have to. There's paperwork you have to sign, and she has to sign."
Rick drafted some memo confirming I would receive everything I'd been promised, and I had forwarded it to Kelly for her review.
"I hope to God you didn't send this memo over to Blister," Kelly and Barnum tell me on a phone call the minute they receive his legalese.
"No, he said he wanted to, but I wanted you to see it first."
"Don't. Don't send them anything. No shenanigans with the district. I'm not even sure what they did is legal, and they basically—I've been led to believe—have to slip it by the board and hope they don't notice. I'm not even sure Pointdexter knows."
"Got it." Now I'm thinking *I* had them; they settled this so fast, and everything's so hush-hush. It went almost immediately from "you're going to be fired in the next hour" to "hurry up and sign this deal before it goes away."
What I didn't tell her was that I recently found out that Pointdexter is a neighbor of Rick's. He'd seen him at a Christmas party and a barbecue, neighborhood stuff, and I had asked him to see

if there was any benefit to approaching Pointdexter in an informal, neighborly way about my situation.

"None," said Rick. "I don't want him to know I'm anywhere near this thing. I mean, if the opportunity comes up, I could—but no. Bad idea."

I'm thinking that when Pointdexter saw Rick's letterhead, and that he was my financial advisor, he may have thought twice about what they were doing. That would have happened almost simultaneously, right after my phone call to Strickman, and that's when they all caved.

I wonder what that last meeting was like, if anybody got their ass kicked; but the union is sworn to secrecy, and no one else knows anything, particularly Storm.

I go see Blister the next day because everything is rush, rush, rush. I walk into her office, and they say, "Just a second." She rolls out and says, "Oh yes, we have some papers to swap." Like just another item on her to-do list, something of no significance.

She signs a note that says my last payday is August 31, that I am owed *x* amount of money; I have been over these numbers so many times I can see everything is there; I sign and after that, the district and I are finished. It's one paragraph, written in simple language, not legalese as if, yes, they are trying to just stick this in among other paperwork the board must approve and hope my settlement is just routine—but I sense it is not.

"I want to say one thing to you and whoever else was involved in this fiasco," I open, "and I want you to know what you cost me. Not money. The money is minor.

"You cost me closure with my students. You cost me closure with my colleagues. One day I'm there, and the next day, I'm not. Gone. Like I died. Like a piece of tainted shrimp some cook decides is not good enough to serve the patrons. Like I had leprosy in the times of Jesus. That is unfair to me, unfair to the kids, unfair to everybody. Something that will never be fixed. You're part of a pack of mongrel dogs who just pounce and have *no* regard for your teachers, your students, or their parents.

"What would have been better, to be straight with the kids or to do what you did, which was cut me off like some cancerous appendage? Let me tell you something. I grieved, they grieved—some of those kids think they are responsible for this bullshit perpetrated from this fucking office. Well, good for you. You destroy lives. We are supposed to be about the business of changing lives. But for the better!

"Some of these people may heal. I hope I'm one of them. Oh, and tell Strickman I guess he is a fair guy."

And I'm gone. No reaction.

My therapy intensifies with Duke and Canella. They both say I look healthier than ever and that the zombie who walked through their doors years ago previously is not there. But I am still restless and prone to tearing up. And Canella sees it—no, she senses it.

"It's trite, I know," she says, "but you need closure. You need to get it at school. Conrad? No. I think Storm holds your closure."

It's the middle of summer, things are quiet, and I e-mail Storm to ask if I can drop in to chat. He responds, "Sure." So I go in, I'm up, he's up, and he tells me he's going to retire in a year. He tells me I look healthy.

Using one of his lines, I ask, "Do you know why I asked to see you today?"

"No, no, I don't."

"Well"—and I laugh with pseudo-shyness—"this is really from my therapist, my counselor. More than me, to be perfectly honest, but she says for me really to, uh, heal, I guess—really put all this behind me, I need—"

I pause for effect.

"I need some closure." And I look down and laugh.

"Closure, eh? Well, I don't know. I mean I don't really know if I can help you with that. They really didn't talk to me much."

I can't tell if he's conning me, if he's protecting himself.

"Well, you know why they rushed me out of here on May 15, on The Ides of May, if you will."

"Something you said, or did, but no one ever spelled out exactly what that was. I think it was the culmination of everything, or that line—what was it—'are you the kind who likes to be beat up' or whatever, but after that, I wasn't included in many discussions."

"They felt you handed it badly?"

"No, I'm not saying that."

I still can't tell if he's holding back, but if he is, it is because he has to; he's too afraid to tell me what he knows. Or not. I don't know what Storm knows. I assume he knows more than I do. But I don't know. So I go on.

"You told me once that at that time, you were asked to get your four deans together and have them interview ten kids each, a random sample of my students."

"I was *ordered* to do that."

That's the first crack in his public mask, his stoicism, and it's evident he's pissed about this. I'm guessing he was probably chastised about how he handled everything, from the initial double-duo, tag-team request from Drake and Leaffler to "check me out," to his observation schedule, to my various breakdowns, to the notes from my doctors he ignored, to "So you're the kind that likes to be beat first?", to his two-day, no-pay suspension, which obviously the Blisters of the world found insufficient, and then they took over and cut him out. But he can't tell me all this.

And he's pissed about how he was treated. I think back on the notes he sent me, the "I've been asked," the "What can you tell me," the "I take direction from Blister," the whole George Harrison *Don't Bother Me* tone of his communications. So I go on.

"I think you said they told you to do this, and you said you sent the results of the unofficial, haphazard, unscientific interview process over to Blister—*in a sealed envelope!*"

"*That's right*," he says, topping the volume of my previous utterance. Yes, he is pissed. Definitely pissed.

I pause. "Surely you looked at it. I would have."

We are symbolically head-to-head now, with an atmosphere of "who's loyal to whom" hanging in the air.

"I may have glanced at it, but I was ordered to send it over in a sealed envelope."

I pause. "I would imagine that must have felt a little demeaning."

"You're goddam right it did."

Now I don't pause, but speak urgently. "Okay, but think. Somebody must have typed something, and eventually, after the initial fireworks, somebody from over there had to send that something over here. Even if it just came in the mail, your admin or somebody might have just filed it someplace. Or maybe you did without even thinking about what it was or what it meant."

Storm sits, and I see him considering what I said. I've seen this from him before.

I pride myself—if that's the right word—on a memory that's a double-barreled curse. I remember most everything, and I forget almost nothing. Storm is not like that. I've had to remind him of the content of meetings in the past, what was said, what he said, and who-said-what-when. And he has that look on his face now.

He turns to the dark polished credenza behind him, opens a drawer, looks through some files, pulls out a piece of paper, and looks at me. He is unsure of what to do, so I tread with care.

"Is that it?"

He says nothing. Then, "It's like a matrix, a rubric."

"People in boxes?"

"What?"

"You mean the four deans' names are across the top and the ten students are under each, who they are and what they said, in forty boxes."

"Something like that."

"Okay. I have one request. Look for tits."

He looks at me, and I see his mind trying to put shadows into something concrete, but he's not giving anything away either way about what he knows or what he's heard; he's not admitting anything, and if he's acting, he's playing his part well.

"Tits? What do you mean tits?"

"Just any mention of the word tits."

He looks at me like I'm crazy, and maybe I am, but I have piqued his interest. He's going over the boxes, playing seek-and-find just like a little kid. He's pensive, scanning the sheet, gets to the bottom, points at the square and says, "Here."

He reads, "Teacher might have said tits."

"Might have? *Might have?*"

"Yes. Teacher might have said tits."

"Is that anywhere else in that stack of boxes? Tits?"

He looks over the matrix-rubric. He doesn't look up and says, "No. Only once."

"Forty kids. One tits. Thirty-nine no tits." Sounds like an obscene bridge bid.

"Yes."

"And the one is *maybe?*"

"Yes. Well, might have. Might have."

He's guarding the paper, and as much as I want to rip it out of his hands and run to Rick's Attorney-at-Law office, I go slow.

"Okay. One more thing. Follow that string of boxes up and tell me who is the dean who interviewed that student?"

He follows it up and whispers, "Drake."

"Yes. Drake. So Drake writes 'might have said tits.' Now I don't want to know the student's name, but seriously, is this a student talking, or is this Drake talking? Did Drake coax this out of the student, grill the student, or just made the whole thing up. We don't know."

"But let me tell you this," I continue, "I did not say tits. The district lawyer told the union rep I said 'tits,' and he said they had it solid. This is solid? Might have? One out of forty? Did anyone go back and ask the thirty-nine other kids if I said tits, and if they did, and these thirty-nine kids all said no—well, then what? I know you. That's what you would have done. But they didn't let you, did they? They wanted me out, and they needed a way so they invented tits. Hmmm. Makes you think, doesn't it? Again, neither of us was there. I was two days from getting fired over 'might have.'"

Storm sits. I sit. No one says anything. Finally, I say, "Well, I guess I got my closure. And it turned out all right for me. Of course, she still works for you. Or so it seems."

No one says anything. I rise and extend my hand. "Thank you for the closure." And I leave.

Later that summer, I met up with Robert Groden and other JFK people and bought two copies of his latest book. I had him sign

Conrad's with the following: "Anyone who stands on the grassy knoll is not a nerd."

I mail it to him and hear nothing, so I call him, and he says, "I literally got this two minutes ago."

"You read the inscription?"

"Oh, yeah. I get that." He laughs.

I explain that since we had split the cost of the previous book he bought from Groden on the grassy knoll, which I now had in hardcover (he had found the unsigned soft cover), him having this new book evens everything out.

"This book will be used. Trust me. Thank you."

Last time we spoke. I think I called him once for a recommendation for a running shoe, but he never called me back.

Drake became an assistant at a grade school in the district. An obvious demotion; she later left the district entirely for another menial assignment.

A friend called me on Leaffler's behalf and asked me, "Leaffler wants to know if you're done."

"Done with what?"

"Done with whatever it is you're doing behind the scenes."

"Yeah, I'm done. Maybe I'll write a book. Tell her I have no malice toward her. Tell her I think she was over her head. Maybe she still is. Tell her I think I scared her. Tell her not to be so afraid all the time. Tell her I still have a note she once wrote me, and I carry it around with me all the time. It says, 'Sorry I've been such a bitch.' Tell her that."

Storm retired. I saw an interview he did with a student for the school's new TV blog, and when asked if he had any regrets about retiring, he said something like "If I have one regret, it's that I didn't spend the last ten years in the classroom. I think I would have felt more at home there and been more useful there."

I imagine he's building on his land in New Hampshire near Mount Monadnock, so central to the themes in Thornton Wilder's *Our Town*.

Maybe one day I'll visit him.

CHAPTER 34

Hypostatization

Today I stop at Caitlyn's grave. I bring a purple felt pen, which I usually stick in the ground. Students knew me as the guy with the purple ink on their papers. As I approach, the three of them are there: Tom, my father, and Caitlyn.

Tom pokes my father, who leans down to listen and then, quoting the ghost of Hamlet's father says "Mark me" in this deep, dark voice. Tom clasps his hands and opens his mouth in that silent laugh I recall so well.

"Okay, guys," I say, laughing. "You want to cut the Hamlet's father's ghost bit?"

Tom approaches first. Smiling. Rolling his wheelchair over the graveyard grass. Caitlyn hands him a guitar, and he plays the opening notes to Led Zeppelin's "Stairway to Heaven." Flawlessly. He whistles as he plays. He is beautiful. She dances.

When he's finishes, he says, "You were great."

"No, Tom. I wasn't. I wasn't great."

"You were great. Remember that time outside the dorm, in the street they blocked off for some party, and you were dancing, so drunk, and fell flat on your face, and then, in one second, in one swift move, you got back up and started dancing as if that were a planned move, you falling down. You looked like a break-dancer before there were break-dancers. You were great like that."

My father comes next. "I told you I thought you'd make a great teacher. In many ways, you were. But you're not some character in a book. And you tried to be like a certain Aries and you can't do that and you know what I mean. Remember—Imitation is suicide."

I know what he's referring to; a moment from my senior year when I had the greatest teacher and scholarly influence I ever experienced. This man had taught at Rich East since my dad did in the 1950s. He was the kind of teacher who changed a lot of lives, including mine. But, like me, he had little use for the system or his colleagues and focused on illuminating the minds of his students.

One day in 1970, the days of rage, a kid lit up a cigarette in his class. Some people started to cough, and I remember I turned around and the kid told me to turn around. And this man kept on teaching. Right before the bell rang, he said, "Until the school liberalizes its smoking policy, I would prefer if you would not smoke in my classroom."

And he walked out the door. I turned on the kid and said, "How could you put him in that position, forcing him to do something because you're an idiot?"

"Shut up," the kid said.

This teacher's punishment? Three freshman English classes. He didn't even teach English. A waste of his talent. My father and I got in a huge fight over this. You see, by this time, my father was an assistant superintendent at a neighboring high school, but having come from Rich East, he knew all the administrators over there. Hell, he socialized with them, played golf with them, helped them get promoted.

"He got what he deserved," my father said one day. It was then it dawned on me his buddies probably called *him* and asked him for advice on how to handle this "champion of the smarter students." My father had that much clout.

"What happened to him was criminal, and you had something to do with it, didn't you?"

"His problem is your problem," my father says, standing in the graveyard. "You wanted to be cool. You got too close to your students. I think you know that. You wanted to be him. But you're not him."

Nothing for a while, then he says, "Tom is right. You got shafted and you fought for what was right and you won. You stood up for yourself. That's a lesson your students will not forget."

Caitlyn is next. She's holding a paper with some undecipherable characters, or at least it seems that way to me.

"I have been asked to help you understand *you*," she says, kind of smiling and laughing as though she is thrilled to be given this opportunity. "The way you feel, this anxiety, these premonitions are not really psychological triggers—they are genetic. You try to control them through wine and Klonopin and, earlier, through marijuana. The marijuana is better for you, by the way, but is not the final way. But this is what's important. You will understand this more as you go on following your map."

Caitlyn takes out a card. She looks at it and then closes her eyes. She is silent for a moment and then speaks.

"Anandamide. Arachidonoylglycerol. Hypostatization. The map is not the territory."

She hands me the card containing the words.

"Other things I feel will help you, but what you do—*always*—is totally up to you. Walk everywhere. Go to the Rich East Lagoon. Catch a catfish. Kiss it. Then release it."

Suddenly, I am alone with my purple pen. I stick it in the ground. In the days ahead, I think back on all these things and wonder where I will go now.

And now.

And now.

And now.

Appendix:
The Anatomy of a Strike

William J. Burghardt

On the morning of August 28, Allen McWilliams laced an old pair of gym shoes in his west suburban-Chicago Lombard home and prepared to head to Glenbard South High School in nearby Glen Ellyn, one town west. McWilliams was scheduled to walk the teachers strike line at the school starting at 8:30 a.m. Lacing up his shoes is one of the few things he remembers about that day.

The strike had been called a week before by a unanimous voice vote from the 479 teachers, though one teacher remembered that the head football coach at Lombard-based Glenbard East, Dennis Lewik, had voted no. This year's East team was supposedly the strongest in years, and with three key skirmishes against top competitors leading off the season, the coach did not want to forfeit any of the games. The strike, indeed, forced them to forfeit their opener with Willowbrook (the Rams finished the season at a disappointing 3-5).

McWilliams, thirty-five, who taught math at South and was also the head wrestling coach, was, like Lewik, looking forward to this year's sports season. As head wrestling coach, he had one grappler, Chris Kersten, who had a chance to be the state champion at 189 pounds. Kersten was also an outstanding football player and would go on to be named an all-area lineman. But wrestling didn't start until later in the year, and McWilliams, like the great majority of the District 87 teachers, consisting of the entire faculties at the four Glenbard high schools, understood the need for the strike. He believed there was a point to be made; and the strike, followed a long and heated confrontation between the teachers union (the Glenbard Education Association) and the seven-member District 87 board, in McWilliams mind, was warranted.

He arrived at the school and determined his spot was along the north side of Butterfield Road, a four-lane divided highway, by Raider Lane, which was a traffic-lit intersection that linked Butterfield Road to the school. Another street, Abruzzo Lane, linked the other side of the school with Park Boulevard—South is tucked on a parcel of land just northwest of the intersection of Park and Butterfield. An office building and the Village Theater Guild, a community theater situated in a former one-room schoolhouse from the 1890s, separate the school from the actual intersection, which is heavily driven during school hours. The speed limit along Butterfield Road is fifty miles per hour. The school's location, insulated from the busy intersection, facilitated easy drop-offs for the students at peak rush-hour times, but the teachers wanted full exposure to the strike and had determined a Butterfield Road display of pickets would draw more publicity to their cause. At the Park-Butterfield intersection, they would distribute fliers outlining their position on the strike to drivers.

McWilliams found his place on the north side of Butterfield Road, just west of the Raider Lane intersection. He was walking with another teacher, Jim Snyder, a sophomore football coach and Industrial Arts teacher, though what they were discussing is, again, something McWilliams does not remember.

At that time, a 1994 Saturn driven by Maryse Manelli, fifty-five, of Elgin, was traveling eastbound on Butterfield, moving toward the Park Boulevard intersection. Manelli was driving without a license; she had lost her driving rights when the license was canceled by the secretary of state in March after a March 16 accident at Route 59 and Helen Avenue in unincorporated Winfield township. A medical condition apparently caused her to lose consciousness in the March accident, and her vehicle left the roadway and hit a snow bank.

Apparently, on the morning of August 28, Manelli again blacked out at the wheel. The Saturn began to swerve, and two tire marks were left on the Butterfield Road meridian as the maroon four-door turned sharply left, heading for the embankment on the north side of Butterfield, 150 feet west of Raider Lane. The car, traveling at approximately forty-five miles per hour, continued on its path, and witnesses later stated that at no time did the car slow down.

"They never saw her coming, and the car never braked," said Social Studies teacher Kurt Tillman, who was walking the picket line about thirty feet behind the two coaches.

"We were hit from behind. My head hit the windshield," said McWilliams, whose bright-red hair gives him an almost all-American boyish look. The Saturn continued on and struck a traffic standard, turned 180 degrees, and ended up facing south, toward Butterfield Road, coming to rest just a few feet north of a concrete drain in the embankment by the road. Snyder was struck and thrown into a ditch. McWilliams, who was on the car, was thrown an additional thirty feet or so when the car hit the traffic standard. McWilliams's body ended up near Raider Lane.

"My gym shoes flew off my feet," said McWilliams. "The first people to me thought I was dead. They rushed over to Jim because they could see he was still alive. They thought I was gone. They thought I was another teacher because they couldn't recognize me because of all the blood. I later described to a friend of mine, who is a paramedic, what happened to me, and he said I had a 2 percent chance of surviving an accident of this magnitude."

Both teachers and the driver were taken to Good Samaritan Hospital in Downers Grove. Manelli was charged with two counts of aggravated reckless driving and one count of driving without a license. McWilliams suffered a bruise on the brain, a broken fibula, a fractured left ankle, and tendon damage in both knees. He was in intensive care for almost four full days. Snyder, thirty-six and a resident of Sugar Grove, had minor surgery.

There are many teachers—like Kathy Coyner of Glenbard North in Carol Stream, who teaches English—who felt the accident was just that, an accident, and had little or nothing else to do with the strike story. Gail Ellenbaum, a math teacher at South, and one of ten members of the teachers Professional Negotiating (PN) team also felt that "it was just an unfortunate accident." But another PN team member, Jim Jacobson, strongly feels that the accident was the turning point in the settlement, which came three days later. "The accident woke everybody up and put pressure on the school board to end this thing," he said. "I think we would have been out ten days or more without that happening."

That evening in room 2800 of the Student Resource Center at the College of DuPage, located less than half a mile down Park Boulevard from Glenbard South, the teachers gathered for a 6:00 p.m. rally. There was undeniably a massive union of spirit in the room in large part due to the accident. At the front of the room, on a raised platform, sat the PN team. Bill Wright, the spokesperson and president of the union, and a nonvoting member of the PN team who teaches history at Glenbard North, gathered the group together, and there was a microphone set in the aisles for teachers to respond. "A few days ago, the board of education drew a line in the sand, and we didn't walk across, *we thundered across it!*" said Jacobson, who was described as the most fervent and "radical" of the members of the team. In fact, it was the Glenbard North teachers, in general, who had the most passion for standing up to the District 87 board, and who were often described with that word. "We have a lot of radicals at North," said Bill Beggs, who teaches math, "and we are tired of hearing from the school board that we somehow have to explain why we deserve the money we earn." Later on that night, Wright hammered home time and again the theme, "Don't apologize for the money you make. You earn it. You deserve it."

An Issue of Trust

The money was both the issue and not the issue in this strike. The bigger issue was trust—the teachers, by the time they called the strike, had lost total faith in the board. "They were flat-out lying to us, I have no doubt," said Jacobson. "They were hiding money. They were deceptive about the finances they had available."

From the teachers' point of view, the makeup of the school board was indeed conservative. Joy Talsma was the president who had garnered a reputation, even during her tenure on the District 41 elementary school board, as someone who felt that teachers' salaries were too high. Tom Voltaggio was a member of IRATE, a local group of residents who steadfastly fought tax increases. Sandy Pihos owned her own business and approached the running of the school district that same way. Lois Hince, who had a son attending Glenbard North, was a former journalist and was seen as a key swing vote. Donna France and Randy Church were new board members as was a minister, Dave Brown, whom the negotiating team saw as the most reasonable member of the board.

"He attended the information meeting at Grace Lutheran Church where we took our case to the public," said Ellenbaum. "After the teachers were hit in the accident, Dave went to the hospital."

The aforementioned information meeting was held the evening of Wednesday, August 26 (the strike vote came on Friday, August 21), and did, indeed, have some members of the community speak who were not at all happy with the teachers and did think they could have negotiated while the schools remained open. That was the biggest factor in alienating the community. While there were feelings on both sides of the issue—Teachers are overpaid vs. The unreasonableness of the board—the bottom line for the public, since no new taxes were involved, was keeping the schools open.

"My daughter's senior year is starting, and every day this goes on is one more day I'm concerned that she won't be ready for college or at least will be delayed going," said Mary Miller, who works as a youth coordinator for St. Petronille's Catholic Church in Glen Ellyn. "The money, the salaries, who cares, I want the schools opened." Most students obviously relished the extension of their summer vacations, but there were pockets who vocally demanded the schools open. On the last weekend of the strike, a group of students banded at the District 87 headquarters at Main Street and Crescent Boulevard in Glen Ellyn, holding signs that said, "Honk if you support the students. Open the schools."

Sara Marsh was a National Honor Society student as a junior, and when the strike delayed the opening of her senior year, she and many of her friends were not happy. "This is the last year of high school, and mentally, many of us are looking ahead and want to complete this year and move on with our lives. I have friends who are athletes who are concerned if their scholarships would somehow be in jeopardy. As it turned out, the strike only lasted a few days, but we still have lost several half days needed to complete projects. It looked like the teachers were just being stubborn."

Renee Ferguson, whose daughter was enrolling as a freshman at Glenbard West, led a group of parents who wanted to tie yellow ribbons around all the trees at the high school as a sign "that our children were being held hostage." They were prevented from doing that by the Glen Ellyn police.

The teachers knew they were facing an uphill public relations battle and worked hard to get their side of the story out, but had trouble, in part because the details of the story were so complex. Many were furious at education writer Casey Banas of the *Chicago Tribune*, who appeared to have a "pro-board/anti-teacher" bias. Indeed, Banas's stories often led with the board's point of view; the teachers' positions were listed at the end after all the board quotes had been stated. Banas also used the board's data in quoting the amount of dollars offered, printed the teachers' salaries, which, although a matter of public record, needed a longer explanation to give accurate analysis—many were retiring and receiving a severance bonus in their last year. So the top salaries quoted, many of which reached near one hundred thousand dollars with that bonus added, were, from the teachers point of view, "misleading." At the same time, a website, published in the newspaper, listed the teachers' salaries, but they were inflated due to miscalculations in the raise rate. Much of this information was technical and would take a long time to explain. The salaries ran in both the *Tribune* and Lisle-based *Daily Herald*, and the teachers were never able to accurately explain their side of the salary issue.

The lowest blow from the teachers' perspective was when Banas used the board's analysis of a dollar-per-hour figure, ignoring the fact that all teachers put in extra time grading papers at home, among lots of the other outside classroom activity. Banas, like the board, took the hours the teachers teach per week and divided their salaries out to give an inflated weekly rate, making it look like most were earning over $2,200 per week. Banas's coverage so angered the union that they complained to Banas's editor and at one time were contemplating some kind of legal action.

Matt Nickerson, the reporter for the *Daily Herald*, was seen as giving a much more balanced view. For example, Nickerson carefully explained the differentiation in the teachers' salary figures, which were calculated from the "base," versus the board's figures, which incorporated bumps for years of experience and additional schooling. The *Herald*, with a heavy suburban audience, ran the strike story on page 1 every day. They also printed extensive interviews with Talsma and Wright on facing pages.

"I saw Banas at the district office using their fax, using their phone, and huddling with them—he was very much in their corner. He would spend little time with us but a lot of time with them, using their facilities," said Jacobson. "Nickerson, on the other hand, did a very good job."

The hours a teacher works varies. For many, like PN team member and spokesperson Mike Kolodziej, who coaches a large forensics team at Glenbard West, hours accumulate rather quickly. "I figured out that I work over fifty hours per week counting summer," he said. "Many tournaments go all day Saturday, and we compete almost every week." Ellenbaum, who coaches a math competition team at South, agreed. "These contests have become very competitive and a sign of the school's reputation, and I have been devoting more and more time to it." The teachers are compensated for their extracurricular commitments.

But is every teacher involved in extracurricular activities? How many teachers are involved in assignments of some sort outside of the classroom? Ellenbaum estimated that "about three-fourths" of the teachers are involved in extracurricular activities from students, be it drama, forensics, athletics, math olympics, or other kinds of commitment. Sports teams practice almost every day. Jacobson acknowledged that "there are bad teachers" who may abuse the system, but that "it is the job of the school administrators to monitor those teachers and get rid of them."

Another unique factor in this particular negotiation was the unusually high amount of teachers in District 87 who were near or at the top of the pay scale. According to numbers published by the school board, 45 per cent of the teachers in District 87 have twenty or more years of experience with forty-five hours beyond a master's degree, the highest level on the salary schedule. The board published one of their offers during the strike week that said these teachers would have been paid $84,247 a year under their latest offer, and the teachers rejected the offer. Wright, the head of the union, affirmed the figures were correct. But the salary figures were not out of line in comparison to other school districts. In fact, in DuPage County alone, which does not include many of the "big 15" schools the teachers compared themselves to, District 87 starting salaries ranked fourth out of sixth ($31,738 vs. the top salary of $33,274 in Fenton District 100), and the top salary was fifth out of sixth ($76,170 vs. $81,955 for Lake Park's District 108).

While the comparison of salaries and positioning the teachers as overpaid was expected, what ultimately drove a huge wedge between the two sides was the teacher's impressions that they as a group—and their profession—were being treated as unimportant, uninformed, and as "second class citizens." Time and again, teachers described Talsma as "condescending," she and Voltaggio both "lectured us." Pihos was "arrogant." The board's lawyer, Len Himes, was "smug." Board member Lois Hince called the teachers "greedy." During the strike week, the war of words escalated to a fever pitch, which was one reason the rally following the accident had all the emotion of an evangelical revival.

What drove the two parties to such a position?

Contract History and "WIN-WIN"

The history of the Glenbard teachers' negotiations goes back almost two decades. Negotiations in the late 1970s and the early 1980s were quite different from the way the contracts are negotiated today. Back then, GEA used the local Illinois Education Association UniServ director and the head of the PN team as their spokesperson.

They would make decisions with the rest of the team. The school board used their lawyer as their primary spokesperson, and he conducted all the negotiations. The school board had no face-to-face contact with the rest of the teachers' negotiating team.

This system, which sounds like a way to mainstream the process and keep the number of personalities involved in the discussions to a few, sounds practical but had some pitfalls. In District 87, discussions became confrontational with the board's lawyer. Because the board was removed from the process, their view of the teachers became quite negative as they heard things secondhand. Likewise, the PN team had little direct contact with the board, and as information was communicated from person to person, animosities increased, like a game of "telephone" that got off track.

The issue during the late 1970s and early 1980s was class size. In 1979, class size limits were proposed by the teachers, but the board did not wish to negotiate the issue. In 1981, the issue was again raised, and a compromise was reached. An agreed-upon written policy was adopted, and the board agreed to notify the teachers of any change in the policy if warranted—this policy was called a "memo of understanding." In 1983, the board agreed to put the "memo" in the actual contract. In 1985, salaries and the class size issue resulted in the teachers actually calling for a strike on September 6. Last-minute negotiations and concessions by both sides averted the walkout. Board figures for 1985 stated the average teacher's salary in the district at $34,947, with the ceiling pay at $44,050. Beginning Glenbard teachers made about $20,000, The Illinois average teacher's salary was $25,829, and the national average was reported as $23,456.

Part of the compromise was the creation of fifteen "relief sections" allocated for all schools to help balance the size of classes. This meant that if a class reached a certain size—say thirty students—other classes would be broken up to create a new class. Two years later, when the WIN/WIN process agreed to by both the board and the teachers was implemented, the number of relief sections was increased to thirty-two.

The rising number of confrontations over salary and class size issues caused both sides to re-evaluate how negotiations could be improved. Studying other union-district methodology, District 87 adopted the WIN-WIN Negotiating Model, which did several things. First, it brought both sides—the PN team and school board—face-to-face during negotiations. One of the goals of WIN-WIN was to anticipate problems and solve them before they occurred.

The first WIN-WIN contract, for 1987-89, was a new experience for both sides. Mutual problems were agreed to: salary and contract language. This contract also resulted in a computer deal, where the district would buy every teacher and staff member a Mac Classic computer. Every teacher and staff member that voluntarily participated was required to take seventy hours of staff development tech hours, over a three-year period. After successfully completing the hours, the teachers were given ownership of the computer.

The 1989-91 contract signaled a change not just in the WIN-WIN model but in the attitude about property taxes across the country. Proposition 89 passed in California, reducing property taxes, and locally, a movement to reduce the tax levy was headed by Glen Ellyn resident Tom Voltaggio. Downsizing was rampant among middle managers in the private sector, and raises that might have been 4-7 percent were becoming 1-3 percent. This three-year contract was negotiated in the context of the taxpayer revolt, and this agreement signaled, in the teachers' minds, the beginning of "losing ground" vis-à-vis other districts in the area.

At the end of this contract, the board told the teachers that the district was indeed in dire financial straits. Why it is not clear: there are some who believe that the board did not tax to the fullest extent allowed by law before the locked-in property tax cap took effect in 1991, which put a lid on property taxes without the passing of a referendum. "Even though the board may have felt they didn't need these funds immediately, you try to get as much as you can because you're locked in, once the cap is in place, to a 5 percent annual increase," said Ellenbaum. "It was there, they just didn't go after it." And during the next several years, the district was looking at some very difficult financial choices.

In the fall of 1991, the board asked the community for a huge commitment in building a fifth high school in the district in

Glendale Heights. This would have alleviated overcrowding issues and most importantly to the residents of Glendale Heights, given the village their own high school (probably called Glenbard Central). Education enthusiasts in all towns worked hard for the passage, but in April 1992, a referendum to seek funds to build a new school was defeated by a 2-1 margin, and a separate referendum to raise money to operate the school lost 5-1. It was apparent that people in Glen Ellyn, Lombard, Carol Stream, and Bartlett could not support the building of a fifth high school despite the strong support the new school concept received from residents of Glendale Heights. Students in the community would continue to be split up to North, West, and East.

With the cap in place, the district began to have some serious financial obligations and asked the teachers for help. The 1991-93 contract was one of the lowest ever negotiated with increases falling in 0.9 percent to 1.1 percent range during the three years. In 1992, the first wave of budget cuts took place, with twenty "group 7" coaching positions lost. Voltaggio, who had been a vocal anti-tax proponent in Glen Ellyn, was elected to the board that spring.

Following the 1993 contract, something unprecedented occurred—the board and the union opened up the existing contract and agreed to roll it over for one additional year. The teachers realized that the district faced shortages in tax dollars, and the board asked for help. The teachers made, in their eyes, major concessions: they agreed to supervise study halls as a way to help the district. This was supposed to be a temporary responsibility, but has remained in later contracts. The teachers also agreed to reduced sabbatical leave. This contract was also negotiated in the WIN-WIN procedure, and it was apparent that both the teachers and the board realized there were serious cash-flow problems resulting from the tax cap.

"Opening the contract was a major concession from the teachers' point of view," said Wright. "It's as if the board came to us and said, 'Look, we need your help,' and we responded. It was something we didn't have to do, but we did it."

In 1994, Superintendent Stevens was awarded a 16 percent salary increase by the District 87 board.

The last three-year contract negotiated between the board and GEA—prior to the one concluded in August of 1998—was for the three school years of '95-'96, '96-'97, and '97-'98. The board painted a picture that the district was again in dire financial trouble, and the teachers conceded and agreed to a three-year contract for 1.2 percent raise the first year, 1.2 the second year, and 1.3 the third year. Even though this was an improvement over the 1991-93 numbers, the District 87 teachers realized that they were beginning to drop in comparison to other school districts, most notable the "big 15," the school district from the North Shore, and even other DuPage high schools in Hinsdale and Downers Grove.

From the teachers' point of view, in this contract, they again gave up substantial benefits. They changed from a comprehensive major medical insurance program to a PPO, which raised teacher payments. "Changing the insurance program saved the board millions of dollars," said Jacobson. Each teacher agreed to an additional day of subbing, increasing that number to three days per instructor.

In April of 1995, a major point of trust erupted. At that time, five of the present seven board members were on the board: the top three of Talsma, Voltaggio, and Pihos, as well as Hince and France. The board had projected, during the negotiations of the latest three-year contract, that District 87 would finish the present '95-'96 school year with a deficit of $1,900,957. This was used as a negotiating point in the recent contract settlement. But the following July, when the property tax dollars rolled in, the school district ended up $3.1 million in the black.

"Well, that got our attention," said Wright. "That's a swing of about $5 million. We just had settled the contract in May, and a few months later, this unexpected windfall came in. And of course we waited patiently for the board to open up the contract and perhaps give us back some of what we had given earlier. And of course it didn't happen. Many teachers felt we'd been had."

"They didn't open the contract up, but we did. We bit the bullet on the last one," said Kolodziej. "We settled for less than a cost-of-living raise."

A five-million-budget projection error can result from several scenarios. New growth in the village always adds some money, but like most boards, it appears two things happened: District 87 business manager Lisa Beckwith had drawn a worst case scenario picture, perhaps at the board's insistence—many boards like to play it as safe as possible with public funds—and add that to the unexpected surge in tax revenues, and there's five million dollars. Just an oversight or deception? Other teachers weren't so sure.

"Deception? Well, budgets are complex things and monies move from account to account," said PN member Julie Dagnon from West. "But yes, we weren't sure. It looked funny."

"I think the first time around, you might be able to say it was a case of conservative assumptions and anticipating the worst," said Kolodziej.

More tensions followed the next year. The board projected a deficit of $6,825,255 for 1996-1997 and ended with a surplus of some $2,612,536, with $4,652,504 in the working cash fund. In 1997-1998, the board projected a deficit of $13,126,819 and ended up $12 million in the black.

"That's about a $20 million mistake," said Kolodziej. "Now that is either deception or stupidity." The board had projected deficits of $40,015,353 through 2000-01.

In this atmosphere, the 1998 contract sessions were to open in April, with the board $12 million in the black. There was no doubt in the teachers' minds it was payback time. Before that occurred, there was a school referendum to be voted on in March.

The March Referendum

At 7:30 p.m. on March 3, 1998, one in a series of informational meetings was held in the library at Glenbard West, conducted by the superintendent of schools for District 87, Robert Stevens, and four board members, to inform the public about an upcoming school referendum on March 17. Board President Talsma informed the crowd of about fifty that this referendum was being brought to the public after a long process of evaluation and study. It affected the future of all Glenbard students at the four high schools; the board had hired experts to help them plan what to do. The meeting was to last one hour and they handed index cards out to the audience for questions.

The board was concerned about the number of students in the "pipeline" feeding into District 87 schools. Projections indicate a much higher number of students attending all four high schools into the year 2000 and beyond. Talsma said the board looked at a number of options, including one that called for $71 million in renovation. The board turned that proposal down.

The current proposal—to be voted on March 17—called for approval of a $16 million referendum that would not raise anyone's taxes, because of the "retirement" of a previous bond the same year. Another $18 million was available from alternative revenue bonds, which brought the total of dollars coming in, if the referendum is passed, to $34 million.

"Each school is different," Stevens explained at the meeting. North rests on 14.2 acres and is 30 years old. East rests on 30 acres and is 39 years old. South rests on 40 acres and is 26 years old. And West, which rests on 14 acres (should be 40, according to state recommendations), is 76 years old and has gone through seven additions. All four schools are now at capacity. If the referendum does not pass, programs would be cut, mobile classroom brought in, or a staggered start time considered for the beginning of the school day.

Talsma went over the improvements to be made at each school in detail, which mostly included new classrooms, classroom renovations, labs, a new gym at West, moving the library to the old Hilltopper gym at West, and other patching and fixing.

The board members reiterated time and again that this would be done "without an increase in taxes" because of the retirement of one bond and tapping alternative revenue funds in others.

There was a very vocal group from the town of Glendale Heights in the audience who did not want the referendum to go on the ballot, but were instead interested in reviving the issue of a fifth high school to be built in their town. Currently, Glendale Heights students go to North and West mostly, some to East. The board replied that there was a referendum to build a fifth high school in 1992—as mentioned earlier, the referendum to seek funds to build a new school lost 2-1, and the referendum to operate the new school lost 5-1.

The board said these changes covered by the new referendum, if adopted, would take the district comfortably through the year 2017.

The audience was upset at not being able to jump up and ask questions as things were being discussed. They were told to fill out cards. This squashed much of their ire. They kept yelling out, "Answer our cards!" Talsma and Pihos controlled the meeting by taking the cards and then reading a question and answering it. The people in the audience kept trying to interrupt the board members with specific questions—they were instructed to "fill out cards," which many did, though it was never determined if all the questions were answered.

The lion's share of the Glendale Heights residents' questions revolved around the selling of land the district once held but sold after the fifth high school referendum went down to defeat. Residents wanted to know where the money from the sale of that land, in Glendale Heights, was distributed.

Other questions focused on a big problem for the district, which is bus service, with some kids riding about an hour to and from school. The board replied they were studying that problem. There is a state law that no student can be on a bus over an hour, a major problem for the district.

If the proposed referendum passed, the project would be done in two years. Other questions raised included "Why move the library?" and "Where will the cafeteria go?" The meeting eventually dissipated with the Glendale Heights contingent feeling their voices had not been heard.

With a minuscule turnout of the registered voters, the referendum passed on March 17, 1998, by about thirteen thousand to nine thousand.

The 1998 Contract Negotiations

A steering committee was formed between the board and the PN team to resolve basic negotiating issues for the 1998-99 contract. The WIN-WIN format was again agreed to—the teachers began their demands with eleven issues, the board four. The teachers' key point: they wanted to talk about the money first and not wait until the end of the negotiating, when things were often rushed and thrown together in a haphazard way. In an April 9 issues meeting, the board presented their four major points, which included compensation and the pool of available dollars as well as other side issues such as extracurricular compensation and looking to move the dental plan to a new supplier. They wanted to "see more student-teacher interaction during the resource period," which was the one period per day the teacher uses to see students who need help. There were other issues, but the salaries were the driving edge for both parties.

On Tuesday, April 14, the first substantial negotiating meeting was held, and PN team chair Kolodziej asked for the board's opening offer. It was the teachers' belief that in the steering committee it was agreed the board would open the negotiations with an offer. The lawyer for the board, Len Himes, addressed the PN team in what Wright later documented as "confrontational terms." Himes stated that the board is quite happy with the present contract. It was the union's desire to open the contract, he said, and therefore the union should give the board their proposal first. Kolodziej asked Himes if he had any proposal with him and he said no. The PN team went into a caucus to determine their response.

"It was then I knew we were in for a long, drawn out battle," said Wright. "In effect, we asked them for their first offer, and their first offer was zero."

"I was reminded of a student who had not done his homework," said Kolodziej. "They didn't have anything. We assumed zero."

The PN team caucused and decided: the board and the union had agreed to the WIN-WIN collaborative model for negotiations, and in order to have an open discussion, they needed the board's figures. The current contract was negotiated in this way, the team reasoned, and since the board had nothing in terms of figures, the union would leave and see the board on Thursday. Talsma and Voltaggio tried to move the focus off the money and on to large areas of philosophy. "This board has a mandate from the community,"

Voltaggio is remembered as saying. "The board is obviously not ready to negotiate," said Wright, and he said they would meet Thursday.

On Thursday, April 16, the PN team proposed the board a one-year contract at 7.3 per cent on the base. PN team member Brian Loynachan from Glenbard North explained the team's position and offered comparisons to comparably sized school districts—including those in the so-called "big 15," which dominated the North Shore as well as other schools in DuPage County, and why the number was realistic. The board responded they couldn't afford the proposal. Pihos wondered where the schools were chosen to compare District 87 to, and Loynachan said the schools were taken from the District 87's report card, distributed to the public, that compared the district's scores with others. "Teachers cannot compare themselves in the profession," said Talsma, a refrain should we revisit in subsequent meetings. She said that District 87 could not be compared to the schools residing in more lucrative communities on the North Shore, and that her constituents would require only a comparison to DuPage schools.

Talsma stated that the Naperville and Wheaton unit districts should be included in the comparisons—unit districts are those who combine the salaries of teachers from kindergarten through 12, versus just 9-12 like the Glenbard schools—the result is that the high school teachers salaries in the unit districts are lower. The PN team claimed that this would be an apples and oranges comparison. The board offered a counter proposal—1.05 percent on the base for each year the next three years. Both sides agreed there were a lot of numbers on the table and agreed to meet again the following Tuesday.

The Tuesday, April 23 meeting opened with Kolodziej outlining in detail the financial history of the union and the boards of District 87 and why the teachers deserved a greatly improved package. The board continued to pick at the information presented and the usually quiet Brown stated that the negotiations should just focus on this particular contract. When the two past contracts were brought up, Talsma continually used the phrase, "That's all water under the bridge."

"If these other districts you're comparing yourselves to want to spend themselves into financial ruin," said Talsma, "that is their business. The Glenbard district won't do that." Added Voltaggio: "Your numbers are not based on any sort of reality." There was then a PN team caucus, and Kolodziej told the board, "We don't control the purse strings." He stated the PN team expected the board to bring back a better offer at the next meeting, "substantially better than what the board offered the last two contracts."

"We wanted them to open the eyes of our membership with a substantial offer," recalls Jacobson.

The two sides began to meet less frequently. There was a meeting on Saturday, April 25, when the board said they had new information to share. Finance Manager Gary Frich passed out a "scattergram," which is a computer generated graphing of numbers showing various salary ranges. "As far as we were concerned, it was a rehash of the same information we had been hearing," said Wright. Kolodziej asked the board if they had a new proposal. Talsma replied that she was under the impression that the PN team would start to lower their proposal. The PN team refused. The board went into a caucus, and it was at this time Jacobson insisted that the entire PN team walk out. "We should have walked the minute they didn't have an offer," he said. The other PN team members felt they should at least listen to what the board was going to offer. The board returned and offered a new proposal—1.32 percent on the base for each of the next three years. The board would also add $50,000 of money from new tax revenues each year of the contract. The board also asked the union to knock percentage points off their proposal. Kolodziej informed the board that this was not even a new offer that "one quarter of a percent is not an increase."

At this meeting, the board's lawyer Himes stated, "We are not going to meet you in the middle." A meeting was scheduled for the next Tuesday.

At the May 5 meeting, the PN team handed out their new proposal, which they reduced by $51,000. Kolodziej said, "We do not want to get into a long series of nickel and dime increases and decreases that are a waste of time." Talsma responded with what Himes had said at the previous meeting: "We will not meet you in the middle." Business manager Frich handed out more supportive materials showing what meeting the teachers' demands would do to the financial health of the district. At the same time, the board's projections showed them being in the black clear out to 2002.

What followed was hours worth of discussion between the PN team and the board about the financial history of the district. Voltaggio stated that the board "did not know there was going to be a tax cap" put in place in 1992. Wright asked, "When was the last time an educational fund referendum for new tax dollars was requested by the district?" The answer was 1987. The PN team continued to explain why they needed an increase from the 1.32 percent. The PN team asked the board for a new proposal. The board went into caucus. The board came back and asked what new proposal the PN team had. "We have given you ours," said Wright. The board did not have a new proposal. "When you have one, give us a call," said Wright. It was at this time that board called for a federal mediator to resolve the dispute.

The PN team caucused and agreed that this seemed to be the only direction to go. Bob Ray, who is the Illinois Education Association representative for the teachers union, and Himes, the board's lawyer, were to work out the details as to who would be the best choice for the federal mediator. There was no date set for the next meeting.

Federal mediators are offered free to school boards and teachers unions to resolve contract disputes. They travel all over the country and are sometimes difficult to schedule. The choice of who the mediator is key, and both Ray and Himes felt comfortable with Jim Schepker. Working around his schedule, a meeting was set for Thursday, May 28.

Schepker met with the teachers first, for about forty-five minutes. The money issues and the longevity of the contract were highlighted as stumbling blocks. Kolodziej gave Schepker an information packet summarizing all the information the PN team had given the board. Ray summarized the contract history and asked about meeting procedures.

The previous contract, signed by the board and the PN team, specified that there would be no negotiations over the summer if the contract was not settled by the end of May. The first date that the contract specified a summer negotiation could be held was August 15, which happened to be a Saturday. This became a sticking point—the board telling the community that the teachers would not negotiate over the summer, and the teachers replying that the contract, signed by both parties, specified that date as the earliest talks could begin.

Schepker asked about meeting dates and the fact that the contract specified an August 15 date, noting that it was odd to have a starting date in a contract, but it was important that date be honored. Schepker then met with the board for forty-five minutes, and both teams met together. Schepker emphasized the following points:

- He is a neutral third party. It is his job to get both parties to sign an agreement.
- He is not an advocate for either side. He asked that both sides come to the table with an open mind.
- When he meets with each group he would like them to identify their priorities. He wants each group to be open with him, and discussions with him would be held in confidence.
- He suggested small groups and/or committees to discuss things.
- He suggested that the teams needed to be open to different possibilities when dealing with financial information.

After that, the PN team showed some new information, showing that the amount of money in the Education Fund, which is used to pay the teachers' salaries, had dropped from 67 percent to 58 percent over the last eight years. Talsma responded that the fund had dropped because the district had hired more new teachers at a lower salary, which is why those number had dropped. PN team member Dagnon said that the number of full-time equivalent positions—moving part-timers to full-timers—have increased over the last eight years as well.

Schepker wanted the Steering Committee, which was the subgroups who initially lined out procedure, to meet and discuss changes in protocols and dates. Each team met separately to caucus. There was a very heated exchange among the PN members about when to go back and meet with the board. The discussion revolved around meeting over the summer—which would be, in effect, opening up the old contract to a change—which could have been done, but it was finally agreed that August 15, the contractual date, was one the teachers needed to stick with.

"We felt we would be hearing the same things over and over again," said Wright. "At this point, we had been lectured to and condescended to and not treated as equals but subordinates. The team had become polarized by the board's refusal to budge."

"We wanted to see how the fiscal year would end," said Kolodziej. "Trust was shot at this point. We wanted to be competitive with the other teachers in the 'Top 15.' Many people didn't realize that districts like Hinsdale have their Teacher Retirement Service fees paid 100 per cent by their districts—District 87 teachers have to pay their own. As a result, Hinsdale salaries are less, but overall, they come out better. We needed to be taken care of, and we needed to make up for lost ground."

The Steering Committee met and dropped a section requiring all members to be at all meetings. The board wanted the steering committee members only to meet with the board. As Wright noted later, "At the time, it was unclear why the board would push this option, but as discussions went on, it was evident that Talsma, Pihos, Voltaggio, and Himes thought they might be able to 'divide and conquer' the PN team."

These meetings—with the three board members and their lawyer—were to take place in late June and early July. Talsma explained that they didn't need all the board members to negotiate the contract. They trusted their representatives to the Steering Committee. Kolodziej explained that the teachers came from four different schools, and they all need to be part of the negotiations.

A clause stipulating that only the board president and the president of the union would be spokesperson to the media in terms of joint releases was dropped. Both sides would need to get their messages out separately.

The hot issue of meeting dates was raised next. The board wanted to meet in small groups during June and July. The PN team said no, as most members had vacations and classes that conflicted. Himes said the PN team was refusing to meet during the summer. The PN team responded that they would follow the language in the current contract signed by both sides.

The PN team then said that August 15 was a Saturday and that they would meet with the board on that date and any or all dates afterward to ensure a settlement. Himes was on vacation. The first date both sides could agree to was Tuesday, August 18. It was agreed both sides would set aside August 18, 19, and 20 to meet with the federal mediator, Schepker—all three parties also set aside Saturday, August 22, and Sunday, August 23, for meeting dates. The first day of school for the students of District 87 was scheduled to be Monday, August 24. The PN team strongly stated that they would not return to work without a contract.

The PN team met separately to discuss their next moves. Wright was to meet with Superintendent Stevens during the first week of August to inform him and the board that the teachers union would be filing an intent to strike notice on August 10. It was felt that Wright should stress that this is just a legal procedure and that the union will be negotiating in good faith to avoid a strike.

The PN team decided to meet at Julie Dagnon's home on August 17 to prioritize issues and strategies. On Friday, August 21, the union would hold an all-membership meeting to discuss the status of the contract. If no contract package was finalized, then the membership would ask to take a strike vote. Finally, the PN team decided to name one spokesman—Wright—as the liaison to the media.

The August Sessions

As the negotiation time approached, there began a fervor in the community that had not existed before. The media began to report more heavily on "what might happen" as the August 18 meeting approached. As things stood at this point, the union was at 7.3 percent one year increase and the board was at 1.34 percent. And the board had stated time and time again they would not meet in the middle.

The sessions began with neither side budging, and at this point, the two groups separated with Schepker and Assistant Supt. Ron Smith working between the two groups.

"We were still far apart," said Wright. "We started putting together a three-year package. All kinds of number were flying. With any three-year deal, it appeared the first year would be the problem."

One PN team member stated that the board at one time was waving a five-year contract with increases between 2-3 percent each year. The sessions with the federal mediator represented some give and take, but there was very little movement. Tuesdays and Wednesdays five-hour sessions featured positioning and some proposals swapped but, initially, nothing concrete. It was the first day back after the summer, and the two sides were both testing the ground to see where the other might yield.

Kolodziej stated that during the week, "the federal mediator could have put a little more pressure on both sides. He could have been a little more aggressive. He did come to us at one time and said, 'You're making a good case.'"

On Thursday, with a strike vote called for the following day at 6:00 p.m., there was a movement within the PN team to go for a one-year 5 percent increase to open the schools the following Monday. The 5 percent figure the first year became an immovable point, particularly to the more "radical" corps at Glenbard North. The board finally moved Thursday and offered a three-year deal with 4 percent the first year, followed by 3 percent and 3 percent.

The PN team was divided, and there was a lot of tempered talk. "There were some knockdown, drag-out battles," said Wright. "Even within the team, we were all showing the strain the negotiation process had on all of us." The board rejected the one-year 5 percent increase offered by the teachers to keep the schools open.

Wright stated to the board: "Had you come to us in April with this 4-3-3 package, at least we would have had something to talk about." But the emotions were running so high with the teachers at this point that the PN team unanimously rejected the package. Friday morning at 12:30 a.m., talks broke off. It was too late to stave off the emotions that had built up over months of frustration and ill will.

On Friday at 6:00 p.m., the vote was taken, and the teachers went on strike. It was the first strike in the eighty-two-year history of the Glenbard schools.

Federal mediator Schepker secured agreements from both Talsma and Wright to agree to a 6:00 p.m. session Sunday to try for one last attempt to avoid closing the schools on Monday. The session merited no progress. Of note to the teachers—Voltaggio didn't show for the session due to other commitments.

"The angriest I got throughout the whole negotiation process when the one-year 5 percent offer to keep the schools open was rejected," said PN member Dagnon. "We could have gone to work, and the school's would open."

On Monday, which was to be the first day of school, the teachers marched. The public's concern was most noted in the upcoming forfeits for the boy's football teams at the four Glenbards. As stated earlier, Glenbard East had what they considered to be the best team in years, and their first game was against Willowbrook, a team they felt was an easy win. Glenbard West played Wheaton-Warrenville, the state champs two of the last three years (they would win the state championship again in late November), and while considered a long shot at best, the players wanted that one crack at an upset. Glenbard West's Mitch Novack, who blamed the school board for the impasse, said, of the WWS game, "I just want to play them and beat them." There was little chance his team would get another opportunity to play them.

Students organized protests at all the schools to vent their frustrations and to try and move the negotiations along. Many marched with the teachers in support of the strike. At Glenbard South, twenty students marched behind a sign that said "Students strike against the strike."

Two dozen football players from Glenbard East, donned in their jerseys, attended the rally Monday at the district headquarters in Glen Ellyn. They had worked out all summer and were convinced they could go to the play-offs if there was no strike.

The two sides were waiting for the federal mediator to schedule a negotiation session. The public became impatient that the two sides would not meet without the negotiator, but by this time, there was no way the two sides could get together without the input of the third party. Some felt the mediator was letting the strike go on for a few days to build pressure and let emotions subside and give everyone a higher motivation to settle.

Tuesday and Wednesday provided town meetings and no movement. Teachers went out into homes in the district to explain their positions. Parents at one meeting asked Wright if it was illegal to meet with the board without the mediator present. He said he would check. Students marched again Wednesday at both Glenbard West and Glenbard South. Brandon Chrisman, a senior at South, organized the march and said, "Our purpose today is to show both our striking teachers and the board of education that this strike hurts us the most." Of the four schools, students at South were the most active.

The teachers saw that a one-year package was not going to go, and at 8:10 p.m. on Wednesday, August 26, offered a three-year deal consisting of 5 percent, 4 percent, and 4 percent.

"At that point, both sides saw the one-year package wasn't going to go anywhere," said Wright. The 5 percent figure for the first year was still seen as key to the teachers. The board took the offer into a caucus and made a counter offer at 12:26 a.m. Thursday morning. The board moved one-quarter percent in the last year of their previous three-year package—to 4, 4, and 3.25—and the union did not see that as significant.

On Friday morning, McWilliams and Snyder were hit in the car accident at South. Friday night, the very mobilized teachers united in the spirited rally at COD. It did seem that the accident not only fully galvanized the teachers but gave impetus to end the impasse on the board's part. At the rally, Glenbard South math teacher Bob Doboscz spoke passionately about the accident—walking back to his car after the collision, he felt furious at the board for having caused this to happen, but then he paused and said, "It was not their fault. I was feeling hostile towards them, and it was not right. I needed and maybe we all need to lose some of our feeling of hostility."

The next meeting was Saturday at 3:00 p.m. at the district office. At this point, several key people stepped up: Assistant District Superintendent Ron Smith, finance manager Frich, and lawyer Himes began to move between the two groups. It became clear that the two sides were now going to do what the board had promised they would never do—move toward the middle. The priority for the teachers was a 5 percent first year raise and a 14 percent three-year total. The board was at 4 the first year and 10 percent for the three years.

"Ron Smith came down and asked us what was absolutely crucial," said Jacobson. "We told him 5 percent the first year, and 14 over 3. He stated, 'You are not going to get both.'"

It was apparent the board seemed hesitant to give in to the 5 percent first year offer—after all, they had been offered that to open the schools the week before.

Finally, in the early hours of Sunday night—many PN team members felt it was only because of fatigue—the board's compromise came: 5 percent the first year, 4 the second, and 3 the third. This was the proposal that finally came to the PN team.

There was still dissension among the PN team. "Again, things became tense. Some thought we could do better," said Wright. "Some thought that this was as good as it was going to get." The teachers at North wanted the 5-5-4 and were adamant not to give that up. One PN team member said, "I told a fellow teacher to finally shut the fuck up and that is something I never thought I would do to a fellow colleague." Loynachan stated, "While I personally favor this, I know the teachers I represent do not, so I vote no." Jacobson, the other North teacher, also voted no. Dagnon did not like the fact that the teacher's resource period had not been settled further, and she voted no. But the others agreed to accept the pact by a 6-3 vote (7-3 if you count Wright, who technically couldn't vote).

The signing of the contract was next. One PN team member recalled Talsma raising a point of discussion and Smith snapping at her, "Just sign it."

It appeared the strike was over, but there was still more to do. On Wednesday, the teachers ratified the contract. It was over. But not really, it had just started.

A strike fifteen years ago in a Glendale Heights elementary school district still harbors hard feelings. Teachers remember parents who crossed the picket line to go in the school and "supervise." Parents respond that it was the only way to take care of the children. They had no other way to do it.

And there are hard feelings from this strike that will hold over.

"I feel this school board has dismantled this district," says Dagnon. "These teaching jobs in District 87 are the plum of DuPage County, and they should be paid at that rate. I fear for the future of the teachers in this district if the makeup of this board does not change. The strike settlement is not the end. It is only the beginning."

The board formerly ratified the contract at their Monday, September 13 meeting. In published reports, Talsma said, "I am not happy. I am concerned about the financial implications." She expected a lengthy strike if the board did not settle.

Voltaggio called the contract talks between the board and the union were called negotiations but "the process amounted to little more than a unilateral series of demands (by the union)." He added that approving the contract "serves to reinforce that brinkmanship tactics are the norm. The settlement places most, if not all, teachers well ahead (in salary) of the average private sector taxpayers who must support this contract (with their property taxes)." He said "these kinds of settlements will ultimately serve as the catalyst" to harm public education with more restrictive legislation.

Pihos said the top priority was getting the students back in school: "However, I cannot support a contract, which while more than generous to the teachers, did not reflect fairness to the students and the parents and community members who pay the taxes that will generate the income for these ambitious salaries."

Hince said, "The students' excitement of starting a new year and meeting new challenges, their hopes, their dreams were put on hold."

Voting for the contract were Brown, Church, France, Hince, and Talsma. Voting no were Pihos and Voltaggio.

Internet Links

https://www.google.com/?gws_rd=ssl#q=prayer+man+oswald

https://www.youtube.com/watch?v=73_ds1xQmD4

https://www.youtube.com/watch?v=mnl5X5MQKTg

About the Author

William J. Burghardt is the author of two produced plays, *Just Before the Snow Melts* and *Shadow Stock*. A former journalist and theater critic, his articles and reviews have appeared in several Chicago-area publications, including *The Chicago Tribune*, and he is a winner of the Peter Lisagor Award for Outstanding Journalism, an honor bestowed annually by Chicago Headline Club to candidates in the seven-county Chicago area. He is an actor, director, and a former radio host for a theater-related program at a Chicago-area radio station.